CONSERVATIVE CRISIS AND THE RULE OF LAW:
ATTITUDES OF BAR AND BENCH, 1887-1895

Published under the direction of the American Historical Association from the income of the Albert J. Beveridge Memorial Fund.

For their zeal and beneficence in creating this fund the Association is indebted to many citizens of Indiana who desired to honor in this way the memory of a statesman and historian.

Conservative Crisis and the Rule of Law:

Attitudes of Bar and Bench,

1887-1895

BY ARNOLD M. PAUL

PUBLISHED FOR THE

American Historical Association

CORNELL UNIVERSITY PRESS

ITHACA, NEW YORK

92463

CORNELL UNIVERSITY PRESS

First published 1960

PRINTED IN THE UNITED STATES OF AMERICA
BY VAIL-BALLOU PRESS, INC.

To the Memory of

OLIVER WENDELL HOLMES, JR.

Acknowledgments

IT is a pleasure to write out my appreciation to the many persons helpful during the course of this work. My primary obligation is to Professor George E. Mowry of the University of California, Los Angeles, in whose stimulating seminar in 1953 I first tried out some ideas on the courts and the 1890's, and who has generously supported this project through many stages. Professor Mowry's guidance was especially valuable in taking out the "rough" from the first draft.

Professor John Higham, now of Rutgers, consulted with me in the planning period and provoked my thinking on American conservatism and majority rule. Professors Brainerd Dyer and David G. Farrelly of the University of California, Los Angeles, Lawrence A. Harper of the University of California, Berkeley, and Douglass Adair of the Claremont Graduate School read various drafts, and each made many important criticisms. Judge Philbrick McCoy of the Superior Court of Los Angeles County gave the manuscript the benefit of a truly judicious reading, and I am grateful for his encouragement and suggestions. My good friend Ralph House of Tujunga, California, spent many arduous hours helping me with clarity of style in the later versions. I should add that my recurrent obstinacy exempts any of these gentlemen from responsibility for the statements and opinions herein.

I wish to thank Mrs. Esther Euler of the Interlibrary Loan Office at U.C.L.A. for kindly permitting exceptional use of her time and facilities. The staffs of the Law Library of the University of Southern California and the County Law Library of Los Angeles were also very co-operative. I am grateful to the Albert J. Beveridge Committee of the American Historical Association for sponsoring the publication of this book.

Last, but surely not least, I am forever indebted to Thomas C. Cochran of the University of Pennsylvania, who, as my teacher at New York University, first inspired me with the study of American history, and then, years later, as Visiting Professor at U.C.L.A., confirmed my commitment to the historian's way.

ARNOLD M. PAUL

Pasadena, California
June 1960

Contents

I   Introduction 1

II   Conservatism at the Crossroads: The Late Eighties 19

III Concerns of the Legal Progressives 39

IV The Hardening of Conservative Attitudes . . . 61

V Democracy and the Judiciary: Problems of the
Moderate Center 82

VI The Courts and Labor before the Pullman Strike . 104

VII The "Debs Rebellion" and Legal Conservatism . . 131

VIII Development of the Income Tax Crisis . . . 159

IX The *Pollock* Case and the Triumph of the New
Judicialism 185

X Conservatism and the Judiciary: An Appraisal . . 221

Bibliography 238

Table of Cases 248

Index 253

CONSERVATIVE CRISIS AND THE RULE OF LAW:
ATTITUDES OF BAR AND BENCH, 1887-1895

If I were asked where I place the American aristocracy, I should reply without hesitation that it is not among the rich who are bound by no common tie but that it occupies the judicial bench and the bar.

The more we reflect upon all that occurs in the United States, the more we shall be persuaded that the lawyers, as a body, form the most powerful, if not the only, counterpoise to the democratic element.

ALEXIS DE TOCQUEVILLE,
Democracy in America

I

Introduction

THE period 1886–1896, from the Haymarket riot to the Bryan election campaign, was a time of social tension in the United States. Widespread outbreaks of labor militancy, agrarian crusades for free silver, demands for progressive taxation of large incomes, and incessant agitation against the "trusts" troubled the times. An economic depression that began in 1893 intensified social protest, creating an atmosphere of class antagonism. The growth of Populism, the Coxey "armies," the Pullman strike, the enactment of a graduated income tax—all seemed to portend a serious challenge to prevailing economic relationships. American industrial capitalism, raw and not yet really respectable, was experiencing a major crisis.

The social protests of the post–Civil War era stemmed from the great pace of industrialization, and, more particularly, from the swift concentration of economic power in the large corporation. Midwestern and Southern farmers, unable to control their marketing through organization and suffering from a long-term international price decline, complained bitterly of monopolistic rates by railroads, grain elevators, and banks. Factory workers and miners, crowded in slums with insecure status in a rapidly changing economy, periodically rebelled at low wages, long hours, and bad working conditions. Small businessmen, faced with the more efficient, and frequently more ruthless, competition of the large corporation, charged that the continued consolidation of capital was destroying individual opportunity. And many professional and white-collar people, uneasy over the accumulation of great wealth and the growing disparity of rich and poor, feared that the traditional fluidity of American society was fast disappearing. The near-unanimous passage of the Sherman Anti-Trust Act in 1890 revealed the pervasiveness of popular dissatisfaction with many aspects of the new industrialism.[1]

As popular discontents grew more menacing in the 1890's, and conservative alarm for the security of property increased accordingly, the role of the courts assumed a new importance. Gradually at first, and then with rapid strides, the judiciary emerged in the mid-1890's as the principal bulwark of conservative defense. The transformation of the due process clause into a substantive check upon legislative regulation, the development of the labor injunction as an antistrike weapon, the near-emasculation of the Sherman Anti-Trust Act in the *E. C. Knight* case, and the overthrow of the federal income tax in the *Pollock* case were related aspects of a massive judicial entry into the socioeconomic scene. American constitutionalism underwent a revolution in the 1890's, a conservative-oriented revolution which vastly expanded the scope of judicial supremacy, with important consequences for American economic and political history.

[1] Edward C. Kirkland, in the first edition of his *A History of American Economic Life* (New York, 1939), p. 566, put it this way: "In short, public opinion by the end of the eighties was well-nigh unanimous that big business ought to be severely regulated. If there was ever an illustration of the operation of the 'general will' of Rousseau, this policy afforded it." See also Hans B. Thorelli, *The Federal Anti-Trust Policy: Origination of an American Tradition* (Baltimore, 1955), chs. iii and iv. A recent reinterpretation of social conditions and reform movements in this period, emphasizing concepts from social psychology rather than economics, is Samuel P. Hays, *The Response to Industrialism, 1885–1914* (Chicago, 1957).

The nature of the legal doctrines and court decisions that comprised what we may call the "new judicialism" of the mid-nineties has been previously analyzed by constitutional scholars,[2] though I have attempted fresh clarification after re-examination of the cases in conjunction with other source material. The chief contribution of this book is a study of the relationships among the doctrines and decisions of the courts, the social tensions of the time, and the changing attitudes of lawyers and judges.

As tensions mounted after the Haymarket riot, and the leading cases establishing the new judicialism passed in review, lawyers and judges appeared before the bar associations, contributed articles to the law journals, made speeches at commencement exercises, and otherwise made known their views on the great problems of the day. What issues loomed largest in the minds of these articulate members of the legal profession? How far did they think it wise for courts to go in interposing judicial blocks between the demands of reform and the interests of conservatism? How did they regard the growing conflict between capital and labor, and what role did they think proper for the judiciary in that conflict? And most important perhaps, how did they evaluate the implications for the democratic process in the expanded concept of judicial review then being developed? [3]

[2] For the rise of substantive due process, a valuable survey is in Charles G. Haines, "Judicial Review of Legislation in the United States and the Doctrines of Vested Rights and of Implied Limitations on Legislatures," *Texas Law Review*, 3 (Dec., 1924), 1–43. For the new uses of the injunction in labor disputes, Felix Frankfurter and Nathan Greene, *The Labor Injunction* (New York, 1930), is the standard authority. For the *E. C. Knight* case and the commerce power, see Edward S. Corwin's *The Twilight of the Supreme Court* (New Haven, 1934), ch. i. And for the income tax cases, see the same author's *Court over Constitution* (Princeton, 1938), ch. iv.

[3] Besides the pertinent cases, I have used as my principal source materials the papers and addresses printed in the annual reports of the national and state bar associations and the articles and editorials printed

4 Conservative Crisis and the Law

On these and other questions, wide diversity existed among lawyers and judges.[4] Dissent and disapproval were far more frequent at this early date than has been generally supposed. A tradition of Jacksonian equalitarianism, of antimonopolism, was still quite strong in the profession. And, as will be seen, the legal progressives waged a great debate over many phases of the new judicialism.

Of major significance were important differences within the general framework of what may be called the conservative point of view. Two main streams of legal conservative thought could be distinguished: a laissez-faire conservatism, drawing heavily on the antipaternalism doctrines of Herbert Spencer and dedicated to the utmost freedom for economic initiative and the utmost restriction upon legislative interference;[5] and a more traditional conservatism, which, while assigning the protection of

in the law journals. The categories chosen offer the advantages of manageability, permitting examination of nearly complete universes in order to estimate representativeness, and professionalism, significant for revealing opinion expressed "in church" as it were.

[4] Pioneer work in this field, the study of the social attitudes of American lawyers in the late nineteenth century, was undertaken by Benjamin R. Twiss, *Lawyers and the Constitution: How Laissez Faire Came to the Supreme Court* (Princeton, 1942), in his chapter entitled "Priests of the Temple of the Constitution." Analyzing the principal speeches at meetings of the American Bar Association in the 1880's and 1890's, Twiss noted the doctrinaire laissez-faire ideology they often manifested and concluded that these views were probably typical for the legal profession as a whole. From the standpoint of representativeness, however, conclusions drawn from the segment of professional opinion analyzed by Twiss are apt to be misleading. See Richard Hofstadter, *The Age of Reform: From Bryan to F. D. R.* (New York, 1956), pp. 155–163, for a discussion of some factors making for occupational differentiation and dissatisfaction within the legal profession at the turn of the century.

[5] Clinton Rossiter in his *Conservatism in America* (New York, 1955) has also used the term laissez-faire conservatism, but in a more general sense, to denote the American Right from 1865 to 1933 (see esp. pp. 132–163). The standard work on Spencer's philosophy, including its close linkage with classical economics, is Richard Hofstadter, *Social Darwinism in American Thought, 1860–1915* (Philadelphia, 1945).

private property to a high status in the hierarchy of values, was especially concerned with the problems of maintaining an ordered society in a world where the forces of popular democracy might become unmanageable. From the professional standpoint, legal conservatism as a whole, and particularly traditional legal conservatism, set great store by precedent and the proprieties of judicial procedure.

Within all these categories of opinion there were wide variations from moderate to extreme—or, as may be said, from center to left (for the progressives) and from center to right (for the conservatives). And in tracing the changing attitudes of lawyers and judges from 1887 to 1895, when court intervention reached its climax, we shall find that it was a significant movement to the right within traditional legal conservatism that finally determined the triumph of the new judicialism.

Before turning to developments in 1887, a review of the constitutional background is pertinent. Under the pressure of social discontent, legislators had begun to act in the 1870's and 1880's in regard to railroad and grain elevator rates, labor relations, and other matters affecting large business concerns.[6] In turn, corporation lawyers had been pressing the courts to protect more vigilantly the rights of property against legislative regulation. The newly adopted Fourteenth Amendment, with its general phraseology prohibiting the states from abridging the

[6] The latest analysis of the Midwestern legislative movements of the 1870's is by Charles Fairman, "The So-called Granger Cases, Lord Hale, and Justice Bradley," *Stanford Law Review*, 5 (July, 1953), 592–620. The most recent general survey of social and economic legislation in this period is in Sidney Fine's *Laissez Faire and the General-Welfare State: A Study of Conflict in American Thought, 1865–1901* (Ann Arbor, 1956), pp. 357–359. The movement for labor legislation in the 1880's and 1890's still awaits full research. The chief types of labor laws were "store order" acts, often called "scrip" or "truck" acts, aimed at prohibiting or restricting payment of wages in company scrip; "coal screening" laws, designed to assure a fair accounting to miners paid on a piecework basis; and weekly-payment laws.

"privileges and immunities" of citizens of the United States, or from depriving "any person of life, liberty, or property, without due process of law," or from denying to any person "the equal protection of the laws," was repeatedly offered as a suitable constitutional vehicle for judicial interposition. The due process clause especially, corporation lawyers maintained, should be understood as embodying guarantees of fundamental private rights against legislative infringement—especially in regard to such matters as the labor contract and the rate schedules of railroads and other public service corporations. The claim made was threefold: that the legislature had no power to intervene in these matters; that if the legislature did have the power, it had to exercise it "reasonably"; and that the final arbiter of reasonableness was the judiciary. And the interpretation of reasonableness urged upon the judges by corporate counsel often meant at the very least a substantial diminution of the legislative power, and in some types of cases—the freedom-of-contract cases for example [7]—the impressment upon the Constitution of a laissez-faire ideology.[8]

But "due process of law" historically had connoted procedural and not substantive restrictions upon the powers of government,[9]

[7] By "freedom of contract," or "liberty of contract," was meant the supposed right of both employer and employee to contract at will on the terms of employment, unhampered by legislative prohibitions or requirements. Freedom of contract was said to be part of the "liberty" and/or "property" of which no person could be deprived without due process of law. See Roscoe Pound's well-known article, "Liberty of Contract," *Yale Law Journal*, 18 (May, 1909), 454–487. Freedom of contract passed into virtual oblivion in the late 1930's.

[8] The role of leading corporate counsel in blocking out the constitutional interpretations most appropriate for a laissez-faire ideology is the main topic of Twiss's *Lawyers and the Constitution.*

[9] "Due process of law" was another term for the phrase "law of the land" in Magna Charta; the one or the other had been incorporated in colonial charters, in state constitutions, and in the Fifth Amendment to the federal Constitution. Both phrases had been used almost exclusively in reference to procedural safeguards governing common-law trials, such as the right to counsel, the right to call witnesses in one's

and to adopt the interpretations of the corporation lawyers would mean a drastic extension of judicial review beyond its traditional limitations.[10] The courts were cautious; the United States Supreme Court in particular, which must ultimately set the pattern for constitutional trends throughout all American courts, was yielding very little, formally at least, to the arguments of corporation lawyers. To be sure, the Court had acceded in January, 1886, to the claim of Roscoe Conkling that the word "person" in the Fourteenth Amendment was intended to apply to corporations as well as to natural persons.[11] But as

defense, etc. In a few cases before the Civil War, however, due process of law had been held to imply a general limitation upon the legislative power over private property, that is, upon the content or substance of the legislative act. Edward S. Corwin, "The Doctrine of Due Process before the Civil War," *Harvard Law Review*, 24 (March and April, 1911), 366–385 and 460–479. Abolitionists also made frequent use of "due process" in their attempts to frustrate federal enforcement of fugitive slave acts. Howard J. Graham, "Procedure to Substance— Extra-Judicial Rise of Due Process 1830–1860," *California Law Review*, 40 (Winter, 1952–1953), 483–500. And Wallace Mendelson has shown recently that a number of state courts had been expanding the term "law of the land" before the Civil War to invalidate legislative acts which were, in effect, judicial decrees or retroactive law, e.g., special dispensations to or burdens upon particular railroad companies ("A Missing Link in the Evolution of Due Process," *Vanderbilt Law Review*, 10 [Dec., 1956], 125–137). Despite these preliminary manifestations of substantive due process, the great weight of judicial precedent prior to the 1870's still favored a strictly procedural interpretation.

[10] Prior to the 1880's judicial review had been generally confined to the determination of whether the legislative act complained of was or was not within the exercise of a power specifically granted (in the case of Congress), or not specifically forbidden or withheld (in the case of state legislatures)—the periodic appearance, in some courts, of "higher law" dicta having been insufficient to effect any change in the scope of judicial review. The traditional judicial review was thus far removed from the theory of substantive due process, that an act, even if falling within a power properly belonging to the legislature, say the police power, was invalid if infringing unreasonably upon the rights of liberty or property. See Charles G. Haines, *The American Doctrine of Judicial Supremacy* (2d ed.; Berkeley, 1932), esp. pp. 400–421.

[11] *Santa Clara County* v. *Southern Pacific R.R.*, 118 U.S. 394.

a leading authority has pointed out, this alone was only of potential value to corporations seeking relief from state regulatory laws;[12] for on the critical issue of whether the Fourteenth Amendment should be regarded as imposing substantive restraints upon state social and economic legislation, the Court was firmly upholding the legislative power.

The basis of the Court's position had been established in 1877 in the great case of *Munn* v. *Illinois*,[13] one of the famous "Granger" cases resulting from the reform movements of the 1870's. Rendered by a 7-2 majority of the Court, Justices Field and Strong dissenting, *Munn* v. *Illinois* seemed for many years an impregnable barrier to the new constitutionalism.[14] Long the bête noire of laissez-faire conservatism, the case merits restatement here.[15]

At issue was an Illinois law of 1871 requiring a license for the operation of public warehouses in cities of not less than 100,000 population (Chicago was the only city affected) and prescribing a maximum schedule of rates for the storage and handling of grain. Chief Justice Morrison R. Waite for the Court,[16] rejecting the contention of the plaintiff that he was

[12] Howard J. Graham, "An Innocent Abroad: The Constitutional Corporate 'Person,'" *U.C.L.A. Law Review*, 2 (Feb., 1955), 160–165.

[13] 94 U.S. 113.

[14] "New constitutionalism" is used here, as by many writers, synonymously with "laissez-faire constitutionalism," both referring specifically to the rise of substantive due process. It should be distinguished from the term "new judicialism," which I have coined to refer to the broad range of new powers assumed by the judiciary in the 1890's.

[15] For conservative reactions shortly after the decision, see Charles Warren, *The Supreme Court in United States History* (Boston, 1923), III, 303–306. The most recent full-length study of the *Munn* case is Fairman's "The So-Called Granger Cases," which emphasizes the role of Justice Bradley in the preparation of the opinion that Chief Justice Waite delivered.

[16] The only major study of Waite is Bruce R. Trimble, *Chief Justice Waite—Defender of the Public Interest* (Princeton, 1938). Though a successful railroad and corporation lawyer in Toledo, once on the Supreme Court Waite consistently upheld state power over corporate business.

being deprived of property without due process of law, sustained the law as a legitimate exercise of the police power. Under this power, continued the Chief Justice,

the government regulates the conduct of its citizens one towards another, and the manner in which each shall use his own property, when such regulation becomes necessary for the public good. In their exercise it has been customary in England from time immemorial, and in this country from its first colonization, to regulate ferries, common carriers, hackmen, bakers, millers, wharfingers, innkeepers, etc., and in so doing to fix a maximum of charge to be made for services rendered, accommodations furnished, and articles sold.[17]

Thus, regulation of private property was not per se a deprivation of property without due process of law. But what were the circumstances which governed the determination of whether such regulation was or was not a deprivation? Here Waite had recourse to the 200-year-old common-law treatise *De Portibus Maris* by Lord Chief Justice Hale, wherein it was stated that when private property is "affected with a public interest, it ceases to be *juris privati* only." Said Waite, in what was to be the most oft-quoted passage of his opinion:

Property does become clothed with a public interest when used in a manner to make it of public consequence, and affect the community at large. When, therefore, one devotes his property to a use in which the public has an interest, he, in effect, grants to the public an interest in that use, and must submit to be controlled by the public for the common good, to the extent of the interest he has thus created.[18]

The grain storage business in Chicago, lying squarely astride the great stream of interstate commerce in grain, was thus affected with the public interest. And the elevator facilities in Chicago, having always charged agreed-upon rates and able to

[17] 94 U.S. 125. The "etc." in this paragraph was hardly calculated to reassure laissez-faire conservatives.
[18] *Ibid.*, p. 126.

"take toll from all who pass," constituted therefore a "virtual monopoly."

Possibly the critical hinge of the whole opinion was in regard to the claim of appellant that in any event the owner of the property was entitled to a reasonable compensation for its use, and "reasonable" was a matter for judicial and not legislative decision. To this Waite answered:

The controlling fact is the power to regulate at all. If that exists, the right to establish the maximum of charge, as one of the means of regulation, is implied. . . .

We know that this is a power which may be abused; but that is no argument against its existence. For protection against abuses by legislatures the people must resort to the polls, not to the courts.[19]

The Chief Justice was adhering firmly to judicial restraint: the reasonableness of public regulation would remain a political question, and not become a legal one.

In subsequent cases the Court upheld and expanded further its broad acknowledgment of legislative power,[20] reaching close to its high point in this line of decisions with the 1886 case of *Stone* v. *Farmers' Loan and Trust Co.*[21] In that case a railroad's charter granted in 1884 specifically empowered the company to fix its own rates and charges. Nevertheless, Chief Justice Waite, again speaking for the Court, sustained the application to the company of a newly established railroad commission's findings as to what rates the company should charge. Since the company had conceded that its power to set rates was limited by the common-law rule that all charges must be reasonable, it could not complain, said Waite, if the legislature determined for itself in the first instance what was reasonable, for this was simply

---

[19] *Ibid.*, p. 134.

[20] The principal cases were *Beer Co.* v. *Massachusetts*, 97 U.S. 25 (1878); *Fertilizing Co.* v. *Hyde Park*, 97 U.S. 659 (1878); *Stone* v. *Mississippi*, 101 U.S. 814 (1880); and *Butchers' Union Co.* v. *Crescent City Co.*, 111 U.S. 746 (1884).

[21] 116 U.S. 307, also known as the *Railroad Commission Cases.*

another example of statutory implementation of the common law, always a recognized practice.

Having thus refined away the charter rights in respect to rates almost to the vanishing point—and weakened further the protections of the *Dartmouth College* case [22]—the Chief Justice felt obliged to insert this concession:

From what has thus been said, it is not to be inferred that this power of limitation or regulation is itself without limit. This power to regulate is not a power to destroy, and limitation is not the equivalent of confiscation. Under pretence of regulating fares and freights, the State cannot require a railroad corporation to carry persons or property without reward; neither can it do that which in law amounts to a taking of private property for public use without just compensation, or without due process of law.[23]

In extreme cases then, the Court agreed, it might set aside an act as contrary to due process. In ensuing years this passage was much quoted by railroad counsel, and it has since been regarded by many scholars as an important springboard for substantive due process.[24] At the time, however, no such favorable prognosis was foreseen by corporation lawyers or by laissez-faire conservatives generally, who saw only continued judicial obeisance to the legislative will. Nor did the two dissenting opinions

[22] The celebrated case of 1819 (*Dartmouth College* v. *Woodward*, 4 Wheat. 518), where Chief Justice Marshall held that a legislative grant of a corporation charter was a "contract" within the meaning of the term as used in Article I, Section 10, of the Constitution, prohibiting the states from passing laws "impairing the obligation of contracts." Although the *Dartmouth College* doctrine was for decades a major bulwark for corporations, it had been steadily shorn of effectiveness by court interpretations, by the "reserved" clauses in new state constitutions, and by the passage of general incorporation laws (Benjamin F. Wright, *The Contract Clause of the Constitution* [Cambridge, 1938], pp. 247, 251, 258).

[23] 116 U.S. 331.

[24] Thus, Haines, "Judicial Review of Legislation," p. 9; and Warren, *op. cit.*, III, 591. But see Fairman, "The So-Called Granger Cases," p. 669, n. 380, for a different reading.

of Justices Harlan and Field, the former on narrow, the latter on broad grounds, seem sufficient to promise an early reversal of the Court's position.

In contrast to this continued insistence by the United States Supreme Court upon the flexibility of legislative discretion, matters affecting the state courts had already produced a basis for possible restrictions on the legislative will. For by 1887 the doctrine of freedom of contract had been developed, and its initial applications established.[25] The first great step toward this end after the Civil War was the publication by Thomas M. Cooley in 1868 of his famous *Constitutional Limitations*,[26] wherein he gathered together the scattered constitutional law of the different states into a convenient, organized whole which could serve as a principal source for citation in the state courts. In his preface Cooley said he had written "in full sympathy with the restraints" that the Fathers had imposed upon government in America.[27] Although Cooley was conscientious enough to mark out areas of state power as well as restrictions upon states,[28] the over-all emphasis of the book was on "Limitations."

But Cooley did not merely collect for exposition; in the process he also enlarged upon and created afresh. His discussion of "law of the land" and "due process of law" was a contribution of considerable importance to laissez-faire constitutionalism; [29]

[25] The course of this evolution has been carefully examined recently by Clyde E. Jacobs, *Law Writers and the Courts: The Influence of Thomas M. Cooley, Christopher G. Tiedeman, and John F. Dillon upon American Constitutional Law* (Berkeley, 1954), pp. 23–63. Jacobs' main emphasis is upon the contributions of the textbook commentators to the doctrines of the new constitutionalism.

[26] *A Treatise on the Constitutional Limitations Which Rest upon the Legislative Power of the States of the American Union* (Boston, 1868). For Cooley's background, and evaluations of his work and influence, see Jacobs, *op. cit.*, pp. 27–32 and *passim*; and Twiss, *op. cit.*, ch. iii.

[27] *Op. cit.*, p. iv.

[28] See especially his broad statement of the police power, *ibid.*, p. 572.

[29] "The principles, then, upon which the process is based are to determine whether it is 'due process' or not, and not any considerations

so also was his impugnment as "class legislation" of laws which unwarrantably infringed the "capacity to make contracts." [30] These and other passages of his writings were to be frequently quoted by counsel, and by judges, as authority for judicial invalidation of state regulatory acts.[31]

Cooley's path-breaking work on the state level was soon supplemented from an entirely different source, the individualist opinions of Justice Stephen J. Field of the United States Supreme Court.[32] Not the least fascinating of the many unusual elements of the rise of the new constitutionalism was the acceptance of Field's ideas on the state level before they finally attained sanction from the majority of his colleagues on the supreme federal bench.

In the famous *Slaughter-House Cases*,[33] Field's dissenting opin-

---

of mere form . . . When the government . . . interferes with the title to one's property, or with his independent enjoyment of it, and its act is called in question as not in accordance with the law of the land, we are to test its validity by those principles of civil liberty and constitutional defence which have become established in our system of law, and not by any rules that pertain to forms of procedure only" (*ibid.*, p. 356). See Rodney L. Mott, *Due Process of Law* (Indianapolis, 1926), pp. 183–187.

[30] *Op. cit.*, p. 393.

[31] Jacobs, *op. cit.*, has counted up the number of Cooley citations in each of the important freedom-of-contract cases of the late nineteenth century.

[32] The story of Field's life, together with an analysis of his major opinions, is well told in Carl B. Swisher's biography, *Stephen J. Field, Craftsman of the Law* (Washington, 1930). Also pertinent are Ralph H. Gabriel, *The Course of American Democratic Thought* (New York, 1940), ch. xviii, and Robert G. McCloskey, *American Conservatism in the Age of Enterprise* (Cambridge, 1951), chs. iv and v. McCloskey offers an exceptionally penetrating analysis of Field's role as the outstanding spokesman of laissez-faire philosophy on the Supreme Court in the 1870's and 1880's but estimates too highly Field's influence upon the ultimate triumph of laissez-faire constitutionalism.

[33] 16 Wall. 36 (1873). In the *Slaughter-House Cases*, the first cases to arise under the Fourteenth Amendment, the Court refused to accede to a broadly nationalistic view of the Amendment. The privileges and immunities clause was given a narrow interpretation, an attempt to ex-

ion extolled as inalienable the right of the citizen "to pursue his own calling" and arrogated to the judiciary operating through the Fourteenth Amendment the obligation to protect that and all the other "inalienable rights" against hostile state action.[34] Then, in 1884, in the *Butchers' Union* case,[35] Field had the opportunity to invest these same sentiments with the added weight of a concurring opinion.[36] Field's assertion that the Declaration of Independence guaranteed "the right of men to pursue their happiness, by which is meant the right to pursue any lawful business or vocation in any manner not inconsistent with the equal rights of others which may increase their prosperity or develop their faculties," [37] became a standard quotation in freedom-of-contract decisions.

It was partly on the basis of this authority that less than one

---

pand the procedural meaning of the due process clause was abruptly rejected, and the equal protection clause was declared applicable only to Negroes. Although the *Slaughter-House* decision is often regarded as a predecessor of the *Munn* case and was of great importance for the future of the Fourteenth Amendment, it never became a center of controversy like the *Munn* case and as a matter of fact was seldom mentioned in the 1890's. Partly this was because the act sustained in 1873, involving the grant of a slaughtering monopoly by the carpetbag government of Louisiana, had no relation to the new movements for economic and social reform, and concerned no new exercise of the police power (the act was held to fall under the sanitary laws); and partly because the opinion of the Court, though elaborate in construing the effects of the Fourteenth Amendment on the federal system, had little to say about the police power itself, or the role of judicial review.

[34] The Fourteenth Amendment, proclaimed Field, "was intended to give practical effect to the declaration of 1776 of inalienable rights, rights which are the gift of the Creator, which the law does not confer, but only recognizes" (16 Wall. 87). Field's language in his dissent to *Munn* v. *Illinois* was only slightly less sweeping. See 94 U.S. 141–142.

[35] *Butchers' Union Co.* v. *Crescent City Co.*, 111 U.S. 746.

[36] For the concatenation of circumstances that led to this—for laissez-faire constitutionalism, fortuitous outcome, see Walton H. Hamilton's essay, "The Path of Due Process," Conyers Read, ed., *The Constitution Reconsidered* (New York, 1938).

[37] 111 U.S. 756–757.

year later, in January, 1885, Judge Robert Earl of the New York Court of Appeals delivered the widely noticed "freedom of the sweatshop" opinion in the *Jacobs* case.[38] Here the Court struck down as a deprivation of the rights of liberty and property a New York law of 1884 prohibiting under certain conditions the manufacture of cigars in tenement houses. While the case did not turn upon freedom of contract, the principle upheld, of economic individualism untrammeled by state regulation,[39] was readily applicable to a wide variety of subsequent cases.

Although the idea of freedom of contract found its first judicial application in two closely related Illinois cases,[40] it was in Pennsylvania in October, 1886, that the doctrine received its most signal affirmation. At issue in the case of *Godcharles* v. *Wigeman* [41] was the Pennsylvania Store-Order Act of 1881 prohibiting the payment of wages in other than lawful money by mining or manufacturing companies. In an opinion containing but two-thirds of a page on the constitutional questions, and with no citations, Judge Isaac M. Gordon for the Court delivered a bold stricture upon legislative power in the area of labor.

Said the Court:

The first, second, third, and fourth sections of the Act of June 29th, 1881, are utterly unconstitutional and void, inasmuch as by them an attempt has been made by the legislature to do what, in this country, cannot be done; that is, prevent persons who are *sui juris* from making their own contracts. The Act is an infringement alike of the right of the employer and the employee; more than this,

[38] *In the Matter of Jacobs*, 98 N.Y. 98.

[39] After enumerating a long list of supposedly likely extensions of regulatory power if sustained in the present instance, Earl made this declaration: "Such governmental interferences disturb the normal adjustments of the social fabric, and usually derange the delicate and complicated machinery of industry and cause a score of ills while attempting the removal of one" (*ibid.*, p. 115).

[40] *Jones* v. *People*, 110 Ill. 590 (1884), and *Millett* v. *People*, 117 Ill. 294 (1886).

[41] 113 Pa. St. 431.

it is an insulting attempt to put the laborer under legislative tutelage, which is not only degrading to his manhood, but subversive of his rights as a citizen of the United States.

He may sell his labor for what he thinks best, whether money or goods, just as his employer may sell his iron or coal, and any and every law that proposes to prevent him from so doing is an infringement of his constitutional privileges, and consequently vicious and void.[42]

Freedom of contract had surely "arrived." [43]

The closing episode in this first period of laissez-faire constitutionalism was the publication late in 1886 of Christopher G. Tiedeman's *Limitations of Police Power*.[44] Gathering together the latest precedents and elaborations of judicial doctrine, Tiedeman in a sense formalized the current state of laissez-faire constitutionalism. Throughout the book, Tiedeman was at pains to emphasize the narrowness of the police power. Its use was confined to the enforcement of the legal maxim, *sic utere tuo ut alienum non laedas* (so to use your own as not to cause injury to another's). According to Tiedeman, this meant that all laws seeking to protect the party from the consequences of his own act, so long as those consequences had no direct effect upon third parties or the public interest, were constitutionally null and void. And this principle, insisted Tiedeman, should be strictly interpreted by the judges: "The unwritten law of the

[42] *Ibid.*, p. 437.

[43] See Pound, *op. cit.*, p. 471, for an indication of the far-reaching influence of this case. That the *Godcharles* case rose so rapidly in popularity is particularly surprising in view of the fact that it had to contend with the well-considered case of *Shaffer* v. *Union Mining Co.*, 55 Md. 74 (1880), where a similar law was upheld on the ground that "being protective in its character, it cannot have been intended as restrictive of the employees' rights." The explanation of the *Godcharles* phenomenon, however, is not to be found in purely legal factors.

[44] *A Treatise on the Limitations of Police Power in the United States* (St. Louis, 1886). See Twiss, *op. cit.*, pp. 122–127, and Jacobs, *op. cit.*, pp. 58–63. Only twenty-nine years old at the date of publication of his book, Tiedeman was Professor of Law at the University of Missouri.

country is in the main against the exercise of police power, and the restrictions and burdens imposed upon persons and private property by police regulations are jealously watched and scrutinized." [45] Tiedeman's chapters on "Police Regulations of Trades and Professions" and "Police Regulation of the Relation of Master and Servant," which hemmed in the legislative power at every point, became rich source grounds for citations justifying judicial invalidation of state regulation. [46]

But the most remarkable part of Tiedeman's book was its preface. With astonishing directness he announced there the rationale for the new constitutionalism and the motivation for his book. It is worth extended quotation:

The political pendulum is again swinging in the opposite direction [from the days when *laissez faire* presumably reigned supreme], and the doctrine of governmental inactivity in economical matters is attacked daily with increasing vehemence. Governmental interference is proclaimed and demanded everywhere as a sufficient panacea for every social evil which threatens the prosperity of society. Socialism, Communism, and Anarchism are rampant throughout the civilized world. The State is called on to protect the weak against the shrewdness of the stronger, to determine what wages a workman shall receive for his labor, and how many hours daily he shall labor. . . .

Contemplating these extraordinary demands of the great army of discontents, and their apparent power, with the growth and development of universal suffrage, to enforce their views of civil polity upon the civilized world, the conservative classes stand in constant fear of the advent of an absolutism more tyrannical and more unreasoning than any before experienced by man, the absolutism of a democratic majority. . . .

If the author succeeds in any measure in his attempt to awaken the public mind to a full appreciation of the power of constitutional limitations to protect private rights against the radical experimenta-

---

[45] *Limitations of Police Power*, p. 10.

[46] As he did in respect to Cooley, Jacobs has counted up the numerous citations of Tiedeman in the state courts after 1886.

tions of social reformers, he will feel that he has been amply requited for his labors in the cause of social order and personal liberty.[47]

By the end of 1886, then, not only had the patterns of the new constitutionalism been clearly described, but, equally important, their utility for assuring order during a period of social agitation was being impressed upon legal conservatism generally. Tiedeman's preface may be said to be the link between the strict laissez-faire conservatism that had fought its way alone in the earlier period and the more traditional conservatism that was now becoming aroused to the presence of unsettling forces.

[47] *Limitations of Police Power*, pp. vi–viii.

II

Conservatism at the Crossroads:
The Late Eighties

THE year 1886 was a notable one in the history of American labor and in the history of American radicalism. The recession of 1883–1885, though mild in comparison to the major depressions of 1873 and 1893, had left a residue of discontent and restlessness with much of the general public. Farmers, laborers, mechanics, and small merchants showed growing antagonism toward monopoly, blaming loosely "corporate monopoly" for the hardships of the mid-1880's.[1]

The signal for the translation of this unrest into something close to outright class conflict was the victory of the Knights of Labor in September, 1885, in forcing the Gould railway organization to arbitrate differences and end discrimination against the Knights. Attended by wide publicity and speculation as to the supposed awesome power of the Knights, the triumph over Gould was followed by a surge in labor organization. Unskilled

[1] John R. Commons and Associates, *History of Labor in the United States* (4 vols.; New York, 1918), II, 361–362; Samuel Rezneck, "Patterns of Thought and Action in an American Depression, 1882–1886," *American Historical Review*, 61 (Jan., 1956), 284–307.

as well as skilled were swept up in the movement, as labor solidarity temporarily became a reality in America. Strikers, confident of their power, refused arbitration, and violence accompanied many of the strikes. Selig Perlman writes:

This movement, rising as an elemental protest against oppression
and degradation . . . bore in every way the aspect of a social war.
A frenzied hatred of labour for capital was shown in every important strike. . . . Extreme bitterness towards capital manifested itself
in all the actions of the Knights of Labor, and wherever the leaders
undertook to hold it within bounds, they were generally discarded
by their followers, and others who would lead as directed were
placed in charge.[2]

The movement of the Knights reached its climax in another,
more violent strike on the Gould lines in the spring of 1886. The
Knights failed to win this strike which came to an end on May
3, having made, however, "a profound impression on the public
mind." [3]

On May 4, the day after the close of the Gould strike, the
labor movement of the 1880's, which was already being weakened by internal divisions,[4] received its worst blow of the decade
when a dynamite bomb was thrown in Haymarket Square,
Chicago, killing one policeman and wounding many others. The
Haymarket riot, with its repercussions of panic, anger, and reaction, not only seriously affected the contemporary labor movement, but left a lasting imprint on middle-class attitudes. For
years afterwards, lower-class radicalism still ran the risk of association with "anarchism" and "communism." [5]

2 "The Great Upheaval," in Commons, *op. cit.*, pp. 373-375.

3 *Ibid.*, p. 384.

4 The gravest problem within the labor movement was the growing
friction between the traditional craft unions of skilled workmen and
the policy of the Knights, who organized on a mass basis and appealed
to unskilled as well as skilled. Partly as an outgrowth of this conflict,
the American Federation of Labor was organized nationally in 1886.

5 Henry David, *The History of the Haymarket Affair* (New York,
1936). Also contributing to the social tension of 1886 was Henry George's

Lawyers and judges assessing the problems of the times in 1887 showed awareness of the current social excitements. Waitman T. Willey of Morgantown, West Virginia, one of the founders of West Virginia in 1861 and its first United States Senator, delivered the Annual Address at the July, 1887, meeting of the West Virginia Bar Association on the lawyer's role in a modern republic.[6] Defending the lawyer's traditional conservatism as "a valuable characteristic in popular forms of government," Willey held this conservatism "a wholesome check upon those tendencies to licentiousness and disorder incident to popular institutions."

Applying this view directly to contemporary events, Willey predicted that "the conservative power and influence" of the profession was "soon to be severely tested in this country." As probable factors in this coming test, Willey pointed to the increase of "lawless violence and banditti," such as the Mollie McGuires, Ku-Kluxers, and Boycotters; "the secret conclaves of socialism, agrarianism, and anarchism, conspiring for the subversion of our American institutions"; "the fraud and violence by which the ballot has been overthrown in some of our cities, and indeed, practically nullified in whole states"; and finally, the "labor question." Willey's comments on the latter are worth noting:

I think it is becoming a very serious question. . . . The advancement of the laboring classes in education and intelligence, has revealed to them a broader conception of their rights and relations.

---

strong showing on a third-party ticket in the New York mayoralty election of 1886. See Commons, *op. cit.*, pp. 446–454, for a description of the class antagonism precipitated by the campaign.

[6] "Law and Lawyers. Their Relation to a Republican Form of Government," *Proceedings of the* (First) *Annual Meeting of the West Virginia Bar Association* (1887), pp. 114–122. Willey was Secretary of the Association at the time. For Willey's role in the West Virginia separatist movement of 1861 and his subsequent political career, see Allen Johnson, ed., *Dictionary of American Biography* (20 vols.; New York, 1929), XX, 246–247.

. . . We would better not ignore the fact, that a revolution has been inaugurated in this country, which will abate none of its intensity until the relations of capital and labor have been better adjusted, and the power of monopoly has been reduced within just and proper restraints, and the control of public affairs more distinctly conformed to popular will; or until upon a failure to secure those results, the country is engulfed in a merciless despotism, or falls into utter anarchy and confusion.[7]

Former Senator Willey, conscious of the role of the bar as a balancing factor in the tension between populism and conservatism, had correctly prophesied the coming of a crisis which would crystallize that tension. But he had also recognized that changing social relationships necessitated progress and adjustment and had called upon the lawyers to keep in mind that larger perspective.

That this broadly constructive point of view would not be uncontested, however, was soon made clear in a paper read one month later at the Georgia Bar Association by I. E. Shumate of Dalton, Georgia.[8] "Seldom, if ever," announced Shumate to his colleagues of the Georgia bar, "has there been greater need in this country for the exercise of conservative influences than now." The urgency that underlay this conservative need, he explained, was the changing public attitude toward government. Whereas laissez-faire principles had previously prevailed in Georgia, now the philosophy of regulation was "affecting the conduct of almost every branch of business and controlling the private conduct of men in all relations of life." [9]

To show the evils of regulatory legislation, Shumate quoted from Herbert Spencer,[10] especially his attacks upon the public

[7] *Op. cit.*, p. 119. As an instance of the latter, Willey cited the Haymarket riot.

[8] "Professional Responsibility," *Report of the Fourth Annual Meeting of the Georgia Bar Association* (1887), pp. 99–108.

[9] *Ibid.*, pp. 103–104.

[10] Although Spencerian Social Darwinism was doubtless an important ingredient in the ideology of laissez-faire conservatism, only a very few

schools and factory acts. Shumate next criticized the courts for having failed to restrain the new tendencies. They had "discovered a wonderful elasticity in those provisions of our written constitutions conferring and limiting legislative powers."

Deploring such measures as the recently passed Interstate Commerce Act and various state laws affecting freedom of contract between employer and employee, Shumate warned against the "tendency to extremes." In a society where political parties catered to the votes of the populace, politicians were too often "mere weathervanes sensitive to the slightest changes in the drift of public opinion." [11]

Like Willey, Shumate called upon the bar to fulfill a conservative function in the years just ahead, but he put it in a different framework:

As the possibilities for class legislation, and legislation infringing upon the personal freedom and property rights of the citizen increase, the responsibility of those who infuse the element of conservatism into public opinion increases in like measure. . . . Without the leaven of conservatism, which it is the peculiar office of the legal profession to infuse into society, a government of the people, by the people and for the people tends towards the government of enthusiasts, led by extremists, and its laws tend to reflect the popular sentiment of fanatics.[12]

Shumate then was already seeing the pattern of events in terms of extreme positions, and was rallying legal conservatism to the defense of the *status quo*. But apparently he still thought of the struggle largely in terms of politics and public pressures.

A more sophisticated approach to the problems of laissez-faire conservatism was set forth at about the same time before the Missouri Bar Association, where Christopher G. Tiedeman, author of the *Limitations of Police Power*, delivered the Annual

---

of the hundreds of bar association speeches examined for this study contained specific references to Spencer.

[11] *Op. cit.*, pp. 105, 106. [12] *Ibid.*, p. 106.

Address for 1887.[13] That Professor Tiedeman would not shrink from exploring his position to its utmost limits the preface to his book had made clear. But even that could hardly have prepared his audience for Tiedeman's candid discussion of the doctrine of natural rights and how, properly manipulated, it could serve as the chief instrument of conservative defense.

The first section of his address consisted of a smoothly reasoned analysis of the proper status of the natural rights doctrine. Tracing its evolution from Greek philosophy and Roman law through medieval scholasticism to its apotheosis in the theory of the social contract, Tiedeman was quite emphatic in delineating the crudeness of its assumptions. Its later manifestations, in postulating that all law and government were in fact derived from the consent of the governed, and that therefore all men had certain natural rights which could not rightfully be alienated by government, he characterized as "the extreme limits of absurdity."

But in the nineteenth century, he continued, the Austin-Bentham school of positive law had swung the "pendulum of modern thought too far in the opposite direction." Their insistence that the will of the law-making power was definitive had failed to consider that law could be enforced only if it accorded ultimately with the "prevalent sense of right." Seeking some viable synthesis for the valid elements in both these philosophies, Tiedeman offered this surprisingly relativistic definition: "It may, therefore, be laid down as a general proposition that a legal rule is the product of social forces, reflecting the prevalent sense of right." [14]

This prevalent sense of right was always in a process of evolution, continued Tiedeman. Often the legal rule failed to keep

[13] "The Doctrine of Natural Rights in Its Bearing upon American Constitutional Law," *Report of the Seventh Annual Meeting of the Missouri Bar Association* (1887), pp. 97–117. Tiedeman later included practically the whole text of this address in his book of essays, *The Unwritten Constitution of the United States* (New York, 1890), ch. vi.

[14] "Doctrine of Natural Rights," p. 105.

pace with the changing conceptions of right, and then popular dissatisfaction resulted. "There is, therefore," Tiedeman concluded on this point, "no such thing, even in ethics, as an absolute, inalienable, natural right. The so-called natural rights depend upon, and vary with, the legal and ethical conceptions of the people." [15]

Thus far, Tiedeman had been formulating a philosophy of law strikingly similar to modern sociological jurisprudence, and apparently one admirably suited as a vehicle for reform. But ideas can serve unexpected purposes, and now Tiedeman began to move on to more directly pertinent considerations.

America had achieved its independence and established its constitutional system, he pointed out, in that period when the doctrine of natural rights was at its height. Accordingly, those formal declarations of right, which at that time did in fact constitute the felt sense of the community, were incorporated into "the organic law of the land"; and at the same time, for various historical and institutional reasons, the courts had been vested "with the power to veto the constitutional aggressions of the other departments." Here then was an instance where, apparently at odds with the relativistic theory just outlined, a legal sanction could obtain in the present in behalf of a legal conception of the past.

It was of course true, Professor Tiedeman continued, that written constitutions were "as much liable to serious modification through the change of public opinion, as any ordinary rule of law or statute . . . if there is any urgent demand for the adoption of a contrary construction." Until recently, however, those formal statements of eighteenth-century natural law doctrine set out in preambles and bills of rights had not come

[15] *Ibid.*, p. 111. Note the contrast between this analysis, delivered to a select group of professional colleagues, and Tiedeman's textbook statement intended for use in law schools and courts: "The private rights of the individual . . . belong to man in a state of nature; they are natural rights, rights recognized and existing in the law of reason" (*Limitations of Police Power*, p. 1).

up for much adjudication. According to Tiedeman, this was because laissez-faire philosophy had "until lately, so controlled public opinion in the English-speaking world," that government had confined itself largely to the punishment of crime, the care of the poor, and the making of public improvements.[16]

But times had changed:

Under the stress of economical relations, the clashing of private interests, the conflicts of labor and capital, the old superstition that government has the power to banish evil from the earth, if it could only be induced to declare the supposed causes illegal, has been revived; and all these so-called natural rights, which the framers of our constitutions declared to be inalienable, and the violation of which they pronounced to be a just cause for rebellion, are in imminent danger of serious infringement.[17]

And Tiedeman here repeated word for word what he had written the previous year concerning the various "paternalistic" demands upon government and the resultant conservative fear of the advent of "democratic absolutism." [18]

Professor Tiedeman then submitted this concluding statement:

In these days of great social unrest, we applaud the disposition of the courts to seize hold of these general declarations of rights as an

[16] Although this assumption concerning the supposed dominance of laissez-faire principles in the ante bellum period was frequently repeated in conservative speeches in the 1880's and 1890's, ultimately finding its way into most accounts of American political history, recent scholarship has shown that a contrary state of affairs existed and that state governments were continually intervening in economic and social matters. See the *Business History Review*, 29 (March, 1955), 81–96, for an informative survey of this scholarship. See also the discussion by Fine, *op. cit.*, pp. 18–23, of the extent of federal and state intervention. Fine does feel, however, that state economic intervention was on the wane in the 1850's as business interests became stronger and more inclined to be suspicious of governmental activity—a development which may help explain the fixity and pervasiveness of the conservative assumption concerning ante bellum *laissez faire*.

[17] Tiedeman, "Doctrine of Natural Rights," p. 115.

[18] Cited *supra*, p. 17, beginning with "The State is called on . . ." through end of next paragraph.

authority for them to lay their interdict upon all legislative acts which interfere with the individual's natural rights, even though these acts do not violate any specific or special provision of the constitution. These general provisions furnish sufficient authority for judicial interference. . . .

The demand for a paternal government will be sure to modify more or less the construction of these constitutional guaranties. . . . We, who believe in the old order of things, and dread the establishment of the new, can only rely upon the popular reverence for these constitutional declarations, and on the efforts of the courts to stem the tide by courageously avoiding [*sic*] all enactments, which violate them in word or in spirit. This is our only means of defense against the inordinate demands of socialism.[19]

Professor Tiedeman had not hesitated in firmly meeting the issues of the day. Already aware by 1887 of the factors making for a growing social crisis, Tiedeman had marked out the course by which conservatism could resist the tides of change and maintain substantially intact the *status quo*. True, the logic of jurisprudence would indicate that there were no absolute systems, no certain guarantees of an unchanging law and ethics. The doctrine of natural rights itself was, after all, but a passing phase in the history of social thought. But, happily, the incidents of American constitutionalism had given special status to natural law formulations; and these in turn could offer sanctuary to the philosophy of *laissez faire* and to the conservative value of the ordered society. If the judiciary would only do its duty, resolutely and uncompromisingly, the line could be held and the programs of popular majorities turned aside, even in an age of rising tension.

Despite such crisis-oriented interpretations as those of Shumate and Tiedeman, it was evident at the end of the year that legal conservatism as a whole had not succumbed to any general pessimism. Addressing the December meeting of the Alabama State Bar Association on the theme, "A Century of American Law,"

[19] "Doctrine of Natural Rights," p. 117.

the influential John F. Dillon, former United States Circuit Court Judge and later a leading corporation lawyer, expressed his confidence in the general state of American constitutionalism.[20] The Founding Fathers, by their "conservative wisdom" in promulgating organic law in the form of a written constitution, had ensured the implementation of the great principles of 1776.

To Dillon, the distinguishing features of American constitutions were their limitations. The purpose of these limitations was plain: "Having secured to every adult citizen an equal measure of political power—the right to vote—obviously, the foregoing provisions [the limitations] were intended to prevent in times of excitement or of passion, the unjust exercise of popular power."

But the mere setting down of limitations upon majority rule was not enough: "To prevent any miscarriage of the scheme, they provided in the several State Constitutions and in the Federal Constitution for a truly independent judiciary,—viz., judges whose tenure was during good behavior and whose compensation could not be diminished." [21] Here Dillon did note that a possible weakness in this system had been developing in the trend to an elective judiciary in many of the states. Judges whose office depended on the popular vote might not always be sufficiently firm in resisting unconstitutional measures.[22]

[20] *Proceedings of the Tenth Annual Meeting of the Alabama State Bar Association* (1887), pp. 107–138. The identical address was read to the New York State Bar Association at its 1890 meeting. Dillon was one of the most prominent members of the legal profession in this period. After eight years on the Supreme Court of Iowa and ten years as United States Circuit Court Judge, he had left the bench in 1879 to accept a professorship at Columbia University. He soon built up a large corporation practice, including among his clients the Missouri Pacific and the Union Pacific, and left the University in a few years. He was widely known for his scholarship and writings on legal subjects, especially his *Law of Municipal Corporations*. See Twiss, *Lawyers and the Constitution*, pp. 182–189; Jacobs, *Law Writers and the Courts*, pp. 111–112.

[21] Dillon, *op. cit.*, pp. 112, 113.

[22] *Ibid*. A similar fear concerning the weakness of elective judges had

But all things considered, Judge Dillon thought American institutions continued uniquely stable. The nation's unencumbered land system, he felt, was chiefly responsible for this phenomenon. America was a nation of proprietors, whereas England was still a nation of tenants. "In many of the countries of the old world," he continued, more prophetically than he knew,

the landless poor are the natural enemies of the government. Here, every proprietor, however small, is the natural ally of government and of law. There may be some reasons for the various forms of socialism, communism, anarchism, among the struggling and oppressed peoples of the old world. They are the unreasoning and desperate remedies of caste, and hunger and despair. But here, and amongst us, such ideas are baneful exotics, which can take no root, and which attract no notice except when their wild or bad adherents seek to propagate them by illegal violence or murder.[23]

The excitements of 1886 having passed away and a more equable trend having shown itself, traditional conservatives like Judge Dillon had been reassured. True, majority rule always held elements of danger; but thus far constitutional restraints had largely confined these dangers within bounds. And so long as the social equilibrium of the past apparently still prevailed, there seemed no cause for serious concern.

On December 5 of that same year, 1887, an important decision affecting the police power was handed down by the United States Supreme Court in the case of *Mugler* v. *Kansas*.[24] The case turned upon two principal questions: (1) whether the Kansas prohibition law of 1881, by forbidding the manufacture of intoxicating beverages even for personal use, was in violation

---

been voiced earlier in 1887 in an address before the New York State Bar Association by Henry Hitchcock of St. Louis, "Recent Changes in American State Constitutions," *New York State Bar Association Reports* (1887), pp. 47–80, at 77–79. Hitchcock cited the fate of Judge Lawrence of Illinois who had failed of renomination after invalidating the Illinois Rate Act of 1871. See Fairman, "So-called Granger Cases," p. 597, for some notes on this incident.

[23] *Op. cit.*, p. 117.   [24] 123 U.S. 623.

of the rights of liberty and property secured by the Fourteenth Amendment; and (2) whether, by forbidding Mugler the use of his property, purchased prior to the act, for the manufacture of beer, and thereby largely destroying its value to him, the act was not in effect a taking of private property for public purposes without compensation and a deprivation of property without due process of law.

On the first proposition, Justice John M. Harlan speaking for the Court pointed out that the brief for plaintiff admitted that the right to manufacture drink even for personal use was subject to the condition that the rights of others were not affected thereby. But how was this determination to be made? Harlan answered:

Power to determine such questions, so as to bind all, must exist somewhere. . . . Under our system that power is lodged with the legislative branch of the government. It belongs to that department to exert what are known as the police powers of the State, and to determine, primarily, what measures are appropriate or needful for the protection of the public morals, the public health, or the public safety.[25]

Harlan at once qualified this by a warning that courts would not be "bound by mere forms, nor . . . misled by mere pretences . . . but would . . . look at the substance of things." Although in subsequent adjudication less friendly to legislative power this statement was frequently quoted as a peg for substantive due process, at the time it gave little solace to worried conservatives.

On the second proposition, the contention that property was being taken without compensation and without due process, Justice Harlan was far more emphatic and even abrupt in his dismissal of the claim. "This interpretation of the Fourteenth Amendment is inadmissible. It cannot be supposed that the States intended, by adopting that Amendment, to impose restraints

25 *Ibid.*, pp. 660–661.

upon the exercise of their powers for the protection of the safety, health, or morals of the community." Nor could the police powers of the states, he concluded, be "burdened with the condition that the State must compensate such individual owners for pecuniary losses." [26]

Four months later, in April, 1888, in the case of *Powell* v. *Pennsylvania*,[27] with Justice Harlan again rendering the opinion, the Supreme Court went even further in sustaining new exercises of the police power. This time the issue involved was a Pennsylvania law prohibiting the manufacture of oleomargarine or other butter substitutes. The legislature had labeled the act as one designed to protect the public health, but it was no secret that it was the dairy industry the act was designed to protect. In fact, the plaintiff had attempted to introduce evidence from an independent expert that the butter substitutes he manufactured were in no way unhealthful or fraudulent, but the state courts had refused to admit the proffer.

The essence of Harlan's opinion was simply that the Court, on the basis of judicially cognizable facts, could not rule that the legislative statement of intent was in fact unrelated substantially to the real object of the law or the necessities of protecting the public health and preventing fraud. These were "questions of fact and of public policy which belong to the legislative department to determine." [28]

Although Harlan repeated his assurance given in *Mugler* v. *Kansas* that there were limits to the police power, its exercise not extending to the impairment of fundamental rights under the "pretence" of guarding the public health, morals, or safety, the Court's refusal to invoke those limits in the instant case seemed to presage an almost unrestricted latitude for legislative discretion. To the argument of counsel that nothing would now stand in the way of legislative destruction of the constitutional guar-

[26] *Ibid.*, pp. 665, 669. Justice Field filed a separate opinion, agreeing with most of the decision but dissenting on minor issues.
[27] 127 U.S. 678.   [28] *Ibid.*, p. 685.

antees of liberty and property, Harlan replied, "But the possibility of the abuse of legislative power does not disprove its existence." [29]

Justice Field submitted a vigorous dissent, in the manner of his *Slaughter-House* and *Munn* dissents, attacking the act as an invasion of the inalienable rights of the citizen. Field's objections covered such broad grounds that it was never perfectly clear which of those rights he considered most in jeopardy. Liberty and property, certainly: but at one point Field said, "I have always supposed that the gift of life was accompanied with the right to seek and produce food"; and at another point, "The right to procure healthy and nutritious food . . . is involved in the right to pursue one's happiness." [30] Apparently, the whole preamble to the Declaration had been wrecked by the act.

Before examining some reactions to these decisions, notice should be taken of the progressive point of view in the legal profession, what we may call the left wing of the profession. The right-wing and centrist attitudes have already been explored in connection with the aftermath to the tense year of 1886 when legal conservatism was provoked into articulate interpretation of social trends. But no major statement of the progressive approach appeared until midsummer 1888,[31] when Charles C. Bonney of Chicago, a former president of the Illinois Bar Association, spoke at the annual meeting of the Ohio State Bar Association.[32]

[29] *Ibid.*, p. 687.   [30] *Ibid.*, pp. 690, 692.
[31] That is to say, within the categories of sources used for this study (see ch. i, n. 3). A possible exception was the address of James K. Edsall to the 1887 meeting of the American Bar Association, defending *Munn v. Illinois* and the other Granger decisions, "The Granger Cases and the Police Power," *Report of the Tenth Annual Meeting of the American Bar Association* (1887), pp. 288–316. Edsall had been Attorney General of Illinois at the time the Granger cases were going through the courts.
[32] *Ohio State Bar Association—Reports, Vol. IX* (1888), pp. 153–172. Bonney, well known in professional circles, was on the Executive Committee of the American Bar Association for the year 1886–1887, and in May, 1887, he had been considered for an appointment to the United States Supreme Court.

Although Bonney's address, entitled "Impending Perils," covered a number of topics, including such items as complexities of lawsuits, and the handicaps facing the poor and uneducated in obtaining redress of wrongs, Bonney's principal concern was conflict between capital and labor. And the remedy Bonney advocated for this problem was full-fledged state regulation of the labor contract. Rejecting the argument that this would be a violation of personal liberty, Bonney declared that the liberty guaranteed in American constitutions was

that of organic society, to which all merely personal rights are necessarily subject. *A government which has never hesitated to regulate the relations of husband and wife, parent and child, guardian and ward, cannot be denied the right to regulate the less high and sacred relations of labor, production and trade. . . .*[33]

It was among the highest duties of government, he continued, "to protect the weak against the strong, and to prevent, by stringent laws and their vigorous enforcement, the oppression of the poor and friendless by the rich and powerful." Bonney's specific proposals included a comprehensive plan for the settlement of all labor disputes, beginning with collective bargaining, then mediation, and finally compulsory arbitration.[34]

Like the conservative speakers of 1887, Bonney concluded with a call upon the American bar, but this time to take the lead in behalf of popular rights "in the great conflict now impending between the people and the giant forces that are striving for the practical control of the republic." [35]

The *Mugler* and *Powell* decisions gave added confidence to progressive legal thinking. A. H. Wintersteen, of counsel for the state in the *Powell* case, writing in the March, 1889, issue of

[33] *Op. cit.*, p. 168 (italics in source).

[34] In 1886 Bonney had persuaded the Committee on Law Reform of the Illinois State Bar Association to recommend his proposal. *Chicago Legal News*, 19 (Nov. 20, 1886), 81. See also his speech to the Society for Political Education, urging passage of equivalent legislation by the Illinois legislature (*ibid.* [Apr. 30, 1887], p. 272).

[35] *Op. cit.*, p. 172.

the *American Law Register*,[36] was sure that the recent series of Supreme Court decisions would sustain the widest range of legislative discretion. The state had now been confirmed in its right "to declare not only the extent to which it will exercise its power of redressing a conceded public wrong, but also to declare the existence of the wrong to be redressed."

Justifying the necessity of such powers if democracy was to function effectively in a period of change and growth, Wintersteen said:

It seems more in accordance with the American theory of popular government through representatives, that the legislature, rather than the courts, should determine questions of public policy as to the possession of property and the exercise of personal liberty. . . . In a complex social system, such as ours is getting to be, the tendency necessarily must be towards affirmative exercise of governmental powers. . . .

A *laissez faire* democracy is not a practical democracy. Sixty millions of people must have laws. When interests clash and laws are demanded, the practical question is, not whether a State may act by its legislature for the purpose of declaring or redressing a wrong, but whether it is prohibited from so acting.[37]

In sharp contrast to such optimistic reception of the *Mugler* and *Powell* decisions were the forebodings of right-wing conservatives. David Overmyer, of Topeka, addressing the January, 1889, meeting of the Kansas Bar Association,[38] after reviewing the latest decisions, issued these declarations:

[36] "The Sovereign State," *American Law Register*, n.s., 28 (March, 1889), 129–139. The *American Law Register*, published monthly at Philadelphia, was the organ of the Pennsylvania bar. It carried treatises on law problems and case notes on the leading decisions of the country.

[37] *Ibid.*, pp. 138–139. For a similar point of view, particularly exuberant in tone, see an essay by W. M. Rapsher of Mauch Chunk, Pa.: "Are We Drifting towards Pure Democracy?" *Current Comment and Legal Miscellany*, 1 (Dec., 1889), 447–451.

[38] "The Legal Profession—Its Duties and Obligations to Society," *Sixth Annual Meeting of the Bar Association of the State of Kansas* (1889),

When we see the bill of rights gradually but steadily and surely being consumed by the aggressions of that boundless, irresponsible force called "the police power," it is our duty, at all hazards and at every peril, to step into the breach and shout "Halt!" . . .

A hundred years of constitutional existence should not blind our eyes to the fact that the real test of the constitution is yet to come. If it survives the mighty shock of contending forces whose vanguards we even now can all too plainly see, it will be well. Never in this country, since the days of Otis, the Adamses and Patrick Henry, has there been such a demand for heroism at the bar as now. Can liberty be maintained under a popular form of government? is the issue of the hour.[39]

The excited reactions to the *Mugler* and *Powell* cases were minor themes in 1888 and 1889, however; for these were years of prosperity and comparative calm, and the diminution of tension was readily observable in the moderate trend of professional attitudes. The most notable expression of this moderate conservatism of 1889 was the address of the distinguished Simeon E. Baldwin, then a Professor of Law at Yale University, before the American Bar Association.[40] Speaking on the topic, "The Centenary of Modern Government," Baldwin's address was outstanding for its breadth of approach and temperate appraisal of historical trends. Baldwin's major theme was the spread of the principles of republicanism in the hundred years since 1789.

pp. 30–37. Overmyer was active in Democratic politics in Kansas, and practiced before the United States Supreme Court.

[39] *Ibid.*, p. 35. More restrained, though parallel, comments were voiced by S. W. Williams of Little Rock in "Constitutional Law and Magna Carta," *Proceedings of the Eighth Annual Meeting of the Arkansas State Bar Association* (1889), pp. 5–10.

[40] *Report of the Twelfth Annual Meeting of the American Bar Association* (1889), pp. 235–264. The life and career of this eminent New England jurist are examined by Frederick H. Jackson: *Simeon Eben Baldwin—Lawyer, Social Scientist, Statesman* (New York, 1955). At the time of his 1889 address, Baldwin was a member of the American Bar Association's Standing Committee on Jurisprudence and Law Reform; he became president of the Association for the term 1890–1891.

And the concept of republicanism that Baldwin developed encompassed not only equal participation by all men in the selection of their government, but also the enlargement of the functions of government in the service of its people.

In the course of his review, Professor Baldwin referred often to the initially similar and then diverging histories of the United States and France, the two nations which had held such high hopes in 1789. The French philosophers, he believed, were the common inspirations of both experiments, but it was in America that their ideals had been more effectively realized. Baldwin acknowledged that America was fortunate in having had "no hereditary privileges to attack, no absolute power to check, no classes to harmonize." Moreover, with the tradition of English parliamentarianism to fall back upon, America could match the principles of France with the precedents of England. And yet the problem for America in 1789 was still formidable—"to make and keep a great people free." [41]

Considering the leading factors that had marked the history of modern government since 1789, Professor Baldwin singled out religious liberty as of prime importance. "Modern government began," he asserted, "when the State withdrew from its long alliance with Christianity." Inevitable since the Reformation, this "natural epoch in the history of individualism" had strengthened both government and religion and had worked to the greater benefit of the masses of the people. Here Baldwin offered the interesting suggestion that "the exclusion of the church with its paternal authority and paternal bounty from a voice in government" had been of great importance "in the development of that State socialism, which no civilized country [was] now wholly without." [42] As illustrations of the new state socialism, Baldwin included such diverse items as free schools and free libraries, the construction and regulation of railroads, the inspection of tenement houses and the laying of sidewalks, national and international postal systems, the regulation of the

[41] *Op. cit.*, pp. 238, 239.   [42] *Ibid.*, pp. 243, 249.

hours of labor and the age of labor, the requirement of safety standards from the employer, and the beginnings of compulsory social insurance.

At the root of all these new functions Baldwin perceived the steady rise of popular democracy, "based on a wide and constantly widening grant of suffrage." In contrast to a hundred years ago, now hardly any of the American states had even a taxpaying qualification for voting; and the same was true of most of the nations of Western Europe. Women too would soon acquire full suffrage, Baldwin predicted, and eventually Negro suffrage would return in the South.

But Professor Baldwin then noted that in terms of "the power that goes with it," the expansion of the suffrage since 1789 was less significant than expected. It had been presumed by the French philosophers, and apparently subscribed to by Jefferson, that each generation could be wholly sovereign unto itself, that no previous generation could bind a succeeding generation. But on the contrary, Baldwin declared, the "cornerstone of modern government" had been the promulgation of an organic law which could not be overcome "except through forms and delays prescribed by that law for its own defense." In the development of this conservative constitutionalism, America had made a special contribution:

The problem was to make the legislative power, whether exercised by popular or parliamentary vote, subject to some superior authority, and still leave it free to represent the public will. The American solution is through the judiciary.[43]

Concerning present tendencies, the speaker was optimistic. He saw class lines fading out and class interests becoming less important as republican equalitarianism spread. True, the "new power of property" in the last twenty-five years had perhaps given "the rich too much of public consideration"; but this tendency, thought Baldwin, was still "too slight to affect the

[43] *Ibid.*, p. 253.

main current of American life." On the other hand, the rights of the individual were never more protected, and in no country was property as secure as in the United States. America had been faithful to "the solemn trust" of 1789, concluded Professor Baldwin, and in "leading the way towards good republican government" had led the way toward "the best in modern government of every name." [44]

It remained to be seen, however, whether this confident, even complacent, outlook upon the course of popular democracy would long withstand the successive shocks of the 1890's.

[44] *Ibid.*, pp. 260, 264. Other similarly optimistic, though less broadly considered, analyses of current trends in the late 1880's may be seen in the following addresses by well-known legal conservatives: John H. Butler, "Annual Address," *Proceedings of the Seventh Annual Meeting of the Bar Association of Tennessee* (1888), pp. 173–187, though with a hint of "certain underlying factors at work which could well change this apparent calm"; Thomas M. Cooley, "Comparative Merits of Written and Prescriptive Constitutions," *New York State Bar Association Reports, Vol. 12* (1889), pp. 40–55, wherein the author of the famous *Constitutional Limitations* had words of praise for the American combination of "a conservative constitution and a progressive people"; the commencement address to the graduating class of Columbia Law School by Theodore M. Dwight, printed in the *Columbia Law Times*, 3 (Oct., 1889), 1; and another commencement address, this to the Yale Law School by Chauncey M. Depew, printed in the *Advocate* (Minneapolis), 1 (Aug., 1889), 285.

III

Concerns of the Legal Progressives

IN the opening years of the 1890's a two-fold sequence of events served to clarify as well as to intensify the division of opinion between the left and right wings of the legal profession. On the one hand, the course of judicial decision moved in the direction of increasing interposition against legislative action, thus arousing the legal progressives to forceful criticism. On the other hand, the radical and reform movements gained strength, and labor manifested renewed restiveness, with the result that laissez-faire conservatives re-emphasized their demands for more effective judicial intervention, while many traditional conservatives too began to find themselves steadily driven to the right-wing position.

The new trend of judicial decision was made clear early in 1890 when the decision in *Chicago, Milwaukee & St. Paul Ry. Co.* v. *Minnesota* was handed down on March 24 by the United States Supreme Court.[1] The *Chicago, Milwaukee* case (as it will be called hereafter) involved a Minnesota statute of 1887 establishing a Railroad and Warehouse Commission with power to set schedules of reasonable rates. The rates set by the commission

[1] 134 U.S. 418.

were to be considered final and conclusive, with no appeal to the regular judicial system. Justice Samuel Blatchford, delivering the majority opinion of the Court, held the act unconstitutional for depriving the plaintiff

of its right to a judicial investigation, by due process of law, under the forms and with the machinery provided by the wisdom of successive ages for the investigation judicially of the truth of a matter in controversy, and substitutes therefor, as an absolute finality, the action of a railroad commission.

Blatchford admitted that so far as the case before the Court was concerned, the record disclosed that the commission had conducted an investigation and the company had appeared with counsel; but there was no evidence as to "what the character of the investigation was or how the result was arrived at." He continued:

The question of the reasonableness of a rate of charge for transportation . . . is eminently a question for judicial investigation, requiring due process of law for its determination. If the company is deprived of the power of charging reasonable rates for the use of its property, and such deprivation takes place in the absence of an investigation by judicial machinery, it is deprived of the lawful use of its property . . . without due process of law and in violation of the Constitution of the United States.[2]

Justice Samuel F. Miller, who had been with the majority in the *Munn* case, filed a separate opinion saying he concurred "with some hesitation in the judgment of the Court." The list of propositions he submitted as guides for the consideration of this class of cases offered little enlightenment, however, beyond the majority opinion.[3]

But the dissenting opinion of Justice Joseph P. Bradley[4]

[2] *Ibid.*, p. 458.

[3] *Ibid.*, pp. 459–461. See the discussion in Charles Fairman's *Mr. Justice Miller and the Supreme Court 1862–1890* (Cambridge, 1939), pp. 204–205.

[4] Like Waite, Bradley was a former railroad lawyer who later became a strong defender for public superintendence over corporate busi-

(with Gray and Lamar concurring) laid bare the crucial nature
of the issues involved. Stating at once that the decision practically overruled *Munn* v. *Illinois* and the other Granger cases,
Bradley asserted: "The governing principle of those cases was
that the regulation and settlement of the fares of railroads and
other public accommodations is a legislative prerogative and not
a judicial one." [5] The question of the reasonableness of railroad
charges, he continued, was "preeminently a legislative one, involving considerations of policy as well as remuneration. . . .
This is just where I differ from the majority of the court. They
say in effect, if not in terms, that the final tribunal of arbitra-
ment is the judiciary. I say it is the legislature."

Bradley warned that by this decision state and federal courts
all over the land would now be called upon to review decisions
of state railroad commissions. As for the argument that otherwise there would be no appeal from the decisions of a commission, Bradley said: "There must be a final tribunal somewhere
for deciding every question in the world. Injustice may take
place in all tribunals. All human institutions are imperfect—
courts as well as commissions and legislatures." [6]

The *Chicago, Milwaukee* case can be considered one of the
major turning points in the rise of the new constitutionalism.
For with this decision the uneasy balance that had prevailed
in the late eighties between the old and the new in American
constitutional law was shifting to the latter. Although the *Munn*

---

ness. Charles Fairman, "What Makes a Great Justice? Mr. Justice Bradley
and the Supreme Court, 1870–1892," *Boston University Law Review*, 30
(Jan., 1950), 49–102. Bradley, with Waite and Gray, had also dissented
from the *Wabash* decision of 1886 (118 U.S. 557), which held state
regulation of railroad rates affecting interstate commerce an invasion
of Congressional prerogative, even if Congress had not acted. The decision led directly to the Interstate Commerce Act of 1887.

[5] 134 U.S. 461. Bradley was stretching a point here. The decision in
Munn v. *Illinois* turned primarily upon the general power of regulation,
with the question of judicial review of reasonableness a secondary, though
significant, factor.

[6] *Ibid.*, p. 465.

case was still officially unrepealed, it was now in danger of being outflanked, and the way was being opened for judicial supervision of state regulation on the grounds of reasonableness.

The case was also significant in that it was the first indication of how recent changes in personnel might have affected the Court's views. Chief Justice Morrison R. Waite, a staunch defender of the police power, had died in 1888, to be replaced by Melville W. Fuller of Illinois. And in 1889, Justice Stanley Matthews, a moderate conservative of states' rights leanings, had been succeeded by David J. Brewer of Kansas, already well known for his refusal to follow the *Munn* case as a United States Circuit Court Judge.[7] Both Fuller and Brewer, the latter the nephew of Justice Field, were soon to find themselves within the extreme conservative wing of the Court, reinforcing the position that Field had long held alone. The *Chicago, Milwaukee* decision was thus in part the first fruits of this new alignment.

The legal progressives were quick to perceive the larger implications of the case. The *Advocate*, a short-lived weekly law review published in Minneapolis, printed in its April 15 issue the text of a resolution by the Farmers' Alliance of Minnesota bitterly condemning the Court's opinion,[8] and in the next week's issue offered these comments of its own:

If, as Justice Blatchford contends, the reasonableness, the fairness, justice, equity of a proposed statute on a subject of general public policy, is not within the province of the legislature to determine, what function do the courts propose to leave it? . . . The infringe-

---

[7] *Chicago & N.W. Ry. Co.* v. *Dey*, 35 Fed. 866 (S.D. Iowa, 1888).

[8] The resolution of the Alliance included, among other statements, the following oratorical pronouncements: "*Resolved*, that we appeal from this second Dred Scott decision to the people of the nation, and we ask them to consider whether any other race would submit to have their liberties thus wheedled away from them on technicalities by a squad of lawyers sitting as a supreme authority high above Congress, the President and people . . . In our anxiety to protect the rights of property we have created a machinery that threatens to destroy the rights of man" (*Advocate*, 2 [April 15, 1890], 174–175).

ment of the "Due Process" clause of the constitution is a convenient technicality on which to hang the real ruling of the court. For, in effect, and put briefly, this decision is, that the Federal Supreme Court can pass upon the *reasonableness* of a state statute and declare it void for lack of that quality. If it can so judge of a state statute, why not of a federal statute? [9]

A more comprehensive critique of the decision appeared in the editorial pages of the widely read *American Law Review*,[10] whose senior editor, Seymour D. Thompson, a well-known legal publicist and for twelve years Judge of the St. Louis Court of Appeals, would soon emerge as the leading spokesman for the progressive elements of the American bar.[11] The effect of the Supreme Court's ruling, the editorial asserted, was "to subject the legislation of the States to judicial superintendence upon the mere question of its *reasonableness*." The Court's decision was

[9] *Ibid.* (April 22, 1890), p. 189 (italics in source).

[10] Vol. 24 (May–June, 1890), 516–527. Published bimonthly in St. Louis, the *American Law Review* was at this time perhaps the leading law journal in the country. Among its former editors were Oliver Wendell Holmes, Jr., and John F. Dillon.

[11] Son of a poor Illinois clergyman who died in a prairie fire, Thompson was a self-taught man who worked at a dozen occupations, as well as serving in the Union Army, before admission to the bar in 1869. In 1872 he began practicing in St. Louis, where he soon gained the favor of Judge Dillon of the United States Circuit Court, who appointed Thompson master of chancery. Thompson was elected Judge of the St. Louis Court of Appeals in 1880, winning, as a Republican, in a strongly Democratic district and holding this position till retirement in 1892 to give full time to his publications. His many legal texts included such works as *Homestead and Exemption Laws* (1878), *The Law of Negligence* (1880), and in seven volumes, his masterwork, *Commentaries on the Law of Private Corporations* (1894–1899). Thompson was editor, successively, of the *Central Law Journal*, the *Southern Law Review*, and the *American Law Review*. He was credited in 1897 with having "long exercised a continuous and virile influence upon legal thought." In 1904 President Roosevelt appointed him delegate to an international law congress at St. Louis, but Thompson died before he could attend (*Case and Comment*, 3 [March, 1897], 1–2; *Albany Law Journal*, 52 [July 13, 1895], 31).

thus "an overturning of the fundamental principles upon which all our American governments are founded, . . . that the three coordinate departments . . . are independent of each other." [12]

Thompson climaxed his editorial [13] with this charge:

The more the decision is looked at the more clearly it appears that the court has decided a mere moot case. It is nowhere stated in the opinion of the court that the railroad company was *in fact* denied a notice or a hearing, or that the case against it was decided without investigation and without evidence. The court has decided the case upon a view of *what might have been done,* not on a view of what was done . . . It is highly indecent for courts to render such decisions. No court can be so exalted in character as to escape censure for such judicial action.[14]

But the most fervent attack on the Supreme Court was made by Allan B. Brown of the Chicago bar. Accusing the Court of having thwarted the popular will and elevated the corporation above the state ever since the *Dartmouth College* case, Brown urged this remedy:

Put men on the bench who will not hesitate to defy precedent, and pull down the moldy monstrosities Marshall and his compeers set up. Make your judges elective so you can keep them in touch with the people and you will find them correspondingly jealous of the people's rights.[15]

[12] *American Law Review, op. cit.,* p. 522 (italics in source).

[13] Editorials in the *American Law Review* were generally unsigned, but Thompson's forceful, pungent, often fiercely declamatory, style was unmistakable.

[14] *Ibid.,* pp. 523–525 (italics in source). For further comments by Thompson on the Supreme Court and rate regulation, see his two addresses before bar association meetings in 1890 and 1891: "Annual Address," *Proceedings of the Thirteenth Annual Meeting of the Alabama State Bar Association* (1890), pp. 87–130, at 103; "The Power of the People over Corporate and Individual Combinations and Monopolies," *Proceedings of the Illinois State Bar Association at Its Fourteenth Annual Meeting* (1891), pp. 81–91, at 88.

[15] *Chicago Legal News,* 24 (Aug. 20, 1892), 410. See also *American Law Register,* n.s., 31 (April, 1892), 273–280.

The *Chicago, Milwaukee* case and the insistence upon judicial review of reasonableness were not the only developments that troubled legal progressives in the early 1890's. The doctrine of freedom of contract, although not always sufficient to invoke a judicial negative, took root in these years, and its applications were steadily expanded. A count of the cases turning on freedom of contract, from the *Godcharles* case [16] in late 1886 through 1892, shows a ratio of decision of approximately 2-1 against the legislative power. Among the acts that came up for consideration were "scrip" acts, "screening" acts, weekly payment laws, and the Massachusetts weavers' fines bill.

Two of these cases were decided together in November, 1889, by the Court of Appeals of West Virginia. Both cases involved the state's "scrip" act of 1887: in *State* v. *Goodwill,*[17] the court voided a section of the act prohibiting mining or manufacturing companies from paying wages in other than lawful money; and in *State* v. *Fire Creek Coal and Coke Co.,*[18] the court voided another section which forbade mining or manufacturing companies from selling merchandise to their employees at prices higher than those charged the general public.

One of the grounds of decision stated in the opinion was the alleged partial nature of the legislation. By specifying mining and manufacturing companies, said the court, the act had unjustly cast burdens on some classes of employers but not on others. But more important in the court's view was the very fact of governmental limitation upon the freedom of employer and employee to contract as they saw fit regarding their property or their labor. As Judge Adam C. Snyder speaking for the unanimous court put it in the *Goodwill* case,

No one questions the position that unless the government intervene to protect property and regulate trade, property would cease to exist, and trade would exist only as an engine of fraud; but this does not authorize the government to do for its people what they can

[16] See *supra*, pp. 15–16.   [17] 33 W.Va. 179.   [18] *Ibid.*, p. 188.

do for themselves. The natural law of supply and demand is the best law of trade.[19]

In both cases the court relied upon the *Godcharles* opinion for its principal precedent, quoting it or paraphrasing it, and adding embellishments of its own. Thus, in the *Goodwill* case, Judge Snyder said of the "scrip" act:

It is a species of sumptuary legislation which has been universally condemned, as an attempt to degrade the intelligence, virtue and manhood of the American laborer, and foist upon the people a paternal government of the most objectionable character, because it assumes that the employer is a knave, and the laborer an imbecile.[20]

In the *Fire Creek* case, the court condemned the act as stamping both employer and employee with "the badge of slavery." [21]

A contrary decision was rendered in January, 1890, in the case of *Hancock* v. *Yaden*,[22] where the Supreme Court of Indiana sustained that state's "scrip" act of 1887, forbidding payment of wages in other than lawful money of the United States. In the first half of his opinion Judge Byron K. Elliott for the unanimous court set out a careful enumeration of the many instances where the right to contract had been subject to legislative regulation. "The truth is," said Elliott, "that without law as one of its factors, there is really no such thing as a contract. The law is a silent, but a ruling factor in every contract." [23] The effect of this logic was weakened, however, when the court based its affirmation of the act before it on the surprising ground that the legislature was simply attempting to maintain the standard of value of the medium of payment, which it had the power to do under the *Legal Tender Cases*.[24]

[19] *Ibid.*, p. 184.   [20] *Ibid.*, p. 186.   [21] *Ibid.*, p. 191.
[22] 121 Ind. 366.   [23] *Ibid.*, p. 370.
[24] Roscoe Pound, praising Elliott's opinion, says, "It is unfortunate that the sweeping assertions of *Godcharles* v. *Wigeman* should have been made the model for subsequent cases with this decision at hand in the books" ("Liberty of Contract," *Yale Law Journal*, 18 [May, 1909], 486).

One other case of 1890 involved freedom of contract, the California case of *Ex parte Kuback*,[25] which showed that the Far West was not immune to the new trends of judicial decision. Here, an ordinance of the City of Los Angeles, prescribing an eight-hour day for employees of all companies working on city construction contracts, was declared invalid as "a direct infringement" of the right to make contracts. In its short opinion the California Supreme Court cited neither constitutional provision nor case precedent, contenting itself with a general statement from Cooley on the liberty of pursuing one's calling.[26]

More important was *Commonwealth* v. *Perry*,[27] decided December 1, 1891, by the Massachusetts Supreme Court. The case attracted wide attention mainly because of the dissenting opinion of Oliver Wendell Holmes, already eminent in the legal world for his celebrated *The Common Law*, first published in 1881. *Commonwealth* v. *Perry* involved the Weavers' Fines Bill of 1891, which prohibited any employer from imposing a fine upon an employee engaged at weaving or from making any contract with an employee which provided for the withholding of wages because of imperfect work. Judge Marcus P. Knowlton for the court declared the act unconstitutional as "an interference with the right to make reasonable and proper contracts in conducting a legitimate business." [28] The right to make reasonable contracts, he said, was subsumed under Article I of the Declara-

It was no doubt the odd and excessively narrow grounds of the *Hancock* decision that in part accounted for its failure to attain judicial eminence. On the other hand, the force of the *Godcharles* case, or, better, of the social attitudes underlying it, was also able to overcome the excellent opinion in *Shaffer* v. *Union Mining Co.*, which had sustained a Maryland "scrip" act back in 1880 (see *supra*, ch. i, n. 43).

[25] 85 Cal. 274.

[26] *Ibid.*, p. 276. The ordinance also prohibited the employment of Chinese labor, but this was only incidentally referred to in the court's opinion. The conservative *Chicago Legal Advisor* commended the California decision highly (11 [June 10, 1890], 188).

[27] 155 Mass. 117.　　　　[28] *Ibid.*, p. 122.

tion of Rights in the Constitution of Massachusetts which listed among the "natural, inalienable" rights of man the right of "acquiring, possessing, and protecting property."

Holmes's dissent covered a number of points, including two technical grounds on which he believed the act could have been sustained. But he devoted most of his comparatively brief opinion to the fundamental question of legislative discretion. The act did not interfere with the rights of property, he said, "any more than the laws against usury and gaming." And even if it could be assumed that the State Constitution forbade generally the making of unreasonable laws (on the theory that it granted the right to make reasonable laws), and that "speaking as a political economist" he might agree in condemning the law as unreasonable, the law still ought not to be overturned, he maintained, unless "an honest difference of opinion was impossible, or pretty nearly so." Holmes concluded:

I suppose that this act was passed because the operatives, or some of them, thought that they were often cheated out of a part of their wages under a false pretence that the work done by them was imperfect, and persuaded the Legislature that their view was true. If their view was true, I cannot doubt that the Legislature had the right to deprive the employers of an honest tool which they were using for a dishonest purpose, and I cannot pronounce the legislation void, as based on a false assumption, since I know nothing about the matter one way or the other.[29]

Holmes's dissent gave added prestige to the developing progressive opposition to freedom of contract and helped crystallize the attack upon that doctrine. Comment on these cases had already been offered by Seymour D. Thompson in the March-April, 1890, issue of the *American Law Review*.[30] Reviewing favorably the decision in *Hancock* v. *Yaden*, which, it will be remembered, sustained the Indiana "scrip" act, Thompson had described the abuses of the store-order system and had con-

[29] *Ibid.*, pp. 124-125.   [30] Vol. 24 (March–April, 1890), 328.

cluded: "It is the true office of government to arbitrate between those who must work for their daily bread and those who have the power to oppress them."

Following the weavers' fines case and the Holmes dissent, the volume and intensity of criticism rose sharply. Thompson delivered two censures, one in January, 1892, in an address before the Kansas Bar Association, to be examined shortly in another connection, and the other a few months later in the editorial pages of the *American Law Review*. Noting in the *Review* that laws interfering with freedom of contract between insurers and insured had been held valid in most states, Thompson commented:

But in these cases the insured are respectable people. They are not Hungarian and Italian laborers working in Pennsylvania coal mines for sixty-five cents a day. They are not begging of powerful corporations the poor privilege of being tenants at will, of the right to labor, and hence of the right to live. They do not belong to that species of human nuisance that is asking for charity wherewith to subsist and that gets it, if at all, at the end of a pole. . . .

To talk about freedom of contract between such parties is the veriest sham. It is not even truthful or sincere. No such freedom of contract exists. Every judge knows it; every other man knows it; and it is the duty of judges in framing their decisions to take judicial notice of what everybody knows. . . . Judges who render such decisions are not fit for the offices to which the people have elected them.[31]

Less denunciatory in tone but equally critical was a carefully written article by Herbert H. Darling of Boston in the May, 1892, issue of the *Harvard Law Review*.[32] Directing most of his attention to the case of *Commonwealth* v. *Perry*, Darling saw the crux of the problem turning upon the legitimate extent of

[31] Vol. 26 (May–June, 1892), 404.

[32] "Legislative Control over Contracts of Employment: The Weavers' Fines Bill," *Harvard Law Review*, 6 (May, 1892), 85–97. Darling was a recent graduate of the Harvard Law School.

the police power; [33] and the basic statement of this power as related to property rights had been made by the famous Chief Justice Lemuel Shaw of the Massachusetts Supreme Court in *Commonwealth* v. *Alger:* "Rights of property, like all other social and conventional rights, are subject to such limitations in their enjoyment as shall prevent them from becoming injurious, and to such reasonable restraints and regulations established by law as the Legislature under the governing and controlling power vested in them by the Constitution may think necessary and expedient." [34]

With this as his frame of reference, Darling proceeded to an illuminating analysis of the social background of the now-defunct Weavers' Fines Bill:

On the one hand were the manufacturers; on the other, their employees,—the weavers. The position of the former was by far the stronger, because they controlled the money supplies upon which the latter depended for existence. The manufacturers had the power to punish their employees by levying fines, or, what is the same thing, by withholding wages. This power was of a nature to permit great abuse. It is true that imperfect work was often returned by the weavers. . . . Here there was a standing quarrel to be settled. It seemed necessary to place the two classes on a more equal footing. For this purpose the police power of the State was invoked.[35]

Turning to the principal cases used as precedents by the Massachusetts court, *Godcharles* v. *Wigeman* and *State* v. *Goodwill,* Darling agreed that they were pertinent, but he held them liable to the same general defect—of improperly evaluating the police power. "In every case," he asserted, ". . . conflicts between certain classes in the community seemed dangerous to the

[33] In emphasizing the police power, Darling was seeking a more legalistic defense of the act than that offered by the Holmes dissent. Holmes had not been concerned to rest the act upon the police power or any other power, apparently on the broader assumption that so long as not specifically prohibited or absurd on its face, the act could not be unconstitutional.

[34] *Ibid.,* p. 88, quoting 7 Cushing 85.   [35] *Ibid.,* pp. 91–92.

State; the public interest was that private interests should be reconciled." Of fundamental importance in all these cases, Darling held, was the broader question of legislative discretion:

An ostensible exercise of the [police] power which in reality cannot be sustained *from any point of view* as legitimately within that power is undoubtedly invalid; but if there is any doubt, however slight, that doubt must be resolved in favor of the Legislature. . . . That the Statute assumes that the employer is at times dishonest, and the employee at times an imbecile, is a political question to be discussed in the Legislature.[36]

Here indeed was a clear exposition of the theory of judicial self-restraint in a politically responsible government. And it is just possible that Darling's article, together with Thompson's criticisms, may have had some effect; for, of the five cases involving freedom of contract decided in the second half of 1892, only three were unfavorable to the legislation, and two of these were by the Supreme Court of Illinois, which had been the pathfinder in making use of freedom of contract.

In *Frorer* v. *People*,[37] the Illinois court struck down as "class legislation" and contrary to freedom of contract an act prohibiting mining or manufacturing companies from keeping "truck stores" or otherwise paying wages in goods or merchandise; it was "not admissible," said the court, "to arbitrarily brand, by statute, one class . . . as too unscrupulous, and the other class as too imbecile or timid or weak, to exercise that freedom in contracting which is allowed to all others." [38] A similar fate on almost identical grounds met Illinois' coal "screening" act in *Ramsey* v. *People*.[39] The third of the unfavorable decisions was a striking opinion by the Court of Appeals of Texas invalidating a Texas law requiring railroads to pay all back wages within eight days after termination of employment.[40] Besides the customary finding of class legislation and infringement of freedom of

[36] *Ibid.*, p. 96 (italics in source).   [37] 141 Ill. 171.
[38] *Ibid.*, pp. 186–187.   [39] 142 Ill. 380.
[40] *San Antonio Ry. Co.* v. *Wilson*, 19 S.W. 910.

contract, Judge E. J. Simkins' opinion for the court warned that such legislation could lead "by an easy gradation" to government ownership of railways. Also appearing in the opinion was this interesting piece of social philosophy:

The employer and employee must always deal at arm's length. Their interest in making the contract is always adverse. Unquestionably, so long as men must earn a living for their families and themselves by labor, there must be, as there always has been, oppression of the working classes; yet the law has never undertaken, except in a limited extent and upon principles of pure justice, to lift them above the plane of equality, upon which all should stand alike before the law.[41]

Opposing these cases were the decisions in *State* v. *Brown & Sharp Mfg. Co.*[42] and *State* v. *Peel Splint Coal Co.*[43] In the former case, the Supreme Court of Rhode Island sustained a weekly payment law for corporations as a legitimate exercise of the reserved power of the state to amend or repeal corporate charters. The court also pointed out that the power of corporations, which consisted of large masses of aggregated capital made possible by favorable laws of the state, might be too strong vis-à-vis the individual employees, "frequently being dependent upon their current wages for their daily bread," and that, therefore, it was not improper for the legislature to attempt to minimize the power of corporations "to drive hard bargains with their employees." [44]

In the *Peel Splint* case the West Virginia Court of Appeals upheld in the same decision a "scrip" act and a "screening" act. Judge Daniel B. Lucas rendered a unanimous opinion for the court, sustaining the acts as applied to corporations on the

[41] *Ibid.*, p. 912. The court cited Tiedeman's *Limitations of Police Power* (p. 571) for this passage; but the court's language is more imperative, more absolutist.

[42] 18 R.I. 16.   [43] 36 W.Va. 802.

[44] 18 R.I. 33, 35. Note the similarity between the court's language and Thompson's statement, *supra*, that it was "the true office of government to arbitrate between those who must work for their daily bread and those who have the power to oppress them."

ground that the great power of corporations and their special privileges warranted legislative regulation in the interests of "public tranquillity" and the protection of laborers "against all fraudulent or suspicious devices." In a strong passage the court reminded the defendant company that the state was frequently called upon to protect the rights of property and to intervene in labor troubles; "and it can not be possible," continued Judge Lucas, "that the same police power may not be invoked to protect the laborer from being made the victim of the compulsory power of that artificial combination of capital, which special State legislation has originated and rendered possible." [45]

These decisions of 1892 hardly indicated any major turning of the tide, and progressive dissatisfaction at the close of the year was much in evidence. The progressive view was made clear by Conrad Reno, a well-known Boston lawyer, in the November-December issue of the *American Law Review*.[46] Devoting most of his article to a plea for a system of state arbitration boards which would be empowered, in cases submitted to it by either side, to set minimum wages and maximum hours enforceable at law, Reno gave considerable attention to the doctrine of freedom of contract as a supposed objection to his plan.

At the outset he flatly denied that there was any clause in any constitution which expressly and clearly secured freedom of contract. All kinds of statutes had been promulgated and enforced against individuals and corporations impairing this alleged freedom, and this was especially true, he maintained, where the matter was one of public policy. Noting that in the West Virginia case of *State* v. *Goodwill*, Judge Snyder's opinion had contained the assertions that the government was not authorized to do for its people what they could do for themselves and that

[45] 36 W.Va. 820. On a rehearing, called for reasons not stated, the court split, 2-2, and the acts were sustained by a divided court.

[46] "Arbitration and the Wage Contract," *American Law Review*, 26 (Nov.–Dec., 1892), 837–856. Reno was active in the industrial arbitration and utilities regulation movements in Massachusetts in the 1890's and 1900's, authoring several books and legislative statutes.

"the natural law of supply and demand is the best law of trade," [47] Reno posed this pointed question:

With all due respect to this learned tribunal . . . who shall determine questions of public necessity under our form of government, the legislature or the courts? These cases are based upon grounds of public policy and upon the views of a certain school of political economy. . . . Progress along economic lines must cease, if the courts have the power to seize upon vague clauses in the constitution to perpetuate the economic views of the past, and to fasten them upon the present as matters of constitutional law, of which the courts are the final judge.[48]

The social implications of the new trends in judicial review had been plainly discerned. Thirteen years before Holmes's famous dissent in the *Lochner* case (1905),[49] it was already evident that laissez-faire economics was far along the road to incorporation into American constitutional law.

Thus far, we have been considering progressive reactions to the *Chicago, Milwaukee* case and to the freedom-of-contract decisions. For a broader, more comprehensive examination of the attitudes and opinions of legal progressivism, we may turn to the 1892 meeting of the Kansas State Bar Association, where Seymour D. Thompson, well known in the Middle West as a long-time St. Louis judge as well as a leading law editor, delivered the Annual Address.[50] Entitling his speech "Abuses of

---

[47] 33 W.Va. 179, at 184.   [48] *Op. cit.*, p. 849.

[49] *Lochner* v. *New York*, 198 U.S. 45, was the first and perhaps most widely publicized case where the United States Supreme Court invalidated social legislation because contrary to freedom of contract. "The case was decided," said Holmes in his classic dissent, "upon an economic theory which a large part of the country does not entertain. . . . The Fourteenth Amendment does not enact Mr. Herbert Spencer's *Social Statics*."

[50] In *Ninth Annual Meeting of the Bar Association of the State of Kansas* (1892), pp. 24–47. Thompson had expressed many of the ideas of this address in his two bar association speeches of 1890 and 1891 (see n. 14 *supra*), but in more tentative form.

Corporate Privileges," Judge Thompson undertook a general review of the problems of a corporation-dominated society searching for some point of leverage upon concentrated capital and finding itself frustrated by judicial interposition. The address was a remarkable one: for its clarity of constitutional and legal analysis, for its forthright stand in behalf of popular government, for its wide range of humane sympathies, and, surprisingly, for its singularly prescient insights into the ultimate course of twentieth-century reformism.

Judge Thompson's opening sentence at once posed the problem: "whether the corporation is to rule the State or the State the corporation." Corporations had multiplied everywhere, securing special privileges from subservient legislatures and enjoying thereafter the judicial stamp of immortality. Although corporations were "absolute necessities" for a progressive industrial life, they had abused their privileges and pursued a policy of monopolistic combination; aided "by the Chinese Wall of a protective tariff," corporate monopoly had then succeeded in crushing competition in many lines, and in dictating price to the general public.[51] "At every step in this baleful progress," he charged, corporations had the aid and comfort of that branch of the national government "totally out of touch with the people in its sympathies—the Federal judiciary." Individual justices had "struggled for popular right," but the advance of "usurpation" had been glacierlike:

Jurisdiction has been seized on casuistic pretenses; the right of trial by jury has been set aside in vast reaches of country; the courts have gone into the business of the common carrier; the by-laws of corporations have overtopped in the judicial estimation the legislation

[51] For other expressions of concern in this period over the growing power of consolidated capital, see two well-written papers read at the 1891 meeting of the Tennessee Bar Association: Horace H. Lurton (later Supreme Court Justice), "Is the Trust Dangerous?," *Proceedings of the Tenth Annual Meeting of the Bar Association of Tennessee* (1891), pp. 144–169; John A. Pitts, "State Regulation of Railroads," in *ibid.*, pp. 214–242.

of States which were once called sovereign; and constitutional ordinances earned on the field of battle and intended as charters of human liberty, have been turned into the shield of incorporated monopoly.[52]

Thompson then traced in detail the course of this alleged usurpation by the federal judiciary. An incisive critique of the celebrated *Dartmouth College* case and the resultant corporate immunity to much of state regulation was followed by the reminder that, although eventually a *de facto* repeal of that decision had been effected by new state constitutions, general incorporation laws, and court modifications, the process had consumed "a long reach of time and great labor, worry, and expense." But all this had apparently been of little avail, he continued, for the Fourteenth Amendment was proving an even more efficient guardian of corporate privilege. Thompson was willing to grant Roscoe Conkling's argument that "they builded better than they knew," [53] and that there was nothing inherently improper about including corporations along with natural persons under the protection of due process of law. "But that was not the point," he maintained, in an exceptionally lucid analysis:

There was nothing new in this Amendment, except that it turned a provision which had always existed in Magna Charta, and which was to be found in some form of expression or other in the constitution of every State of the Union, into a Federal prohibition against the several States. . . . But surely the new amendment did not intend to make that due process of law which had never been due process of law before.

[52] Thompson, *op. cit.*, p. 25.

[53] This was Conkling's phrase in his argument to the Supreme Court in 1882 urging the Court to construe the word "person" in the Fourteenth Amendment to embrace corporations as well as natural persons. For the latest—and apparently definitive—word on this question, see Howard J. Graham's " 'Builded Better than They Knew' Part I: The Framers, the Railroads and the Fourteenth Amendment," *University of Pittsburgh Law Review* 17 (Summer, 1956), 537–584.

As a typical instance of the results of this new due process, Thompson cited the *Chicago, Milwaukee* case of 1890 and warned that the determination of the reasonableness of rate regulation would be henceforth not merely a judicial question but a *"Federal judicial question."* [54] Such would be the inevitable result of a previous usurpation, "more flagrant than . . . any" —the judicial construction of the term "citizen" as used in Article III, Section 2, of the Constitution to mean also "corporation," and thereby gaining for the federal courts jurisdiction in cases involving violations of state laws by corporations organized in other states.[55]

As a consequence of these new powers of the Supreme Court, Thompson predicted, all state legislation under the police power would have to be submitted "to the revision of the superintending bench of appointive lawyers at Washington," whose rule of revision by the judicial process of "inclusion and exclusion" [56] amounted to "mere discretion." "In view of these facts," asked Judge Thompson, "is it not time to pause and inquire whether we have not reached the danger-line, and whether, in fact, we are really a self-governing people?" [57]

But Thompson did not leave the matter on this negative note. This Missourian defender of the rights of states was now ready to advocate that the people abandon attempts at corporate regulation through state legislation and direct their energies instead to the national government. State legislation could no longer cope with great corporations, he explained, while, on the other

[54] *Op. cit.*, p. 39 (italics in source).

[55] Art. III, Sec. 2, provides, among other things, that the federal judicial power shall extend to all cases between a state and citizens of another state.

[56] Thompson was referring here to *Davidson* v. *New Orleans*, 96 U.S. 97 (1878), where Justice Miller had stated that the extent of the police power as subject to the Fourteenth Amendment could only be ascertained by applying to each case the process of "inclusion and exclusion."

[57] *Op. cit.*, p. 42.

hand, it was unfair to subject corporations doing extensive interstate business to differing state regulations.

Certain prerequisites were essential, however. First, the Senate,
"little better than a collection of the lawyers and the agents of
corporations," would have to become a popularly elected body,
something "sure to happen in the near future." Then, the federal
government should be prepared to exercise "plenary power over
the subject of commerce—not merely interstate commerce, but
over the whole subject of commerce. This should include the
capacity to give us a general commercial code, and to regulate
corporations in the interests of the people by uniform laws." [58]

Thompson's best eloquence was still to come. Turning to the
corporation's "relations with the wage-worker," he reviewed
several of the recent freedom-of-contract cases, and exclaimed:
"What mockery to talk about the freedom of contract where
only *one* of the contracting parties is free! What mockery to
talk about the freedom of contract as between the corporation
which has everything and a day laborer who has nothing!" [59]

Nor would Thompson agree that labor was but another commodity, subject to the law of supply and demand:

I grant that such is the general and often the inexorable law: but
I protest that it is within the power of human institutions to mitigate
its rigor. I say again, that if human government has any just office
to perform, it is to arbitrate between the man who has everything
and the man who has nothing; between the man who is up and the
man who is down; between the man who is on top and the man who
is beneath.[60]

---

[58] *Ibid.*, p. 43. Thompson had clearly anticipated here an important
phase of the New Nationalism of Theodore Roosevelt in 1912, and its
partial implementation in the New Deal of Franklin D. Roosevelt. One
result of the constitutional revolution of the late 1930's was the virtual
acceptance by the Supreme Court of this concept of a nationalized commerce (*Wickard* v. *Filburn*, 317 U.S. 111 [1942]). Much water would
flow under the judicial bridge before then, however.

[59] *Op. cit.*, p. 45 (italics in source).   [60] *Ibid.*, p. 46.

The corporation manager, Thompson asserted, had less motive to treat his laborers properly than the owner of a horse or the late slaveowner, both of whom had at least a chattel value in their property. But the worn-out wage earner could easily be replaced by the throngs of "hungry paupers" always crowding forward.

Thompson then noted that the Roman Pontiff too had been touched by "the cry of the laboring man," [61] and he closed his address with this moving plea:

Surely the dignity of manhood is not to be thrown into the economic scale with the beasts of burden, or with inert chattels. . . . Surely the State can find some way, without too much suppressing human liberty, to see to it that every man who is able and willing to work shall get enough to support a family and a house in frugal economy. I admit the magnitude of the problem; I do not countenance visionary crusades; but the evil is not so overwhelming as to be without remedy. I pray you to find it.[62]

With this speech by Seymour D. Thompson, delivered in January, 1892, on the very eve of the period of intensified social unrest, the progressive position on the role of the judiciary in regard to popular reform had been clearly defined. Concentrated capital, while left sufficiently free for the performance of its economic functions, must be made subservient to the needs of the general welfare. And if American courts, far too often the friends of corporate interests, persisted in their interference with the legislative will, then popular government itself would become an empty façade, devoid of substance or vitality.

Although probably a very decided minority within the profession, the legal progressives in early 1892 were of considerable influence, listened-to and respected.[63] More important, they

---

[61] The famous encyclical *Rerum Novarum* of Leo XIII, issued 1891.

[62] *Op. cit.*, p. 47.

[63] Thompson had this address reprinted in the *American Law Review* and, in a note appended thereto, admitted that the orally delivered ad-

could often count on the support of moderate conservatives. As the tension of the times rose steadily, however, these patterns of intraprofessional opinion would be subject to significant realignment.

---

dress had "received a good deal of adverse criticism." The note also said this: "But he [Thompson] takes pleasure in stating that he met among the members of the Kansas Bar Association several learned gentlemen that have both the ability and the courage to speak soundly and sensibly in behalf of the scattered, isolated, ignorant and helpless masses, in their struggle for self-government and for the right to exist, against concentrated money and power. It ought to be added that the more radical portions of this address provoked but faint applause" (Vol. 26 [March–April, 1892], 243). A selection of interesting letters to the editor, commenting pro and con on Thompson's address, may be found in the July-August issue of the *Review* (26:579–583).

IV

The Hardening of

Conservative Attitudes

ON the fourth of February, 1890, the one hundredth anniversary of the United States Supreme Court was celebrated in New York City's Metropolitan Opera House.[1] In keeping with the august status the Court had attained in the American system of government, and perhaps in expectation of an even greater role for the Court in the coming decades, the ceremonials were conducted in an atmosphere of high solemnity. Portraits of the Chief Justices on easels, a vast arch draped with flags, and a large facsimile of the Seal of the Court were among the decorations on stage. The Honorable Grover Cleveland, former President of the United States and Chairman of the Executive Committee in charge of the affair, was in the presiding chair. Arrayed beside

[1] The source for this material is Hampton L. Carson, *The Supreme Court of the United States: Its History; and Its Centennial Celebration* (Philadelphia, 1891), a semiofficial volume prepared under the direction of the Judiciary Centennial Committee. The idea for a celebration was suggested by President Harrison in his Inaugural Address of March 4, 1889. The New York State Bar Association undertook the staging of the affair and formed a committee of arrangements, including former President Cleveland and Vice-President Levi P. Morton.

and behind him on the platform, according to prearranged order, was an assemblage of eminent dignitaries: [2] the Justices of the Supreme Court of the United States; the four scheduled orators of the day; members of the New York Court of Appeals; the Judges of the United States Circuit and District Courts; the Judges of the highest appellate court of each state; members of the organizing committees of the New York State Bar Association; leaders of the American Bar Association; and special guests.

Of the four speeches delivered that day by leaders of the bar upon various aspects of the history of the Supreme Court, the last, by Edward J. Phelps of Vermont, a former president of the American Bar Association,[3] was the most directly oriented to the problems of legal conservatism. Phelps' oration was entitled "The Supreme Court and the Sovereignty of the People," and it was on the basis of his definition of the latter term that Phelps developed his point of view:

The sovereignty of the people is not the arbitrary power or blind caprice of the multitude, any more than of an aristocracy or a despot. It is not the right of any class, small or great, high or low, to wrong or oppress another. It is not a struggle between classes at all. It is simply the recognition of the natural and equal rights of men as the basis of a government formed for their protection by its people, and regulated by law.[4]

Government had as its main function then, continued Phelps, the protection of the rights of the individual. Monarchs and oligarchies, when invested with governmental power, had abused

[2] The President and the Cabinet, invited to attend, did not do so because of the death of Secretary of the Navy Benjamin F. Tracy (*ibid.*, p. 587).

[3] Phelps was one of the leaders of the New England bar. Besides his presidency of the American Bar Association in 1883–1884, he was the first president of the Vermont Bar Association (1880) and Kent Professor of Law at Yale from 1882 till his death in 1900. An active Democrat and Ambassador to England, 1885–1889, Phelps was considered for the Chief Justiceship in 1888.

[4] *Ibid.*, p. 690.

their authority and trampled on the individual, and the parliamentary system had been the outcome. But the fathers of the country, having learned that "even representative government cannot always be depended upon by those it represents . . . [had] . . . placed the protection of personal rights beyond the reach of the popular will, and found in an independent judiciary the true and final custodian of the liberty of the subject."

Thus far, the Supreme Court had been mainly concerned with administering the relations between states and nation. "But new attacks upon individual rights," warned Phelps, "in many forms and under many pretexts, are beginning to be heard of, and are to be looked for in an increasing measure. The accursed warfare of classes is the danger that appears chiefly to threaten the future." And the Court would soon find itself under the necessity of deciding repeated conflicts "involving the protection of property, of contracts, of personal rights." Phelps was sure, however, that the Court would be "equal to the emergencies that are to come." [5]

Assurance that at least one Justice of the Court was in sympathy with the vigorous judicial conservatism declared essential by Phelps was offered by Justice Stephen J. Field, who, as senior Justice, responded on behalf of the Court to the several orations. After discussing generally the nature of the judicial power in America, Justice Field stated his opinion on the new responsibilities of the Court:

As population and wealth increase—as the inequalities in the conditions of men become more and more marked and disturbing—as the enormous aggregations of wealth possessed by some corporations excites uneasiness lest their power should become dominating in the legislation of the country, and thus encroach upon the rights or crush out the business of individuals of small means—as population in some quarters presses upon the means of subsistence, and angry menaces against order find vent in loud denunciations—it becomes more and more the imperative duty of the Court to enforce

[5] *Ibid.*, p. 693.

with a firm hand every guarantee of the Constitution. . . . It should never be forgotten that protection to property and to persons cannot be separated. . . . Protection to the one goes with protection to the other; and there can be neither prosperity nor progress where either is uncertain.[6]

Stephen J. Field's policy for the years of crisis was clear. The discontents of restless majorities, the possible justifications for their protests notwithstanding, would have to be everywhere restrained by the judiciary, in the interests of social order and the rights of property.

Less than two months later, almost as if in specific response to these pronouncements of judicial conservatism, came the decision in the *Chicago, Milwaukee* case, with its holding that the reasonableness of rate regulation was ultimately a judicial question. Laissez-faire conservatism was not reassured, however, especially in view of rising social unrest and political agitation;[7] and a survey of this class of conservative opinion in the years 1890 and 1891 [8] shows a continuing pessimism among both moderates and extremists, ranging from a kind of generalized un-

---

[6] *Ibid.*, p. 717.

[7] A renewed campaign in the labor movement for the eight-hour day, the emergence of the Farmers' Alliances as activist protest organizations, and a wave of state and federal regulatory legislation were the principal political developments. In the elections of 1890 the Alliances gained control of a dozen state legislatures and elected some fifty Congressmen and four Senators (John D. Hicks, *The Populist Revolt* [Minneapolis, 1931], pp. 178–181). For the legislation of 1890 and 1891, see the surveys by William B. Shaw in the *Quarterly Journal of Economics*, 5 (April, 1891), 385–396, and 6 (Jan., 1892), 227–242; and the article by Richard T. Ely and L. S. Merriam, "Report on Social Legislation in the United States for 1889 and 1890," *Economic Review*, 1 (April, 1891), 245–256. Edward Bellamy's utopian socialist novel, *Looking Backward*, was published in 1888, immediately attained wide popularity, and was followed by the organization of hundreds of Bellamite "Nationalist" clubs.

[8] In 1888 and 1889 the sources of legal opinion show a generally equal balance between the pessimism of laissez-faire conservatives and the confidence of traditional conservatives; in 1890 and 1891, however, laissez-faire pessimism clearly predominates.

easiness over the course of social change to a professed belief that even the judiciary could no longer protect adequately the rights of property.

The frame of reference underlying this pessimism was made evident in the address of William M. Ramsay, of Cincinnati, speaking to the 1890 meeting of the West Virginia Bar Association on the topic, "The Future of the Legal Profession." [9] Elaborating upon the problems confronting the lawyer in his capacity as "statesman" and molder of "right judgment," Ramsay thought that the biggest problem of the day stemmed from the drive toward the organization of capital into vast industrial aggregations and the consequent attack upon these as dangerous monopolies inimical to the general welfare. In contrast, others believed that such organizations, even if not ultimately beneficial, could not be injurious enough to warrant court or legislative interference with the right to contract. Ramsay then stated where he stood on this question:

The right to contract and be contracted with . . . is sacred, and lies at the very foundation of the social state. . . . Shall we say that seventy millions of people are in danger of "monopoly" because a handful of men, or a dozen corporate bodies unite to refine sugar or oil, or to make whiskey, or furniture, or any other commodity, while all others are equally at liberty to engage in precisely the same pursuit? . . . I believe in freedom of contract and of action, everywhere in the industrial world, as fully as in freedom of thought and speech touching all questions as to which the opinions of men are divided.[10]

The attempts at control over these supposed monopolistic organizations, Ramsay continued, constituted only one phase of

[9] In most of the law libraries of the country, the first part of this address will be found bound in with the *Report of the Thirteenth Annual Meeting of the West Virginia Bar Association* (1899) at pp. 75–80, with the remainder of the address bound in with the *Report of the Proceedings of the Fourth Annual Meeting* (1890) at pp. 81–87.

[10] *Report of the Proceedings of the Fourth Annual Meeting* (1890), p. 81.

the general problem of the revival of "paternalism" in government, as shown by demands for government ownership of railroads and telegraph lines, laws forbidding purchase and sale of commodities on margin, oleomargarine laws, and provisions for the printing or purchase of school books by the state. Allied with the move toward paternalism was the "so-called conflict between capital and labor, the discontent of large masses of men —men earnestly and laudably seeking an improvement in their condition but not always well advised in the employment of methods to effect that improvement." [11]

Central to the consideration of all these questions, Ramsay concluded, was America's

heterogeneous population—mighty in numbers and rapidly increasing—restless, active, enterprising, generally intelligent and upright, but with a large infusion of ignorance and viciousness rapidly recruited from the worst elements of the population of the old world —with increasing wealth and increasing discontent, with new ideas developing and old ones being revamped . . . and all of this in a land governed by the ideas of the majority. It is a time of real crisis, and we know that events of tremendous significance are impending, peaceful, no doubt, but not less significant for that reason.[12]

Another analysis of contemporary developments affecting the rights of private property, equally doctrinaire with Ramsay's in its concern for unrestricted freedom of contract but somewhat more reconciled to the inevitability of limitations upon that freedom, was presented by Frederick N. Judson, a prominent corporation lawyer in St. Louis, in a paper read to the American

[11] *Ibid.*, p. 83.
[12] *Ibid.*, p. 84. For a similar coupling of immigration and social tension by legal conservatism in 1890, see John H. Doyle, "Presidential Address," *The National Bar Association of the United States—Proceedings of the Third Annual Meeting* (1890), at pp. 38–40. John Higham, *Strangers in the Land* (New Brunswick, 1955), pp. 68–105, shows through a variety of other sources the close connection in the 1890's between widespread nativism and social tension.

Bar Association at its midsummer meeting of 1891.[13] Judson began by pointing out that the social and economic conditions which had developed within the past few years had called into question "as never before, the relation of the fundamental rights of the individual to the police power of the State." To what extent could "legislative discretion as to the requirements of the public welfare" abridge the citizen's liberty or deny him the use of his property "without any process"? Among the "potent factors" sharpening this issue were

the stress of competition in business, the prevailing social unrest, the distinct trend of a certain class of social agitators in the direction of State socialism, the superstition that legislation is a sovereign cure-all for social ills, and last, but by no means least, the competition of reckless politicians for the unthinking vote.[14]

Judson then set up the problem in terms of opposing juristic concepts. On the one side was "liberty of contract [15] . . . at once an incident and an evidence of a relatively highly advanced civilization"; and the historic progression from "fixed status" to "free contract" was a first essential of rational liberty: "Without it, the right of holding property is worthless, freedom from personal restraint is vain and profitless, and life itself is without hope or happiness." On the other side was the police power, by which government enforced "the necessities of the social state,"

[13] "Liberty of Contract under the Police Power," *Report of the Fourteenth Annual Meeting of the American Bar Association* (1891), pp. 231–259. Besides his large corporation practice in the 1890's, Judson was a lecturer at the law school of Washington University and the author of several law treatises. Rather interestingly, Judson later became active in numerous reform movements of the Progressive Era.

[14] *Op. cit.*, p. 232.

[15] Judson, like Ramsay, was using the term "liberty of contract" as the juristic equivalent of economic liberty generally. The course of constitutional law did not move along this line, however, and the term "liberty of contract" (or "freedom of contract") was soon associated almost exclusively with judicial decisions concerning labor laws.

to which even freedom of contract "as all other individual rights, must conform and yield."

Analyzing the various categories of cases where the conflict between the police power and the liberty of contract had been the subject of judicial decision, Judson indicated his disapproval, if ever so faintly, of every one of those cases which had weakened, in his opinion, the special value of individual liberty of contract: among others, these included *Munn* v. *Illinois* and the cases following it (though here Judson saw a brighter trend in the recently decided *Chicago, Milwaukee* case), the liquor and oleomargarine cases, and the cases sustaining antitrust laws and the regulation of insurance contracts. Only in regard to "the so-called labor legislation" had the courts been effective in protecting the liberty of contract against government regulation; and here Judson quoted with approval the strong language of the *Godcharles* case.[16]

Despite these wide-ranging affirmations of his own preferences, Judson foresaw that legislation abridging freedom of contract "must tend greatly to increase in the near future." American labor agitators, he complained, seemed to look upon the denial of free contract as "the great panacea for social ills," although in England the working classes had made great advances through voluntary association. But admittedly, he agreed, no hard and firm line could be drawn: "We cannot but be impressed with the directly opposing conclusions of eminent judges

[16] A somewhat different defense of the freedom-of-contract cases was offered by Darius H. Pingrey, "Limiting the Right to Contract," *Central Law Journal*, 34 (Jan. 29, 1892), 91–96. Pingrey agreed that many of the laws overthrown by these cases were "well-intentioned" in their efforts to "shield the weak from the strong." But once begun, he complained, the process continued, "only to invade one class of rights today and another tomorrow, by which the complicated machinery of industry is thrown out of gear, thus disturbing the normal adjustment of the social fabric." Pingrey finally rebelled against the harsh logic of his own position in the spring of 1895, when freedom of contract reached its extreme, and he vigorously denounced the doctrine (infra, ch. x, n. 3).

in applying the same constitutional guarantee to the same state of facts." He concluded:

We are between the "Mighty Opposites," involving opposing fundamental forces of society. Upon this question . . . whatever our written constitutions may provide, it is inevitable that our juristic conception must harmonize with the subtle yet all-powerful influences of public opinion, and with the conception of individual liberty which that public opinion sustains. If that is suffered to decline, no written constitution can in the end preserve it against the only power which in this age threatens it, the power of majorities.[17]

More direct in its pessimism was an article in the *American Law Review* by Charles C. Marshall of the New York bar, exploring anew the significance of *Munn* v. *Illinois* in the light of recent trends.[18] Marshall's essay came to the conclusion that the principles of the *Munn* case were probably on solid ground, and that, therefore, conservative interests had no alternative but to begin an agitation for a constitutional amendment which would establish once and for all the sanctity of private property. Otherwise, the applications of the *Munn* case might be extended to a large variety of businesses and occupations, with "prodigious consequences" in store. Marshall averred:

It is apparent that against the whim of a temporary majority inflamed with class-prejudice, envy or revenge, the property of no man is safe. And the danger is even greater in an age teeming with shifting theories of social reform and economic science, which seem to have but one common principle—the subjection of private property to governmental control for the good—or alleged good—of the public.[19]

If the first great struggle in American history concerned the question of personal liberty, he continued, the second great

---

[17] *Op. cit.*, p. 259.

[18] "A New Constitutional Amendment," *American Law Review*, 24 (Nov.–Dec., 1890), 908–931.

[19] *Ibid.*, p. 912.

struggle would be over the question of private property. The slavery question, however, "was a struggle between sections. The property question must be a struggle between classes." [20]

The temper of right-wing laissez-faire conservatism in these years is best revealed in the address of Justice David J. Brewer at the June, 1891, commencement exercises of the Yale University Law School. Justice Brewer, who even prior to his Supreme Court appointment in 1889 had been known as one of the most dedicated defenders of the rights of private property, would soon be equally famous for his frank discussions of public issues —both off and on the bench.[21] Entitling this Yale address, "Protection to Private Property from Public Attack," [22] Justice Brewer made his central thesis clear at once:

From the time in earliest records, when Eve took loving possession of even the forbidden apple, the idea of property and the sacredness of the right of its possession has never departed from the race. Whatever dreams may exist of an ideal human nature . . . actual human experience, from the dawn of history to the present hour, declares that the love of acquirement, mingled with the joy of possession, is the real stimulus to human activity. When, among the affirmatives of the Declaration of Independence, it is asserted that the pursuit of happiness is one of the unalienable rights, it is meant that the acquisition, possession and enjoyment of property are matters which human

[20] *Ibid.*, p. 931.

[21] An able study of Brewer's moral philosophy and legal opinions is Lynford A. Lardner's unpublished doctoral dissertation, *The Constitutional Doctrines of Justice David Josiah Brewer* (Princeton, 1938). The manuscript contains a listing of Brewer's out-of-court speeches and writings. No full-length biography of Brewer has appeared in print, however, partly no doubt because of the attention centered on his more colorful uncle, Stephen J. Field. But Brewer's importance was considerable, perhaps in a sense equal to that of Field, for in the critical decade of the 1890's Brewer became the foremost proselytizer of the doctrines of the new judicialism at a time when Field, a very old man by then, had little direct influence.

[22] Substantial excerpts of this address were reprinted in the *New Englander*, 55 (Aug., 1891), 97–110, and in the weekly *Railway and Corporation Law Journal*, 10 (Oct. 10, 1891), 281–283.

government cannot forbid and which it cannot destroy; that, except in punishment for crime, no man's property, nor any value thereof, can be taken from him without just compensation.[23]

property of Labor-production

From this singularly materialistic exposition of the great Declaration, Justice Brewer moved readily to the admonition that popular governments had the special obligation of preserving intact the rights of property. But, continued the Justice, the contrary had been occurring in recent times, as private property was steadily subjected to a variety of governmental attacks, of which the most dangerous was through the police power, a power from its very nature "undefined and perhaps undefinable":

It [the police power] is the refuge of timid judges to escape the obligations of denouncing a wrong, in a case in which some supposed general and public good is the object of legislation. . . . I am here to say to you, in no spirit of obnoxious or unpleasant criticism upon the decision of any tribunal or judge, that the demands of absolute and eternal justice forbid that any private property, legally acquired and legally held, should be spoliated or destroyed in the interests of public health, morals or welfare without compensation.[24]

extreme

Having thus come near to impugning the integrity of those judges who had refused to interfere with the legislative discretion in certain recent cases,[25] Justice Brewer turned to the case of *Munn* v. *Illinois.* The central issue raised by that decision, he said, was whether public regulation of common carriers and warehousemen could so reduce the charges of the owner that revenue would be insufficient to equal operating expenses, thus compelling an accumulation of debts and loss of the property. This question had been finally answered, continued Brewer, in the *Chicago, Milwaukee* case, which would "ever remain a strong and unconquerable fortress in the long struggle between

[23] *Ibid.,* p. 281.   [24] *Ibid.*
[25] Presumably *Mugler* v. *Kansas* and *Powell* v. *Pennsylvania.*

individual rights and the public good. I rejoice to have been permitted to put one stone into that fortress." [26]

After repeating the ringing stand of his opening statement upon the necessity for unqualified protection to private property, Justice Brewer closed his address on an urgent note:

To accomplish this . . . we must recast some of our judicial decisions; and if that be not possible we must re-write into our constitution the affirmations of the Declaration of Independence, in language so clear and peremptory that no judge can doubt or hesitate, and no man, not even a legislator, misunderstand.[27]

Justice Brewer for the ultraconservatives, like Thompson for the progressives, had become pre-eminently their most articulate spokesman. Like Thompson, who had sounded a loud alarm against judicial interposition when it was just getting under way, Brewer from the other side was demanding the utmost vigilance in behalf of private property although the social crisis of the 1890's was still in its early stages. And again, as Thompson had castigated in the most vehement language the judges who showed tendencies toward intervention, so Brewer, his delicate position as Supreme Court Justice notwithstanding, had condemned in no uncertain terms the judges who felt bound by self-restraint. The polarization of the two extremes was complete.

The year 1892 saw a sequence of events which were to have decisive effects upon the movement of conservative opinion. Early in the year, on February 29, the United States Supreme Court by a division of 6-3 affirmed the principles of *Munn* v. *Illinois* in the important case of *Budd* v. *New York*.[28] The *Budd* case was significant, not so much for any contribution to constitutional law but for its relation to rapidly crystallizing legal attitudes. The case involved a New York act of 1888, which imposed regulations, including schedules of maximum prices,

[26] *Railway and Corporation Law Journal, op. cit.,* p. 282.
[27] *Ibid.,* p. 283.   [28] 143 U.S. 517.

upon warehouses, elevators, and shipping facilities engaged in the transportation of grain along the route of the Erie Canal and the Hudson River to the Port of New York. Constitutionally, the case should have been a routine one, since it was clearly within the pattern of *Munn* v. *Illinois*, which also involved the regulation of grain elevators. Corporation attorneys and laissez-faire conservatives, however, must have hoped that the changing social atmosphere, the new personnel on the Court, and the ruling of the *Chicago, Milwaukee* case would all combine to effect a further narrowing at least, if not a direct overturn, of the *Munn* case. At any rate the *Budd* case attracted much attention as it went through the New York Court of Appeals and the United States Supreme Court.

In October, 1889, the New York court had affirmed the act with a lengthy opinion, standing on the strength of the *Munn* decision and its subsequent approval in a variety of cases. But what made the New York decision notable was the remarkable dissenting opinion of Judge Rufus W. Peckham, who in a few years (1895) would be stepped up to the United States Supreme Court.[29] Peckham's opinion, which simply ignored the authority of *Munn* v. *Illinois*, deserves some quotation:

> To uphold legislation of this character is to provide the most frequent opportunity for arraying class against class; and, in addition to the ordinary competition that exists throughout all industries, a new competition will be introduced, that of competition for the possession of the government. . . .
> In my opinion the court should not strain after holding such species of legislation constitutional. It is so plain an effort to interfere with what seems to me the most sacred rights of property and the individual liberty of contract that no special intendment in its favor should be indulged in. . . .
> The legislation under consideration is not only vicious in its nature, communistic in its tendency, and in my belief, wholly ineffi-

[29] It was Justice Peckham who wrote the Court's opinion in the famous *Lochner* case of 1905 (198 U.S. 45).

cient to permanently attain the result aimed at, but, for the reasons already given, it is an illegal effort to interfere with the lawful privilege of the individual to seek and obtain such compensation as he can for the use of his own property.[30]

With the *Budd* case having already evoked in the New York court so nonjudicially worded a dissent, it was not perhaps unexpected that the further affirmation of the statute by the United States Supreme Court on the basis of the *Munn* principles should see Justice Brewer writing a remarkable dissent of his own. Concurred in by Justices Field and Brown, Brewer's dissent declared the *Munn* case "radically unsound." Only a "legal monopoly" could be subject to legislative control as to price, because anyone could break a "monopoly of fact," and so there was "no necessity for legislative interference." Justice Brewer then made this statement:

The paternal theory of government is to me odious. The utmost liberty to the individual, and the fullest possible protection to him and his property is both the limitation and duty of government. If it may regulate the price of one service, which is not a public service, or the compensation for the use of one kind of property, which is not devoted to a public use, why may it not with equal reason regulate the price of all service, and the compensation to be paid for the use of all property? And if so, "Looking Backward" is nearer than a dream.[31]

The gloomy forebodings of Brewer's opinion may have seemed ominously prophetic to legal conservatives, as they ob-

[30] 117 N.Y. 68–69, 71.

[31] 143 U.S. 551. Seymour D. Thompson paid his respects thus to Brewer's dissent: "His opinion is more rhetorical than judicial, and, like some of his associates, and many of his predecessors, he is evidently laboring under the hallucination that he is a legislator instead of being merely a judge. He indulges in such sentences as this: 'The paternal theory of government is to me odious.' What if it is? He was not put there to decide constitutional questions according to his whims, or according to what was or was not odious to him personally" (*American Law Review*, 26 [Sept.–Oct., 1892], 766).

served the course of social protest in 1892. In that year the newly founded Populist party, catalyzing the rising agrarian unrest, prepared to challenge the major parties in the fall elections. The platform of the party, proclaimed at its Omaha Convention on July 4, 1892, as the "Farmer's Declaration of Independence," served as a rallying point for much of the protest and reformist movement. In addition to such standard agrarian demands as the free coinage of silver and credit inflation, the platform also demanded government ownership of railroads, telegraph, and telephone, a graduated income tax, and the extension of the eight-hour day. The adoption of the platform was followed by a wild demonstration of six thousand people, described by one reporter as "one of the most exciting scenes ever witnessed in a political convention." [32]

Then, on July 6, just two days after the "Omaha Declaration," the widespread labor unrest of the early 1890's erupted violently at the Carnegie steel works in Homestead, Pennsylvania, when strikers of the Amalgmated Association of Iron and Steel Workers of America fought a pitched battle with three hundred Pinkerton guards.[33] Although public reaction to this event turned against labor far less than after the Haymarket riot of 1886 (the Carnegie strikers in 1892 receiving a great deal of sympathy from segments of the public), most conservative opinion, especially in the legal profession, was shocked and dismayed by the bitterness of the Homestead strike and the seeming indifference to law and order on the part of the strikers.[34]

[32] Quoted in George H. Knoles, *The Presidential Campaign and Election of 1892* (Palo Alto, 1942), p. 105. Knoles points out that the nomination for President of the veteran third-party candidate, General James B. Weaver, took the edge off some of the conservative fears.

[33] More workers were on strike in 1890 than any previous year in American history. Commons, *History of Labor in the United States*, II, 495-499, describes the major outbreaks. For the Homestead strike and its aftermath, see Henry David's essay, "Upheaval at Homestead," in Daniel Aaron, ed., *America in Crisis* (New York, 1952), pp. 133-170.

[34] *American Law Register*, n.s., 31 (Oct., 1892), 691-700; *Albany Law Journal*, 46 (July 30, 1892), 81-82. Said the latter publication: "There

As a result of this course of events, a general hardening of conservative attitudes could be seen. Many traditional conservatives, not overly concerned before with the scattered legislative attempts at public control of private property, began now to rally to the defense of the *status quo* against the threatened assaults of lower-class radicalism. The growing pressure of conservative opinion in 1892 was sharply illustrated at the August meeting of the American Bar Association, held at Saratoga Springs, New York. Three speeches warning of the dangers of popular majorities were made at this meeting, as right-wing conservatism moved toward a dominating position in the pattern of legal thought.

Two of these three addresses may be noted briefly. John Randolph Tucker, of Lexington, Virginia, rated an authority on Anglo-Saxon legal and constitutional history, and a Southern conservative of the old school, wound up a disquisition upon the advantages of America's written constitutions over Britain's unwritten system with an indignant attack upon the evils of "Paternal Centralism." [35] Latitudinarian interpretations of the fed-

---

has never been a more impudent and dangerous defiance of the law in this country than the outbreak at Homestead. . . . Even if the corporation's conduct were wrong, the strikers have put themselves in the attitude of law-breakers and murderers, despising and defying the civil authorities."

[35] "British Institutions and American Constitutions," *Report of the Fifteenth Annual Meeting of the American Bar Association* (1892), pp. 213–244. Tucker's two-volume *The Constitution of the United States,* published posthumously in 1899, is said by Edward S. Corwin to have had considerable influence on the subsequent narrowing of the commerce power through the doctrine of "dual federalism" (*The Commerce Power and States Rights* [Princeton, 1936], pp. 38–44). Tucker was a frequent speaker at bar association meetings, addressing the 1888 meeting of the American Bar Association, the 1889 meeting of the Mississippi Bar Association, and the 1896 meeting of the Ohio State Bar Association. He also delivered the presidential address at the American Bar Association in 1893. In all these addresses, Tucker was principally concerned with protection of states' rights against federal power, touching only incidentally upon the freedom of the individual from govern-

eral spending and taxing powers, he drove home to his audience, were resulting in a "paternalistic Democracy" that bade fair to create a government of plundering politicians and a race of "petted parasites." Tucker climaxed his efflorescence with this peroration:

Brother lawyers of America! In all ages, our profession has furnished the trained and skilled champions of right and justice, of liberty and law. Don your armor. Set knightly lance in rest. Demagogues deride and would discard you. The schemes of Paternalism allow you only disinheritance. Be it so. On our burnished shield is the motto: No favorites, no victims, the equal rights of each man to achieve his unhelped and unhindered destiny by brave and self-reliant manhood! Though a disinherited knight, the American Bar enters the lists as the champion of Institutional liberty under Constitutional guaranty. We boldly strike the shield of the proud Templar of misrule, and challenge his power. We will not, cannot, must not fail. The Constitution in its integrity must be restored; political heresies must be exorcised, and our free institutions must be perpetuated.[36]

John W. Cary of Chicago, counsel for the railroad in the *Chicago, Milwaukee* case, read a long, pedantically couched paper, which, nevertheless, took a doctrinaire, extremist position in its contention that private property should be wholly free from legislative limitation as to rates and prices.[37] In the first

---

ment regulation. In his 1892 address, however, when crisis mentality was spreading rapidly, Tucker made the issue of government control his major theme.

[36] "British Institutions and American Constitutions," p. 244. Reporting on Tucker's address, the *American Law Review* noted that Tucker "denounced paternalism in government, to the general satisfaction of his audience. In the words of Irving Browne, 'he tossed, gored, trampled on and rent the detestable doctrine. He stamped and jumped upon it and dealt it ponderous blows with his fists.' This part of his address called forth much applause" (26 [Sept.–Oct., 1892], 746).

[37] "Limitations of the Legislative Power in Respect to Personal Rights and Private Property," *Report of the Fifteenth Annual Meeting of the American Bar Association* (1892), pp. 245–286.

part of his essay, Cary denied that the state legislatures possessed all the ordinary powers of government, except as specifically limited by the federal and state constitutions; instead he resuscitated the doctrine of implied limitations, insisting that laws contrary to the spirit of the Declaration of Independence, with its statement of unalienable rights, could be declared unconstitutional. It was true that judges could not annul laws simply because they thought them opposed to natural justice; but since the bills of rights attached to the state and federal constitutions were worded either in the language of the Declaration or in the equally general language of the English Bill of Rights, the courts, "by a liberal construction of the scope and meaning of those words," [38] could easily find means to protect individual rights from the power of legislative majorities. After a lengthy criticism of the *Munn* case and its subsequent affirmations, Cary gave it as his opinion that "of all the signs of the times which confront us, the most fearful is this disposition of our courts to sanction the lawless violations, by the Legislature, of rights and property secured and guaranteed by the Constitution." [39]

Of far more significance than either Tucker's or Cary's speeches was the presidential address of John F. Dillon.[40] Although a successful corporation lawyer and attorney for leading railroads, Judge Dillon was never a laissez-faire extremist, and, it will be recalled, in his 1887 address at the Alabama Bar Association, expressing the ideas of the more traditional sources of American legal conservatism, he had taken a moderately optimistic point of view.[41] But now, under the impact of advancing social radicalism, Dillon was to urge a philosophy of constitutional conservatism and a standard of judicial review that would arraign him not too far from the most outspoken advocates of *laissez faire*.

[38] *Ibid.*, p. 257. [39] *Ibid.*, p. 274.
[40] "Address of the President," *Report of the Fifteenth Annual Meeting of the American Bar Association* (1892), pp. 167–211.
[41] See *supra*, pp. 28–29.

Dillon, as was customary, devoted the first half of his address to a review of the year's legislation and then moved on to "Comments and Reflections." [42] He began by distinguishing law from legislation. Legislation represented the temporary sense of the populace, "a mere product of sovereignty," the passing creation of the "arbitrary will of the legislator." But law had a more permanent, fundamental nature: in its moral sense, it was the embodiment of the "eternal and indestructible sense of justice and right, written by God on the living tablets of the human heart, and revealed in his Holy Word." This did not mean that law was identical with morality, and it was necessary, for many practical purposes, to distinguish between the two; but the ethical considerations could not be excluded from law, which must ultimately represent "the enlightened permanent justice of the State." [43]

In America, continued Judge Dillon, this sense of underlying justice had been enshrined in written constitutions, which, by guaranteeing the "indestructible" rights of life, liberty, and property, had thereby incorporated the moral law into the organic limitations of government. The provision for an independent judiciary to interpret and enforce these guarantees was the "crowning" achievement in this system of self-imposed restraints. But present-day tendencies, he warned, were straining this system; for the institution of private property, one of these "eternal" rights, was now in serious danger, menaced both openly and covertly:

It is attacked openly by the advocates of the various heresies that go under the general name of socialism or communism, who seek to array the body of the community against individual right to ex-

[42] This portion of Dillon's address was substantially similar to remarks made that spring at Yale University Law School where Dillon had held the William L. Storrs Lectureship for the academic year 1891–1892 (John F. Dillon, *The Laws and Jurisprudence of England and America* [Boston, 1894], pp. 196–215).

[43] Dillon, "Address of President," pp. 200–203, *passim*.

clusive property, and in favor of the right of the community, in *some form*, to deprive the owner of it, or of its full enjoyment.

Property, or its rightful enjoyment, is also covertly invaded, not by the socialist, but at the instance of a popular, or supposed popular, demand; in which case the attack is directed against particular owners or forms of ownership, and generally takes the insidious, more specious and dangerous shape of an attempt to deprive the owners—usually corporate owners—of their property by unjust or discriminating legislation. . . .

The era of the despotism of the monarch, or of an oligarchy, has passed away. If we are not struck with judicial blindness, we cannot fail to see that what is now to be feared and guarded against is the despotism of the many—of the majority.[44]

Dillon then reminded his audience that the founding fathers had been "fully alive" to this danger of popular majorities succumbing to "violent and casual forces"; that it was for this reason that the system of constitutional restraints had been elaborated;[45] and that despite these written limitations, many observers had predicted the failure of the republic. Thus far, those prophecies had proved false, and the constitutional guarantees protecting private property had been generally effective. But these guarantees would have continued value only if "fully and fearlessly enforced by the courts." And Judge Dillon submitted this earnest appeal to the American judiciary:

[44] *Ibid.*, p. 206 (italics in source).

[45] In his Yale lectures, Dillon had been very explicit on this point: "This system of checks and balances which the framers of our government contrived, and which in its totality constitutes our constitutions, has but the single ultimate purpose of curbing the unfettered exercise of the popular will, and it demonstrates how thoroughly they realized the dangerous and destructive force of that will if it were not put under effective restraints" (*Laws and Jurisprudence*, p. 198). In ensuing decades, ironically, it was precisely this argument that was leveled at the Constitution by its left-wing critics. For an acute analysis of this irony and for some pertinent comments on events in the 1890's, see Douglass Adair's article, "The Tenth Federalist Revisited," *William and Mary Quarterly*, 8 (Jan., 1951), 48–67.

If there is any problem yet unsettled, it is whether the bench is able to bear the great burden of supporting, under all circumstances, the fundamental law against popular, or supposed popular, demands for enactments in conflict with it. It is the loftiest function and the most sacred duty of the judiciary. . . . This is the only breakwater against the haste and the passions of the people—against the tumultuous ocean of democracy. It must, at all costs, be maintained.[46]

Right-wing conservatism in America could well gain new confidence from Judge Dillon's address. For it was now clear that important leaders of the older school of traditional conservatism were responding at last to the repeated alarms of laissez-faire conservatives, were at last fully recognizing the deeper dangers inherent in a restless populism. Legal conservatism was still divided between moderates and ultras; and many moderates would still resist, for a while longer at any rate, the claims of the new judicialism. But Judge Dillon had set the pattern; and his finely phrased summoning of the judiciary to a full appreciation of its unique position on the flank of American democracy would serve as an historic landmark for bench and bar in the critical years to come.[47]

[46] "Address of President," pp. 210–211. In his spring lectures at Yale, Dillon had used the term "final breakwater" (*Laws and Jurisprudence*, p. 214); but by late August, after the Omaha Convention and Homestead, it was "only breakwater."

[47] The General Minutes of the Association reports the following resolution offered by W. H. H. Russell, of Michigan: "*Resolved*, that it is the sense of this Association that in printing the proceedings of this meeting, the Executive Committee instruct the Secretary to strike off 2,500 copies of the latter portion of Judge Dillon's address for distribution among the judges of the United States courts and the State courts throughout the United States." After brief discussion on procedural matters the resolution was adopted with an amendment that it be referred to the Executive Committee for such action as it might deem appropriate (*Report of the Fifteenth Annual Meeting of the American Bar Association* [1892], pp. 69–70). I could find no documentary clue as to the final disposition of the matter.

V

Democracy and the Judiciary:
Problems of the Moderate Center

THE year 1893 is remembered in American history for the onset of an industrial depression and a financial panic which in the course of the next few years would exacerbate class antagonism in every sphere of social life, break up regular political allegiances, and bring the national government into the thick of the conflict between capital and labor. For bar and bench these developments would present difficult problems, particularly in regard to the rise of the labor injunction as a new and powerful weapon in labor disputes. In 1893, however, the full effects of the depression were not yet manifest socially or politically. Also, aside from initial federal injunction cases, the significance of which failed to evoke much comment from the profession until 1894, 1893 was a year comparatively devoid of important judicial decisions.[1] Perhaps for these reasons the speeches and

[1] The injunction cases referred to will be discussed in the next chapter. Two interesting freedom-of-contract cases were also decided in 1893. In *State* v. *Loomis*, 115 Mo. 307, the Supreme Court of Missouri, sitting in banc, reversed the opinion of Judge Thomas in Division No. 2, 20 S.W. 332, in order to hold invalid the Missouri "scrip" act of 1889 as unreasonable class legislation and an improper interference with freedom

writings of lawyers and judges in 1893 were chiefly concerned
with the more fundamental aspects of that persistent complex
of problems involving social unrest, majority rule, and the role
of the judiciary.

Although both extremes of legal opinion had their say on
these topics in 1893, including, from the left, an advanced stand
in behalf of state-guaranteed security by Judge John Gibbons
of the Cook County Superior Court [2] and, from the right,
another exhortation from Justice Brewer that the judges protect
fearlessly the rights of private property against the dangers of
majority "coercion," [3] it was the moderate center of the profession that was the most articulate in that year. In one sense, then,
1893 can be seen as a kind of last, and uneasy, interlude before
the waves of conservative fear in 1894 and 1895.

---

of contract. Judge Black for the court condemned the act as intro-
ducing "a system of paternalism which is at war with the fundamental
principles of our government." Judge Barclay filed a strong dissent,
emphasizing the "far-reaching consequences" of the court's assumption
of "reasonableness" as the standard of due process. In *Braceville Coal Co.
v. People*, 147 Ill. 66, the Supreme Court of Illinois, consistent with its
previous decisions, invalidated unanimously a weekly payment law for
corporations as class legislation and impairment of the right to contract.

[2] "Legislation for the Protection of Labor," *Proceedings of the Illinois
State Bar Association at Its Sixteenth Annual Meeting* (1893), pp. 131–
141. Among other things, Gibbons advocated the eight-hour day, the
prohibition of "yellow-dog" contracts, compulsory arbitration including
the setting of wages and hours, and a compulsory insurance system for
industrial accidents. "The old thought concerning the sacredness of
private property must give way to the natural right to live, and it will
soon be established that an honest man, willing and able to work, may
demand from society, not as a favor, sustenance and shelter for himself
and his family" (*ibid.*, p. 134).

[3] David J. Brewer, "The Nation's Safeguard," *Proceedings of the New
York State Bar Association—Sixteenth Annual Meeting* (1893), pp. 37–
47. Brewer went beyond his speech of 1891 (*supra*, pp. 70–72) in his
demands for the most thoroughgoing judicial interposition, warning this
time against the "improper use of labor organization" as well as against
the dangers of legislative regulation of corporate property. Said Brewer
of the strike: "It is coercion, force; it is the effort of the many by the

The outstanding statement of the middle-of-the-road approach in 1893 was made at the midsummer meeting of the American Bar Association, where Justice Henry B. Brown of the United States Supreme Court delivered the Annual Address upon the topic, "The Distribution of Property."[4] Brown had been appointed to the Supreme Court in 1890 from a specialized background in admiralty law (he was considered the country's foremost expert on the subject at the time of his appointment),[5] and thus far his role on the Court had not aroused any unusual interest. He had sided with the laissez-faire conservatives Brewer and Field in their dissent to the *Budd* case, and it appeared likely he would support generally the right-wing point of view. Brown's later course of decision would prove to be a contradictory one, however, as an unexpected independence of mind soon asserted itself.[6] And his address of 1893 was of the same contradictory yet independent pattern: a curious admixture of laissez-faire dogmatism and pragmatic reformism, both interwoven with a materialistic, class-struggle interpretation of his-

---

mere weight of numbers to compel the one to do their bidding. It is a proceeding outside of the law" ("Nation's Safeguard," p. 40).

[4] *Report of the Sixteenth Annual Meeting of the American Bar Association* (1893), pp. 213–242.

[5] *Dictionary of American Biography*, III, 120–121.

[6] In 1894 in *Brass* v. *North Dakota*, 153 U.S. 391, Brown left Field and Brewer to vote with the majority in sustaining a grain elevator act broader than that of the *Budd* case; and in 1895 Brown delivered one of the several forceful dissents to the majority opinion invalidating the income tax (see infra, pp. 175–176, 212–213). In 1898 he wrote the excellent opinion in *Holden* v. *Hardy*, 169 U.S. 366, upholding the Utah eight-hour law for miners, Peckham and Brewer dissenting; but in 1905 Brown sided with Peckham and Brewer, and two other Justices, in the famous *Lochner* case invalidating the New York ten-hour law for bakers. Though an interesting and provocative figure, Justice Brown has been neglected by historians of the Court. The all too brief *Memoir of Henry Billings Brown* (New York, 1915), compiled by Charles A. Kent from an autobiographical sketch written by Brown after his retirement in 1906 and from a number of Brown's letters, shows Brown a perceptive observer of men and events. He thought Theodore Roosevelt's attacks upon "malefactors of great wealth" a good tonic for the country.

tory strangely similar to some of the premises of Marxist socialism.

Justice Brown opened his address with this striking statement: "The history of civilized society is largely a story of strife
between those who have and those who have not." Pointing to
recurrent conflict in successive social structures from ancient
slavery through modern capitalism, Brown found increasing tension "from generation to generation," and this despite the bettered
position of the workingman. The struggle between capital and
labor was an especially old one; for even the Exodus of the
Israelites from Egypt seemed to have partaken of "a national
protest against the oppression of capital, and to have possessed
the substantial characteristics of a modern strike." And all of
these conflicts, ancient and modern, were the direct result of
class interests—"the desire of the rich to obtain the labor of the
poor at the lowest possible terms, the desire of the poor to obtain
the uttermost farthing from the rich. The cause and the result
of it all is the unequal distribution of property." [7]

But with his next sentence, Justice Brown departed irrevo-
cably from his Marxist doctrinal associations: "There is, however, nothing unnatural or undesirable in this." The unequal
distribution of property, he continued, was but the inevitable
result of "differences in our intellectual and physical constitutions," according to which some were "vastly more successful
than others" in the pursuit of wealth.

Brown disputed, however, the charges of those political philosophers who contended that the gulf between the rich and
the poor was constantly growing wider. Private fortunes, to be
sure, were larger than they had ever been; but on the other hand
the condition of the working class had improved "an equal
ratio." Wages were higher, hours of labor shorter, and the
worker was "better housed, better clad, better fed, better
taught," with more opportunities than ever before for himself
and his children. Here Justice Brown apparently let himself be

[7] Brown, "Distribution of Property," pp. 213, 214, 218.

carried away by these newly revealed vistas into this surprising analysis: "Indeed, it is not too much to say that the American working man who does not own his own home must charge it to his own idleness and improvidence, or to other circumstances usually within his own control." [8]

The Justice returned to more solid ground in explaining that the numerous very large fortunes of modern times were the effects of economic centralization and the magnificent opportunities of the American continent. He thought he saw signs that the process might be coming to an end, but this could not be relied on. In the meantime, "the tendency of large fortunes to become larger" meant that the unequal distribution of wealth would remain a pressing problem.

What remedies were available to an enlightened community? Broadly considered, legislation was limited in its possibilities. "It is clear," asserted Justice Brown, "that the fundamental law of supply and demand cannot be set aside." The price of labor went into five-sixths of every item on the market, and wages were thus controlled by what the people were able to buy. Turning to various specific proposals, Brown first examined socialism. He gave it a tight definition: "the total abolition of private property and the ownership of all property by the State —the individual retaining only the right to the enjoyment of his proportionate share." But socialism, even if it could be established in America, would have disastrous results because of its abridgment of all incentive to social progress. Justice Brown's ensuing paean to materialism bears quoting:

It is the desire to earn money which lies at the bottom of the greatest effort of genius. The man who writes books, paints pictures, moulds statues, builds houses, pleads causes, preaches sermons, or heals the sick, does it for the money there is in it; and if, in so doing, he acquires a reputation as an author, painter, sculptor, architect, jurist, or physician, it is only an incident to his success as a money-getter. The motive which prompted Angelo to plan the dome of St. Peter,

[8] *Ibid.*, p. 220.

or paint the frescoes of the Sistine Chapel, was essentially the same as that which induces a common laborer to lay brick or dig sewers.[9]

After further elaboration upon the difficulties with socialism, Brown commented upon and dismissed in turn anarchism, co-operation, compulsory arbitration, and the single-tax plan, all of which would create more problems than they solved.

Then, with these issues disposed of, Justice Brown suddenly veered in the tenor of his address:

Does it therefore follow that legislation can do nothing to improve those relations [labor-capital], or to palliate the evils of the present situation? I think not. It may fix the number of hours of a legal day's work, provide that payment be made at certain stated periods, protect the life and health of the workingman against accidents or diseases arising from ill-constructed machinery, badly ventilated rooms, defective appliances or dangerous occupations, and may limit or prohibit altogether the labor of women and children in employments injurious to their health or beyond their strength.[10]

Having thus in a sentence calmly espoused a good portion of the very items state courts had been striking down for almost a decade under freedom of contract, the Justice must have had his distinguished, and probably quite conservative, audience holding their breaths when he continued: "It may go deeper." In smoothly reasoned succession Brown suggested vigorous enforcement of antitrust laws; municipal ownership of gas, electricity, telephones, and rapid transit; federal ownership of telegraphs, express delivery, and ultimately canals and railways; and, if the accumulation of fortunes continued, the limitation of the inheritance allowed to any one individual "at a million dollars." Interspersed with this program was Brown's key sentence, really his over-all conclusion, that he was "by no means satisfied that the old maxim, that the country which is governed least is governed best, may not, in these days of monopolies and combinations, be subject to revision." [11]

[9] *Ibid.*   [10] *Ibid.*, pp. 235–236.   [11] *Ibid.*, p. 237.

If Justice Brown was inconsistent in his ideas as well as his judicial decisions, he was, after all, only demonstrating thereby his close affiliation with the main stream of American political thought. For whether called moderate progressive or moderate conservative, the essential characteristic of this broadly *liberal* tradition had always been its pragmatic and eclectic approach to the problems of the day. Thus Justice Brown, though still adhering to many of the rigid formulae of laissez-faire ideology, was willing to employ the power of the state at strategic points in the socioeconomic structure. His address was also noteworthy for the conspicuous absence, in a speech entitled "The Distribution of Property," of any references to the dangers of unruly majorities and the need for an alert judiciary.

But the role of the judiciary in its relation to the democratic process could not readily be ignored in this time of tension, and in 1893 the matter was subjected to careful scrutiny. It was of especial importance to the moderate center of traditional legal conservatism—that branch of legal thought not too much aroused to the necessity for social reform and not too much interested in the protection of property values, but concerned primarily, in the strictly professional sense, with the due observance of the precedents and procedures of law, and, in the larger political sense, with the maintenance of a proper balance between the democratic and the restrictive elements of American constitutionalism.

From the juristic point of view, at issue in 1893 was the apparent revival of implied limitations upon the legislative power. In its pure form, the doctrine of implied limitations held that acts of the legislature, even if not directly in conflict with any express provision of the Constitution, could be adjudged invalid as contrary to the "spirit of the Constitution," the "nature of the social compact," or some similar generality. In Federalist times a few expressions of this sort had been ventured by the Supreme

Court [12] and by several state courts; but the doctrine had never received authoritative sanction, and in the Jackson era it had been discarded or permitted to lapse through disuse.[13] Nevertheless, laissez-faire conservatives had been urging since the 1870's that the formulations of the Declaration of Independence, proclaiming as unalienable the rights of life, liberty, and the pursuit of happiness, should be considered as incorporated into the Constitution, and as having attained thereby the status of substantive limitations upon the legislative power. Most courts were more circumspect than to allege the Declaration as the basis for decisions invalidating state legislation—though a few Judges, conspicuously Justice Field, did just that.[14] Such doctrines as

[12] Notably, Justice Chase's statement in his concurring opinion to *Calder* v. *Bull*, 3 Dal. 386 (1798): "An *act* of the Legislature (for I cannot call it a *law*) contrary to the great first principles of the social compact, cannot be considered a rightful exercise of legislative authority"; and Justice Johnson's concurring opinion in *Fletcher* v. *Peck*, 6 Cr. 87 (1810), refusing to rest the decision on an enlarged interpretation of the contract clause, as Marshall had done, but holding instead that "I do it, on a general principle, on the reason and nature of things, a principle which will impose laws even on the Deity." Marshall's opinion had also hinted at this doctrine as a possible alternative to the contract clause (*ibid.*, pp. 135–136). See also Justice Story's opinions in *Terrett* v. *Taylor*, 9 Cr. 42 (1815), and *Wilkinson* v. *Leland*, 2 Pet. 627 (1829).

[13] See, for example, Chief Justice Taney's opinion in *Charles River Bridge* v. *Warren Bridge*, 11 Pet. 420 (1837), at 539. A notable, if isolated, reappearance of the theory of extraconstitutional limitations upon the legislature was *Loan Association* v. *Topeka*, 20 Wall. 655 (1874), where Justice Miller asserted the existence of "implied reservations of individual rights, without which the social compact could not exist, and which are respected by all governments entitled to the name."

[14] Thus, Field's opinions in the *Slaughter-House Cases*, 6 Wall. 36, at 87; *Butchers' Union Co.* v. *Crescent City Co.*, 111 U.S. 746, at 756–757; and *Powell* v. *Pennsylvania*, 127 U.S. 678, at 690, 692. Justice Brewer's dissent to the *Budd* case also emphasized the "unalienable rights" of the Declaration. Although Brewer did not base his opinion on the Declaration per se, he never did allege any specific provision of the Constitution to which he thought the act repugnant, not even deigning to notice the due process clause (143 U.S. 517, esp. at 550).

freedom of contract and requirement of a judicial review of reasonableness tended to be equally effective and more subtle forms of implied limitations.[15]

The commentary in 1893 on these new developments began with an incisive article in the January issue of the *American Law Register* by Richard C. McMurtrie, seventy-four-year-old dean of the Philadelphia bar and an associate editor of the *Register*.[16] Taking as his text Marshall's dictum in *Marbury* v. *Madison* that "the theory of every such government (one having a written constitution) must be, that an act of the legislature, repugnant to the constitution, is void," [17] McMurtrie exclaimed thus upon the history of Marshall's pronouncement: "But how slight has been its capacity to restrain our judiciary from a reckless use of the power thus authoritatively recognized as existing!" [18]

As a prime example of this judicial recklessness, McMurtrie cited the 1886 decision of *Godcharles* v. *Wigeman,* with its holding that the legislature had done "what, in this country, cannot be done; that is, prevent persons who are *sui juris* from making their own contracts." [19] He added these astonished remarks:

[15] As Professor J. A. C. Grant put it in 1931, "In fact, the modern definition of 'due process' is merely the 'natural justice' of Story, Marshall, Miller, Field, *et al.,* under a new name, 'reasonableness' " ("The Natural Law Background of Due Process," *Columbia Law Review,* 31 [Jan., 1931], 65). See also Charles G. Haines, *The Revival of Natural Law Concepts* (Cambridge, 1930), esp. pp. 99–104, 117–122.

[16] "A New Canon of Constitutional Interpretation," *American Law Register,* n.s., 32 (Jan., 1893), 1–9. McMurtrie was admitted to the Philadelphia bar in 1840 and practiced there all his life. Assessments of his character at the bar, which offer a view of him as something of an "old curmudgeon," may be found in Frank M. Eastman, ed., *Courts and Lawyers of Pennsylvania: A History,* 1623–1923 (New York, 1922), III, 832 ff.; and in McMurtrie's obituary in the November, 1894, issue of the *American Law Register* (33: 845–848).

[17] 1 Cr. 49 (1803).

[18] "New Canon of Constitutional Interpretation," p. 1.

[19] 113 Pa. St. 431.

The spectacle of a government that cannot prohibit a contract merely because two grown persons desire to make it, is so utterly absurd as to be quite beyond the region of discussion if government of any kind is to continue. The wisdom of the particular interference may be debatable, but it is simply ridiculous to assert that a State has no right to interfere with the individual's right to contract when courts uphold the power of the state to forbid a harmless wager, the contracting of a debt for whiskey, and a promise to pay a larger price for a risky loan of money than for one as secure as the State itself.[20]

But the "most striking instance" of this "loss of an anchorage in constitutional interpretation," said McMurtrie, was to be seen in *Budd* v. *New York*, "a case fraught with evil incalculable and immeasurable." Although the law had been upheld, McMurtrie thought it a "wonderful thing" that no one who sustained the statute called attention to the failure to allege any specific provision of the Constitution to which the act might be held opposed "or made the point that till this was set up there was nothing to discuss. Not one person, counsel or judge, seems to have been aware that the primary question is that stated in *Marbury* v. *Madison*. To what part of the Constitution is this repugnant?" Dismissing as "absurd" any attempt to hinge the decision on the Fourteenth Amendment, McMurtrie continued with a caustic reference to Brewer's dissent:

The climax is arrived at when the *inalienable right to life, liberty and the pursuit of happiness* is gravely contended to be a ground for refusing to enforce a statute like this. . . . In a country where we alienate life by the halter, and restrain liberty by jails, and prohibit the use of ardent spirits and beer, quite regardless of how fruitless is the pursuit of happiness to many under such restrictions, one cannot but stop to ask what men mean by these words or if they attach any real meaning to their words.[21]

[20] *Op. cit.*, p. 5.
[21] *Ibid.*, p. 8 (italics in source). McMurtrie wrote "inalienable" though Brewer had used the more proper "unalienable" (143 U.S. 550).

McMurtrie concluded his article with this penetration into the meaning of the new constitutionalism:

The importance of all this lies here. At the present time the reasons found in the opinions of judges are accepted as law. The decision of the Court is overlooked. And therefore we shall be met hereafter with the necessary deduction from these opinions—a new canon of constitutional law, viz.: that *a statute interfering with "natural rights" must be shown to be authorized, not that it must be shown to be prohibited*.[22]

Several months later, writing under the *Register*'s "Comments on Recent Decisions," [23] McMurtrie carried his critique further. Under the modern claim of right, he explained, the judiciary had overturned the traditional standard of whether the legislature had the power to do something, and was instead considering "the propriety" of a particular exercise of the power. In the case of the states this standard of judicial review was especially untenable, he continued, for according to generally accepted theory the state constitutions were not grants of power, but restraints upon otherwise sovereign legislatures; and, "a restraint on a sovereignty derived by an inference from notions of right and wrong is essentially not judicial but legislative."

McMurtrie then put the matter in terms of this *reductio ad absurdum*:

Let me attempt to frame a clause of a constitution in the line of this modern notion of constitutional law, e.g., "The legislature shall have no power to enact any statute which is *foolish, unjust or cruel*," and can anything more chaotic be conceived than all future legislation? Still more preposterous, if we attempt to embody the highsounding but meaningless phrases of the Declaration of Independence.[24]

An opposing view to McMurtrie's attack upon the judicial revival of natural law concepts was entered by William Draper

---

[22] *Ibid.*, p. 9 (italics in source).
[23] *American Law Register*, n.s., 32 (June, 1893), 594–596.
[24] *Ibid.*, p. 595 (italics in source).

Lewis, co-editor of the *American Law Register*, in a series of three "Editorial Notes." [25] In a balanced, eminently moderate approach, Lewis affirmed first that the new attitude, that the Fourteenth Amendment prohibited states from passing laws contrary to natural justice or fundamental principles of free government, was associated with the doctrine of the early Marshall period that state constitutions were instruments for conferring, not limiting, power.

But this older doctrine, which emphasized such concepts as the social contract and the unalienable rights of man, had not gone "unchallenged," and Lewis agreed that the mere claim of antiquity for a doctrine did not necessarily "prove its correctness." And thereupon Lewis proceeded to a very ingenious argument. Bills of rights, he assumed, were in the beginning

rather declarations of the nature of government and the rights of man than impassable barriers to legislative power. They were great truths binding on the conscience of the legislature, but which like other bands of a similar nature were . . . easily broken by an act of the legislature.

Their main effect was that of a statement of ultimate principles, upon which the individual could rest, if need be, the resort to civil disobedience or even revolution. Every man was thus his own interpreter of "unalienable rights." But at the turn of the century the judges had asserted their power and had "at once put themselves in the place of the individual citizen as an interpreter and defender of his unalienable rights." The interposition of the courts was, therefore, a device for doing away with the

[25] *American Law Register*, n.s., 32 (Aug., 1893), 782–785; (Oct., 1893), 971–981; and (Nov., 1893), 1064–1071. Lewis was on the faculty of the University of Pennsylvania Law School and later became dean of the school and a well-known legal writer. A supporter of progressive causes in the 1900's, he was chairman of the platform committee at the Progressive Party Convention of 1912 (George E. Mowry, *Theodore Roosevelt and the Progressive Movement* [Madison, 1947], p. 271). In 1923 Lewis was chosen by the American Law Institute to direct its monumental *Restatement of the Law*.

possible necessity of revolution by declaring "unconstitutional" what was inherently invalid. The judiciary was simply acting as the representative of the collective conscience of the people.

Having thus completed his general presentation of the problem of fundamental limitations upon legislative power, Lewis shifted the emphasis as he mounted a stinging offensive against the new uses of this theoretically valid concept:

We must acknowledge, however, that if anything could convince us of the impossibility of developing a constitutional law which will relate to the civil liberty of the individual, it would be some of the expressions of those whom we follow in thinking that the legislature has not all power except where expressly denied. Thus, in *Godcharles and Company v. Wigeman*, . . . we echo Mr. McMurtrie in the criticism of this case. . . .

All this seems to be an attempt to make theories of government, held by only a part of our people, part of our constitutional law. Constitutional law, in so far as it pertains to the civil rights and immunities of the individual, was wisely left by our forefathers to those principles which all parties professed to believe, and only transgressed in moments of political excitement. Had they attempted to fasten the particular ideas of a single party concerning the proper scope of governmental activity, judges would long ago have found it impossible to uphold the constitution.[26]

McMurtrie was not satisfied, however, and in the December issue of the *Register* submitted a forceful rebuttal to Lewis' main contentions.[27] He denied that there were any legitimate grounds whatever for courts to annul legislation except upon direct repugnance to the constitution. Returning again to Brewer's dissent in the *Budd* case and his apparent allegation of the preamble to the Declaration of Independence as reason for striking down the act, McMurtrie commented,

[26] *Op. cit.*, n.s., 32 (Nov., 1893), 1070.
[27] Richard C. McMurtrie, "The Jurisdiction to Declare Void Acts of Legislation—When Is It Legitimate and When Mere Usurpation of Sovereignty?" *American Law Register*, n.s., 32 (Dec., 1893), 1093–1108.

That all this [the assertions in the preamble] is absolute truth to the legislator, though rather puerile, just as it is true that foolish and silly, or cruel and wicked laws should not be passed, is self-evident, but to say that legislation is void if *I think* it silly or foolish is absurd.[28]

If the judges could decide cases on such grounds, continued McMurtrie, there was "no standard more certain than the mere caprice of a tyrant for determining what is and what is not within the legislative power in America." Within its powers the legislature was "the final arbitrator of what is right or proper, and its *power* extends to determining what are the proper limits of the natural rights of pursuing happiness, exercising liberty and even retaining life, or it ceases to be sovereign, and this *legislative* power is transferred to the court." This, concluded McMurtrie, was "the usurpation of sovereignty without even a colorable warrant." [29]

Both McMurtrie and Lewis had perceived the drift of the new constitutionalism, and both had agreed that it was contrary to the first principles of constitutional democracy for judges to read into the generalities of preambles and bills of rights any special theory of the role of government; for this would be to impose a tyranny of the past, or rather of the judges' interpretations of the past, upon the present. Both of these traditional conservatives of the law were thus firmly committed to the philosophy of democratic republicanism. Lewis, however, would have granted the judges authority to invalidate acts of legislatures, even if not repugnant to any specific restraint of the constitution, when on the basis of certain generally agreed-to principles, the act in question would have endangered the personal rights of the individual. But McMurtrie, perhaps shrewder than

[28] *Ibid.*, p. 1101 (italics in source).

[29] *Ibid.*, pp. 1103, 1108 (italics in source). Shortly before his death on October 2, 1894, McMurtrie restated these views in another succinctly phrased article, prophetically entitled "A Last Word on Constitutional Construction," *American Law Register*, n.s., 33 (July, 1894), 506–512.

Lewis, had maintained that once you had allowed this power to the judges you were in the hands of the judges. For once the judges could pass upon the substance of any act in the light of standards not specifically stated in the constitution, the line of demarcation between the legislative and the judicial would be an always shifting one, subject to the changing notions of the judges themselves.

In October, 1893, the high-level discussion over the nature of judicial power, begun by McMurtrie and Lewis in the *American Law Register*, was carried farther by the publication in the *Harvard Law Review* of an important paper by James Bradley Thayer, Professor of Constitutional Law at the Harvard Law School and an active member of the American Bar Association.[30] The essence of Professor Thayer's discriminating analysis was an emphatic caution to the judges that, since the power of judicial review had been largely circumstantial in its origins and, in fact, the result principally of mere assertions of the power by the judges, its scope was severely limited, to be exercised only in the clearest cases.

Professor Thayer traced the origins of the power chiefly to the colonial experience with royal superintendence of charter provisions and to the somewhat off-handed filling of this post-revolutionary vacuum, as applied to the new constitutions, by the judges—judicial review by default as it were. But this new power of the judiciary was not readily assented to, continued Thayer, and he noted numerous instances of disavowal and protest. Nor was the power warranted by the mere fact of a written constitution (with the special exception of the necessity to maintain the structure of federalism); France, Germany, and

[30] "The Origin and Scope of the American Doctrine of Constitutional Law," *Harvard Law Review*, 7 (Oct., 1893), 129–156. In 1893 Thayer served on the Association's Committee on Indian Legislation and its Committee on Publications. Thayer's *Cases on Constitutional Law* was widely used in law schools for many years, and he is credited by Henry Steele Commager with being one of the founders of twentieth-century jurisprudence (*The American Mind* [New Haven, 1950], p. 376).

Switzerland had written constitutions, and no such power was ever asserted in those countries. It was at this point in his analysis that Thayer made his only reference, an apparently casual one, to the currently resurgent doctrine of implied limitations:

It may be remarked here that the doctrine of declaring legislative acts void as being contrary to the constitution, was probably helped into existence by a theory . . . at the time of the Revolution, that courts might disregard such acts if they were contrary to the fundamental maxims of morality, or, as it was phrased, to the laws of nature. . . . It has been repeated . . . as a matter of speculation, by our earlier judges, and occasionally by later ones; but in no case within my knowledge has it ever been enforced where it was the single and necessary ground of the decision, nor can it be, unless as a revolutionary measure.[31]

When at last the power to set aside acts of legislatures had been generally recognized, Professor Thayer explained, its exercise was conceived of as strictly a judicial one; that is, the judiciary could consider statutes of no effect only "for the mere purpose of deciding a litigated question properly submitted to the court." But in doing this the courts were to use exceptional care not to limit the area of legislative discretion and not to intrude upon "that wide margin of considerations which address themselves only to the practical judgment of a legislative body." This primary authority of the legislature was a "momentous" one, insisted Thayer, and entitled to the greatest deference,

and this not on mere grounds of courtesy or conventional respect, but on very solid and significant grounds of policy and law. The judiciary may well reflect that if they had been regarded by the people as the chief protection against legislative violation of the constitution, they would not have been allowed merely this incidental and postponed control. They would have been let in, as it was sometimes endeavored in the conventions to let them in, to a revision of the laws before they began to operate.[32]

[31] *Op. cit.*, p. 133. [32] *Ibid.*, p. 136.

Here Professor Thayer took notice of a curious anomaly in American constitutional history. For while judges usually took formal cognizance of the limits of their power, many of them did so "in a perverted way which really operates to extend the judicial function beyond its just bounds." What courts often did was to pronounce their duty as being simply that of comparing the constitution and the law and, if the two were opposed to each other, of giving effect to the constitution as superior to the therefore invalid law. But such a method, complained Thayer, resulted "in the wrong kind of disregard of legislative considerations. . . . Instead of taking them into account and allowing for them as furnishing possible grounds of legislative action, there takes place a pedantic and academic treatment of the texts of the constitution and the laws."

As a counterpoise to this method, there had developed the "very significant rule of administration," that judicial invalidation of an act duly passed by the legislature was warranted only when the alleged violation of the constitution was so manifest as to be beyond a reasonable doubt. Thayer was at great pains (nine closely reasoned pages) to emphasize the necessity of strict adherence to this rule. The test to be applied by the judges, he declared, was

not merely their own judgment as to constitutionality, but their conclusion as to what judgment is permissible to another department. . . . This rule recognizes that, having regard to the great, complex, ever-unfolding exigencies of government, much which will seem unconstitutional to one man or body of men may reasonably not seem so to another.[33]

Again, even more acutely:

It all comes back, I think, to this. The rule under discussion has in it an implied recognition that the judicial duty now in question touches the region of political administration. . . . The judges were allowed, indirectly and in a degree, the power to revise the action of other departments and to pronounce it null. In simple truth, while this is a mere judicial function, it involves, owing to the subject-

[33] *Ibid.,* p. 144.

matter with which it deals, taking a part, a secondary part, in the political conduct of government. . . . The ultimate arbiter of what is rational and permissible is indeed always the courts, so far as litigated cases bring the question before them. This leaves to our courts a great and stately jurisdiction. It will only imperil the whole of it if it is sought to give them more.[34]

Professor Thayer had thus gone even farther than McMurtrie in delimiting the area of judicial power. McMurtrie had excluded from judicial review any concept of implied limitations upon the legislature, whether or not derived from the generalities of natural law; but otherwise he had simply noted without elaboration that laws repugnant to the constitution could be held invalid. But Thayer had demonstrated that repugnancy too was to be construed in such a way as to leave unhampered the widest range of legislative freedom; for only laws so plainly opposite to the constitution that no possible grounds could reasonably be alleged for them, could properly come under the judicial ban. The course of legal conservatism, however, was moving directly contrary to these views;[35] and Professor Thayer's earnest counsels, though widely respected for their clarity and persuasiveness,[36] would be little heeded in the crisis years of the mid-1890's.[37]

[34] *Ibid.*, p. 152.

[35] Indirect evidence of this movement of opinion is found in the 1894 report of the Secretary of the New York State Bar Association, which noted that Justice Brewer's address at the 1893 meeting of the Association (*supra*, n. 3) had "attracted great attention. . . . It has become a standard work, and the great demand for it is indubitable evidence of its value" (*Proceedings of the New York State Bar Association—Seventeenth Annual Meeting* [1894], p. 55).

[36] Thayer's paper was originally prepared for the Chicago Congress on Jurisprudence and Law Reform, where it was read on August 9, 1893, and quickly attracted public attention. It was soon reprinted in pamphlet form by Little, Brown & Co. of Boston. The *Nation*, though at this time advocating the widest use of judicial power, gave a favorable notice to Thayer's paper. The *Albany Law Journal*, also supporting a broad concept of judicial review, reprinted the *Nation*'s notice without comment (48 [Dec. 23, 1893], 516). See also William Draper Lewis' complimentary remarks in the *American Law Register*, n.s., 33 (Jan., 1894), 73–75.

[37] An interesting case in 1894 decided directly on the theory of im-

We may close this chapter, which has emphasized largely the attitudes of moderate conservatism toward typical problems of the 1890's, with an examination of the Annual Address at the February, 1894, meeting of the Southern New Hampshire Bar Association, an address which clearly displayed the more traditional assumptions of American constitutional conservatism.[38]

The speaker was J. H. Benton, Jr., of Boston, railroad lawyer, pamphleteer, library director;[39] and he began his address by calling attention to the "primary principle" of American government—the political supremacy of the popular majority. The universality of manhood suffrage was unrestricted by educational or property qualifications, Benton pointed out, and it operated by one route or another upon the legislative, the executive, and even the judicial branches of the government. Thus, the original constitutional restrictions upon the popular choice of the President were now meaningless, and the Senate too might soon come under direct popular control. Judgeships in most states were elective for comparatively brief terms, and even the Supreme Court of the United States could "be changed by adding to its numbers."

Benton then recalled that in the formative period of American history "the wisest of the framers of the Federal and State con-

plied limitations was *McCullough* v. *Brown*, 41 S.C. 220, where Chief Judge McIver of the Supreme Court of South Carolina invalidated that state's Dispensary Act, which established a state monopoly of the liquor trade, as "utterly at variance with the very idea of civil government. . . . Trade is not, and cannot properly be, regarded as one of the functions of government." Judge Pope dissenting noted caustically "a growing tendency on the part of the courts to assume a power which the law has never given them, under the guise of some philosophical abstraction that there is some power in them, by reason of some mysterious something, called, for the want of a better name, 'the social compact.'" And he warned the judges they were "leading the way to incalculable mischief, for the mutterings of a coming storm by reason thereof are plainly distinct." Pope quoted McMurtrie as support for his dissent.

[38] "The Influence of the Bar in Our State and Federal Government," *Proceedings of the Southern New Hampshire Bar Association at Its Third Annual Meeting* (1894), pp. 227–255.

[39] *Dictionary of American Biography*, II, 210.

stitutions had serious doubts" that any government thus responsive to the popular will could long continue. They had "evidently felt," said Benton, "that as the country grew in wealth, and social and pecuniary disparity of condition increased, greater safeguards for the security of life and property would be required." And not only had such admitted conservatives as Hamilton and Gouverneur Morris expressed these "grave misgivings," but even the democratic and optimistic Jefferson had "freely confessed his fear of the ultimate tyranny of the many through the legislative branch of the government." [40]

This distrust of the nature of American popular government had persisted, continued Benton, nor had it been dissipated by the recent progress of the country. In fact, from one point of view, the possibilities seemed more foreboding than ever: "Enormous wealth has been rapidly accumulated in a few hands and though on the whole wealth is still more equally distributed than in other countries, disparity of pecuniary and social conditions has constantly increased."

Yet life and property were as secure in America, Benton affirmed, as in any country in the world.

How has this marvellous result been accomplished? What has been the conservative power which has thus reconciled diverse and conflicting interests and held the safeguards of life and property secure amid this surging sea of popular suffrage? [41]

Benton offered as answer "the lawyers of America." It was "the influence of this large and constantly increasing body of cautious and conservative men upon state and federal government" which had so successfully counteracted the disruptive tendencies of popular suffrage. Here Benton quoted with approval Alexis de Tocqueville's well-known passage specifying bar and bench as the American aristocracy.[42]

Benton's comments on the judiciary were especially pertinent:

[40] *Op. cit.*, p. 232.   [41] *Ibid.*, p. 235.
[42] See *supra*, p. x. Benton included with his speech a series of valuable appendices on the participation of lawyers in American state

the judiciary had the "controlling part . . . in the government under our system of written constitutions"; and the Supreme Court by its supervisory power over the federal system, and by its construction of the Constitution, had "largely created the present fundamental law," turning "glittering generalities" into "luminous verities." Then came this significant section:

To this supreme law, as construed and declared by our great national judicial tribunal, and supported by the constant conservative influence of the Bar, the people must look for the ultimate security of person and property.

The judiciary alone can hold the constant conflict of selfish interests, which is an essential element of the growth of society, within the just limitations of the fundamental law,

> "Till jarring interests of themselves create
> The according music of a well-tuned state." [43]

Benton's essay had impressively revealed the historic reliance of American conservatism upon constitutionalism and legalism. Only a watchful judiciary enforcing a written constitution, and an adroit leavening of government by conservative lawyers, could channel within orderly bounds the potential insurgency of popular majorities. Nevertheless, it may be noted, Benton had also postulated a balance-of-power concept of group politics which would leave sufficient room for the necessary interplay of social and economic forces.[44] The judiciary had a vital holding function to be sure—to enforce observance of the rules of the game; but at the same time it was not expected that the judges

---

and federal government. For example, Appendix III, tabulating the number and percentage of lawyers in the House and Senate for every Congress since 1789, showed on recapitulation that lawyers constituted 53 per cent of the total membership of Congress.

[43] *Op. cit.*, p. 242.

[44] The equilibrium concept of group politics, an essential element in modern democratic theory, received its seminal expression, of course, in Madison's famous *Tenth Federalist*, still indispensable for its insights into democratic (then "republican") politics.

would themselves take sides, so to speak, and wind up aiding one or another of the contending parties. As the economic depression deepened steadily in 1893 and 1894, however, intensifying widespread distress and precipitating acute conflict between capital and labor, the philosophy of judicial neutralism would be put to a severe strain.

VI

The Courts and Labor
before the Pullman Strike

THE origins and growth of the labor injunction in the 1880's and early 1890's offer a fascinating study in the evolution of legal doctrine to meet new conditions.[1] Two separate streams of jurisprudence merged in the early labor injunctions: the common law doctrine of criminal conspiracy as applied to American labor cases in the first half of the nineteenth century, that a combination intended to effect an unlawful purpose, or a lawful purpose by unlawful means, was a conspiracy punishable as a crime; and the ancient power of courts of equity to enjoin a nuisance and prevent irreparable injury to property.[2] Neither element in itself was sufficient to meet the problems of the

[1] The standard authority on the use of the labor injunction prior to the Norris-LaGuardia Act of 1932 is Felix Frankfurter and Nathan Greene, *The Labor Injunction* (New York, 1930). For the early development of the injunction, pp. 20–28 are especially valuable. See also Selig Perlman's *A History of Trade Unionism in the United States* (New York, 1922), pp. 146–160.

[2] "Irreparable injury" at equity is injury for which damages are not readily recoverable at law, either because of the pecuniary incompetency of the parties, the difficulty of precise estimation of the loss, or because necessitating a multiplicity of suits.

modern labor dispute, at least from the point of view of the employer. The old procedure of trial for conspiracy, although revived in the 1870's and 1880's, was too delayed, cumbersome, and uncertain: the law could enter the picture only after the damage had been done; criminal trials for large numbers of strikers were not practicable; and in mining and manufacturing towns the attitudes of jurors could not always be relied upon in matters necessitating vigorous enforcement of law and order and the protection of property rights.

A much more efficient remedy was the jurisdiction of equity, by which judges could issue writs of injunction ordering the cessation, or simply the noncommission, of acts threatening irreparable injury to property, upon pain of summary punishment for contempt, with no jury trial needed. But equity jurisdiction could not intervene merely because the acts or probable acts complained of might effect irreparable injury to property— after all, the competition of commercial life resulted in the daily commission of irreparable injury; the acts threatened had to be torts besides, that is to say, wrongful at law and admitting of a suit for damages, before equity could take a hand. If it could be alleged, however, that the injurious acts were to be committed in the context of a criminal conspiracy, that is, if the acts were in furtherance of a combination intended to effect unlawful ends or a combination using unlawful means, then all the necessary requisites would be satisfied. For if an act was unlawful as a crime, and at the same time effected an injury to private property admitting of a suit, it was a tort; and if the injury effected by that tort would be irreparable, then equity could enter to prevent beforehand, by injunction, the irreparable— and unlawful—harm threatened.

But what was "unlawful" with relevance to the modern labor dispute? And what was "property" in the modern sense? An expansion of terms was necessary. The law of property had been concerned primarily with tangible things—in equity, generally land. But this was hardly sufficient for a business economy; and in a series of cases the term was steadily broadened, till by the early 1890's property included such concepts as "probable expectancies" of a continuous labor market and a continuous customer relationship.[3] Property had thus become the equivalent of the continued profitableness of the employer's business; and on this basis the strike itself as well as the boycott, if they could be shown to constitute "unlawful interference" with employer's business, might be subject to judicial interdict. But again, what was "unlawful interference"?

Back in 1842 Chief Justice Lemuel Shaw of the Massachusetts Supreme Court in the famous case of *Commonwealth* v. *Hunt* [4] had declared that the trade union was not in itself unlawful; and in subsequent cases it was generally agreed that combinations to gain higher wages, shorter hours, or better working conditions were not unlawful. *Commonwealth* v. *Hunt* had also held that a strike to secure the employment of only union members was similarly not unlawful. This latter view, however, was not so readily accepted by the courts; and in the 1880's and 1890's strikes and boycotts to compel recognition of the union or the closed shop were frequently condemned as unlawful conspiracies interfering with the freedom of the employer to run his business as he wished.[5] In other cases boycotting per se was often held unlawful conduct, regardless of the ends to be effected.[6] Picketing

[3] Walton H. Hamilton, "Property—According to Locke," *Yale Law Journal*, 41 (April, 1932), 864–880. Cases in point are *Walker* v. *Cronin*, 107 Mass. 555 (1871); *Brace Bros.* v. *Evans*, 5 Pa. Co. Ct. Rep. 163 (1888); *Barr* v. *Essex Trades Council*, 53 N.J.: Eq. 101 (1894).

[4] 4 Met. 111 (Mass.). For an interesting analysis of this celebrated case, see the recent biography by Leonard W. Levy, *The Law of the Commonwealth and Chief Justice Shaw* (Cambridge, 1957), pp. 183–206.

[5] For early expressions of this philosophy by federal judges, see *In re Higgins*, 27 Fed. 443 (N.D. Texas, 1886); *Old Dominion Steamship Co.* v. *McKenna*, 30 Fed. 48 (S.D. New York, 1887); *Casey* v. *Cincinnati Typographical Union No. 3*, 45 Fed. 135 (S.D. Ohio, 1891) at 143; and *Coeur d'Alene Consolidated & Mining Co.* v. *Miners' Union*, 51 Fed. 260 (D. Ida., 1892), at 263.

[6] *Brace Bros.* v. *Evans*, 5 Pa. Co. Ct. Rep. 163 (1888), is a leading case on the use of the injunction against boycotts.

—"marching up and down with intimidating placards"—in the early cases was also frowned upon.[7] As the pattern of cases unfolded in the late 1880's and early 1890's, it often seemed as if the mere fact of "interference" was itself the unlawful conduct and the unlawful end.[8]

Despite this significant groundwork of principles and precedents, the labor injunction by the early 1890's was still on a tentative basis, largely unnoticed by the legal profession and unknown to the general public. But early in 1893 began a series of major federal cases which in the next two years would thrust the labor injunction into national prominence; and a surprised public opinion, both professional and lay, became aware all at once of the critical importance of the injunction in the growing conflict between capital and labor. Two developments were paramount: first, the application to labor organizations of the Interstate Commerce Act and the Sherman Anti-Trust Act, which enlarged the area of "unlawfulness" against which equity could intervene; and, second, a radical extension of the scope of acts prohibited by the injunction, reaching its extreme limit in the spring of 1894 with the forbidding of the mere quitting of work.

The cases of 1893 began with *Blindell* v. *Hagan*,[9] decided February 9 in New Orleans by District Judge Edward C. Billings. In granting the request of a British shipowning company for an injunction *pendente lite* [10] restraining certain defendants from

[7] *Sherry* v. *Perkins*, 147 Mass. 212 (1888).

[8] As Perlman, *op. cit.*, noted at p. 158, the developing view that interference with the employer's business was prima facie unlawful "placed the burden of proof upon the working-man. It actually meant that the court opened for itself the way for holding the conduct of the working-men to be lawful only when it sympathized with their demands."

[9] 54 Fed. 40 (E.D. La.), aff'd 56 Fed. 696 (C.C.A., 5th).

[10] Theoretically, there were three stages in labor injunction proceedings: the preliminary restraining order, usually issued ex parte, without notice or hearing, and supposed merely to maintain the *status quo;* the temporary injunction, or injunction *pendente lite*, after notice and hearing, and issued for the duration of the case; and the permanent injunction, adjudicating indefinitely the rights of the parties. But in many

interfering with the company's business as carriers in the trade between New Orleans and Liverpool, Billings devoted most of his brief opinion to the question of equity jurisdiction in the case. First, he rejected an attempt to invoke an injunction under the Sherman Act, holding that only the United States government could bring suits under that act. But the court could intervene through its general powers of equity, said Billings, since the injury threatened consisted "in the loss of profits which are not susceptible of proof," and was therefore not readily remediable at law. Billings also cited as reasons for accepting the case the pecuniary inadequacy of the defendants and the prevention of a multiplicity of suits.[11]

But, the jurisdiction granted, what evidence justified the restraining of the defendants' actions? The complainant had alleged that it was prevented from shipping a crew "by the unlawful and well-nigh violent combination of the defendants"; but the only evidence offered in the opinion as to violence or other form of intimidation was a finding by the court that, though other companies had been able to secure crews, the complainant company had been unsuccessful until it had obtained "the protection" of the preliminary restraining order. This was sufficient, concluded the court, to indicate an unlawful combination, and therefore to authorize the injunction *pendente lite* enjoining further interference with the business of the employer.

Although in *Blindell* v. *Hagan* Judge Billings had not accepted jurisdiction under the Sherman Act, less than two months later a case was properly presented, and on March 25 Billings became

---

cases, the first stage was the only one; and the third stage was seldom necessary. For the often decisive impact of the preliminary restraining order issued ex parte, and the gross abuses of this procedure, see Frankfurter and Greene, *The Labor Injunction*, pp. 64–66, 77–81, 182–188, 201. Frequently the preliminary restraining orders were not reported or restated in any supplementary proceedings; thus, in *Blindell* v. *Hagan*, evidence as to precisely what the defendants were enjoined from doing is not readily available.

[11] 54 Fed. 43.

the first judge to apply the Sherman Act to labor.[12] The case of *United States* v. *Workingmen's Amalgamated Council of New Orleans* [13] arose out of a general transportation strike in New Orleans called in November, 1892, in aid of a teamster's strike against the employment of nonunion men. The strike largely immobilized the city, and the United States Attorney, F. B. Earhart (who had also represented the shipowners in *Blindell* v. *Hagan*, evidently in a private capacity), sought an injunction on the ground that the through trade at New Orleans was being restrained by an illegal conspiracy in violation of the Sherman Act.[14] Judge Billings granted the injunction ex parte enjoining the Workingmen's Amalgamated Council from interfering with interstate and foreign commerce,[15] and in his opinion of March 25 extending the injunction *pendente lite* said this regarding the Sherman Act:

[12] Shortly before this March 25 case, Circuit Judge Putnam in the course of his opinion in the nonlabor case of *United States* v. *Patterson*, 55 Fed. 605 (D. Mass.), had stated clearly his belief that the Sherman Act did not apply to labor. Explaining a narrow interpretation of the act in regard to certain charges against the National Cash Register Co., the court said: "Careless or inept construction of the statute . . . will, if followed out logically, extend into very large fields; . . . the federal courts will be compelled to apply this statute to all attempts to restrain commerce among the states . . . by strikes or boycotts and by every method of interference by way of violence or intimidation. It is not to be presumed that Congress intended thus to extend the jurisdiction of the courts of the United States without very clear language. Such language I do not find in the statute." Judge Putnam's view was destined for a lonely isolation.

[13] 54 Fed. 994 (E.D. La.), *aff'd* 57 Fed. 85 (C.C.A., 5th).

[14] For some interesting remarks by an "insider" concerning the background of this case, the decision to proceed under the Sherman Act, and the close co-operation between U.S. Attorney Earhart and the businessmen of New Orleans, see the *Report of the Seventeenth Annual Meeting of the American Bar Association* (1894), pp. 21–24. See also Homer Cummings and Carl McFarland, *Federal Justice* (New York, 1937), p. 437.

[15] The text of the ex parte order is not given in the opinion, and again there is no readily available way of knowing just what Judge Billings enjoined.

I think the congressional debates show that the statute had its origin in the evils of massed capital; but, when the congress came to formulating the prohibition . . . the subject had so broadened in the minds of the legislators that the source of the evil was not regarded as material, and the evil in its entirety was dealt with. They made the interdiction include combinations of labor, as well as of capital.[16]

To the argument of counsel that a strike called merely to protest the employment of nonunion men was not intended as a restraint upon interstate commerce, and should therefore be free from the restrictions of the Sherman Act, Billings replied that what was important in the case was the actual effect of the strike upon interstate commerce. Together with certain allegations of intimidation, this was enough ground to effectuate the act and issue the injunction.

While the Sherman Anti-Trust Act was thus receiving its first judicial sanction for use against labor organizations, important litigation was in progress concerning the Interstate Commerce Act. Federal injunctions invoking this act had been issued in the Chicago, Burlington and Quincy strike of 1888,[17] but the first reported case relying mainly on the Interstate Commerce Act

---

[16] 54 Fed. 996. Billings' interpretation receives qualified support from Alpheus T. Mason's analysis in his *Organized Labor and the Law* (Durham, 1925), pp. 119–131. The Senate Judiciary Committee, some members of which favored including labor under the law, substituted broader language in its final report; that the Congress as a whole, however, was aware of the full implications of this change is unlikely.

[17] The background, development, and effects of this strike have been the subject of a recent excellent study by Donald L. McMurry, *The Great Burlington Strike of 1888* (Cambridge, 1956), who includes a chapter on the legal proceedings during the strike, pp. 114–137. It is noteworthy that in the only federally reported litigation of the strike, *Chicago, B. & Q. Ry. Co.* v. *Burlington, C. R. & N. Ry. Co.*, 54 Fed. 481 (S.D. Iowa), the court, while expressing views unfriendly to organized labor, took a narrow view of its own power, holding that the remedy for the evils threatened "must rest mainly with the legislative department." By 1893, however, the judges had been more fully alerted to a broadened conception of their role.

was *Toledo, Ann Arbor & Northern Michigan Ry. Co.* v. *Pennsylvania Co.*[18] (hereafter referred to as the *Ann Arbor* case), decided April 3, 1893. The case is also interesting for what it reveals of the standards judicial conservatism was applying in evaluating the conflicts in these cases between personal rights and property rights, and often between personal rights and the presumed needs of public order.

The precipitant of the dispute was the failure of negotiations for higher wages between the Brotherhood of Locomotive Engineers, the oldest of the four railroad brotherhoods, and the Toledo, Ann Arbor & Northern Michigan Railway Company. The company then hired nonunion men, and on March 7 the brotherhood struck, enforcing against the railroad its Rule 12. Rule 12 provided that it would be a "violation of obligation" meriting expulsion from the brotherhood for any member to handle the property of a railroad against which the brotherhood had called a strike. Accordingly, engineers on connecting railroads refused to haul cars or transship freight from the Toledo, Ann Arbor & Northern Michigan, and on March 11 the struck railroad petitioned the United States District Court at Cleveland for an injunction restraining the connecting railroads and their employees from refusing to haul its freight. The railroad was requesting, in effect, a mandatory injunction, an unusual procedure in a court of equity, but it was asked for on the ground that the third section of the Interstate Commerce Act, requiring common carriers to accept the freight of all connecting railroads equally and without discrimination, was being violated by the employees of the defendant railroads, to the irreparable harm of the petitioner. The restraining order was granted ex parte the same day by District Judge Augustus J. Ricks; and a few days later Circuit Judge William Howard Taft issued another temporary restraining order, this specifically directed against P. M.

[18] 54 Fed. 730 and 54 Fed. 746 (N.D. Ohio). The two phases to this litigation were reported separately; but in recounting the chronology, I have considered both together and cited them as one case.

Arthur, Grand Chief of the brotherhood, enjoining him from enforcing any rule of the brotherhood which would require the employees of railroads connecting to the Toledo, Ann Arbor & Northern Michigan not to handle that company's freight.

The next stage in the litigation began on March 18 when the Lake Shore & Southern Michigan Railway Company, one of the defendant railroads, made application for a contempt citation against five of its employees for refusing to obey the court's order. Judge Ricks thereupon ordered the five to appear March 21 to show cause why they should not be cited for contempt. But sometime between the eighteenth and the twenty-first, counsel for the railroads sought out Judge Ricks again, and, according to the statement of facts incorporated in Ricks' subsequent opinion, represented to the court

that there was great excitement and anxiety among the employees of the railroads involved as to the duties expected from them under the mandatory orders made, and it was therefore suggested that some statement from the court as to the scope and purpose of said orders would not only be very acceptable, but wholesome and beneficial, and might result in preventing the strike from spreading.

So, when the five employees were brought into court on the twenty-first, and before releasing them from day to day during the contempt proceedings, Judge Ricks read to them what he called an "admonition," which included, among other things, these extraordinary statements:

You are engaged in a service of a public character, and the public are interested not only in the way in which you perform your duties while you continue in that service, but are quite as much interested in the time and circumstances under which you quit that employment. You cannot always choose your own time and place for terminating these relations. If you were permitted to do so, you might quit your work at a time and place, and under circumstances, which would involve irreparable damage to your employers, and jeopardize the lives of the travelling public. . . . This court does not assume the power to compel you to continue your service to your employers against your will, but it does undertake to compel you to perform your whole duty while such relations continue.[19]

On April 3 the reported proceedings came to a close with the rendering of two opinions by the court, one by Judge Taft confirming the injunctions *pendente lite,* and one by Judge Ricks on the contempt charge. Both opinions deserve some scrutiny, as well for their strong statements of judicial power as for their near approach to the borderline of ordering specific performance of personal service.

Taft's opinion had three main sections. His first purpose was to establish the criminal conspiracy. By virtue of the provisions of the Interstate Commerce Act compelling every carrier to accept the interstate freight of every other carrier without discrimination, all who conspired to bring about a violation of those provisions, he asserted, were guilty of criminal conspiracy. "But it is said," the future President continued,

that it cannot be unlawful for an employee either to threaten to quit or actually to quit the service when not in violation of his contract, because a man has the inalienable right to bestow his labor where he will, and to withhold his labor as he will. Generally speaking, this is true, but not absolutely. If he uses the benefit which his labor is or will be to another, by threatening to withhold it or agreeing to bestow it, or by actually withholding or bestowing it, for the purpose of inducing, procuring, or compelling that other to commit an unlawful or criminal act, the withholding or bestowing of his labor for such a purpose is itself an unlawful and criminal act.[20]

Taft then delivered this formidable notice to the Brotherhood of Locomotive Engineers: "that, notwithstanding their perfect organization, and their charitable, temperance, and other elevating and most useful purposes, the existence and enforcement of rule 12, under their organic law, make the whole brotherhood a criminal conspiracy against the laws of their country."

The second section of Judge Taft's opinion served to show that

[19] *Ibid.,* p. 747.   [20] *Ibid.,* pp. 737–738, 739.

the complainant railroad would be entitled to damages for any irreparable harm it might endure as a result of the brotherhood's carrying out of Rule 12. The company had rights under the Interstate Commerce Act, and any losses it might sustain as a result of the deprivation of those rights by the illegal acts of the engineers would be recoverable at law—this aside from the fact that the engineers would be subject to the regular processes of the criminal courts.

But since recovery by damage suits was conjectural at best, this brought Taft directly to the third and crucial section of his opinion—what equity could do by preliminary injunction to prevent the loss. Taft's analysis here became quite involved, as he was under the necessity of justifying not merely a mandatory injunction, ordering the employees "to discharge the duties imposed by the interstate commerce law and to exchange with complainant interstate freight," but an injunction not much distinguishable from an order commanding enforced service. The conclusion of his analysis was that since the duties of common carriers could be enforced by mandatory injunction, the same could issue against their employees. But he strenuously denied that this was an enforced specific performance:

It is only an order restraining them, if they assume to do the work of the defendant companies, from doing it in a way which will violate not only the rights of the complainant, but also the order of the court made against their employers to preserve those rights. . . . They may avoid obedience to the injunction by actually ceasing to be employees of the company.[21]

Concerning the specific injunction against Grand Chief Arthur, commanding him not to issue an order to carry out Rule 12, or if already issued, to rescind it, Judge Taft explained that because of Arthur's authority in the brotherhood, Arthur's order to carry out Rule 12 would be obeyed, despite the contrary injunction of the court, with these unfortunate consequences:

[21] *Ibid.,* p. 743.

The interstate business of complainant will be interrupted and interfered with, at every hour of the day, and at every point within a radius of many miles, and all because of Arthur's order. The injury will be irreparable, and a judgment for damages at law will be wholly inadequate. The authorities leave no doubt that in such a case an injunction will issue against the stranger who thus intermeddles, and harasses complainant's business.[22]

If Judge Taft's opinion seemed to concentrate largely on the rights of the employer, to the substantial neglect of the employees' own rights and freedom of action, Judge Ricks's opinion on the contempt charges was even more unfriendly to the strikers: for Ricks coupled to Taft's emphasis on the employer's rights a concept of employees' obligations to the public and then permeated both with a strong antiunion bias less evident in Taft's opinion. Judge Ricks bore down throughout on the matter of the public interest: the engineers were skilled workmen, not easily replaced; the railroads on which they were employed carried thousands of tons of freight per day, sustaining the business of many industries and the labor of thousands of workmen; suspension of this traffic would cause untold hardship, economic paralysis, and numerous other injuries. And all this, continued Ricks,

because of the arbitrary action of a few hundred men, who, without any grievance of their own, without any dispute with their own employer as to wages or hours of service, as appears from the evidence in this case, quit their employment to aid men, it may be, on some road of minor importance, who have a difference with their employer which they fail to settle by ordinary methods.[23]

In the face of such conditions, the Judge continued, courts had the duty and the power to "meet the emergencies" as best they could. He admitted, however, that courts could not ordinarily enforce specific performance of personal service, and dismissed, therefore, the charges against four of the five men, who had simply quit their jobs outright rather than move the cars of the

[22] *Ibid.,* p. 744.   [23] *Ibid.,* p. 753.

Toledo, Ann Arbor & Northern Michigan. Although an employee of a public corporation could not "always choose his own time for quitting," in the present instance, Ricks said, he would give the four men the benefit of the doubt.

But the case of the fifth, one Lennon, was different. Like the others, when ordered to carry the offending cars, he had said, "I quit"; but then, after receiving notice from the brotherhood that the boycott was off, he had remained with his engine and brought the train in, intending to continue in the company's service. This had not been a real quitting of the job, said Judge Ricks, but "a trick to evade the order of the court. . . . It would leave this great corporation, operating 1,500 miles of railing, and moving several hundred cars per day, at the mercy of its employés, and subject the public, with its multitude of interests and rights, to irremediable injuries and losses." He fined Lennon fifty dollars plus costs, and warned all concerned "that the laws and orders having now been fully interpreted and made public, any violations thereof that may hereafter occur will be dealt with in a spirit and purpose quite different from those which have controlled us in this case." [24]

The ultimate step had not yet been taken. No court by injunction had actually ordered any man to remain on his job or face punishment for contempt.[25] On December 22, 1893, with

[24] *Ibid.*, pp. 757, 758. The contempt citation of Lennon was sustained by the Supreme Court in 1897, *In re Lennon*, 166 U.S. 548.

[25] An unusual case, not involving the injunction, but coming close to declaring the strike illegal, was *Waterhouse* v. *Comer*, 55 Fed. 149 (W.D. Ga.), decided by Judge Speer in April, 1893. The Brotherhood of Locomotive Engineers had petitioned the court to direct the court-appointed receiver of a railroad to enter into a contract with the brotherhood regarding wages and other matters. In an opinion well illustrating the public-order concept so characteristic of legal conservatism, the court granted the request, holding that stable labor relations was a matter of great concern to the public and criticizing the receiver for ignoring "the immensity of the changes occasioned by the phenomenal development of commerce and the prevalence of labor organizations." But the court attached the condition that the brotherhood suspend permanently its Rule 12, providing for the automatic boycott of struck railroads. Any

the depression rapidly deepening, and class tension growing, Circuit Judge James G. Jenkins, speaking for the United States District Court at Milwaukee, issued an ex parte order enjoining workmen to remain on the job or face court punishment.[26]

The legal process behind this order began on December 19 with a petition by the receivers of the Northern Pacific Railroad Company requesting authorization from the court for a contemplated reduction in wages,[27] and informing the court that certain of their employees ("whose names the receivers were unable to state") had threatened in the event of adoption of the revised wage schedules to quit the service of the receivers in a body, to prevent by violence others from taking their places, to disable cars and equipment, and in other ways to destroy and prevent the use of the property.[28] The court, responding at once to the re-

---

combination, whether of employees or others, enforcing a restraint of interstate commerce was illegal under the Interstate Commerce and Sherman Anti-Trust Acts, said Judge Speer, and it followed therefore "that a strike, or 'boycott,' as it is popularly called, if it was ever effective, can be so no longer."

[26] Jenkins' injunctions led to an investigation by the House Judiciary Committee to determine whether Jenkins had "exceeded his jurisdiction in granting said writs, abused the powers or process of said court, or oppressively exercised the same, or has used his office as judge to intimidate or wrongfully restrain the employees of the Northern Pacific Railway Company" (*Congressional Record,* 53d Cong., 2d sess., 26 [March 2–6, 1894], 2533, 2534, 2629). The Committee reported on June 8 with a severe condemnation of Jenkins' actions as "reprehensible" and a "gross abuse of judicial authority." A minority report was filed, objecting to a congressional committee attempting to rebuke a federal judge on a point of law (*Receivership of the Northern Pacific Railroad Company,* U.S. 53d Cong., 2d sess., H. Rept., 1049 [1894]).

[27] Railroad receiverships were commonplace in the depression of the 1890's and were often accompanied by reductions in wages. In this case the contemplated reduction was from 5 to 10 per cent, in addition to a downward reclassification of job positions.

[28] The Judiciary Committee revealed that at the time of the petition the receivers showed correspondence to Jenkins which indicated the receivers' fear of being unable to obtain enough replacements to continue operations—but containing nothing to indicate any intent on the

ceivers' petition, authorized the reduced wage schedules; [29] and on the same day it issued its injunction aimed at preventing the strike. Directed to all employees of the receivers, all associations and combinations whether or not of employees of the receivers, and "all persons generally," the court's writ "charged and commanded" that each and every one of its recipients [30] "absolutely desist and refrain" from, among other things, harming or interfering "in any manner, by force, threats, or otherwise" with whoever wished to continue in the service of the railroad or take the places of those who did quit, and from

combining and conspiring to quit, with or without notice, the service of said receivers, with the object and intent of crippling the property in their custody, or embarrassing the operation of said railroad, and from so quitting the service of the said receivers, with or without notice, as to cripple the property, or to prevent or hinder the operation of said railroad.[31]

Upon receipt of a supplemental petition from the receivers, dated December 22, 1893, alleging that strike committees had been set up and that the railroad brotherhoods were about to order a strike to begin January 1, with consequent irreparable harm to the property and great injury to a large portion of the country traversed by the Northern Pacific Railroad, because the area was not serviced by any other railroad or telegraph line or express company, Judge Jenkins issued a supplemental writ, which

---

part of the employees to harm or cripple the railroad by physical means (*Receivership of the Northern Pacific Railroad Company*, pp. 10–12).

[29] Jenkins' prompt acquiescence to the receivers' schedules was a special target of the Committee's ire, the Committee pointing out that under the rules for receiverships the employees were also servants of the court and were entitled to be heard on the proposed rates.

[30] The employees of the railroad were estimated at 12,000, so this was one of the original "blanket injunctions" that formed the precedents for the more famous Debs injunctions of July, 1894.

[31] This text is taken from Jenkins' written opinion of April 6, to be examined shortly. *Farmer's Loan and Trust Co.* v. *Northern Pacific R.R. Co.*, 60 Fed. 803 (E.D. Wisc.) at 807. The italics were used by Jenkins to specify those parts of the injunction being contested by the brotherhoods.

repeated the provisions of the first writ, with the following additional clause:

And from combining or conspiring together or with others, either jointly or severally, or as committees, or as officers of any so-called "labor organization," with the design or purpose of causing a strike upon the lines of railroad operated by said receivers, and from ordering, recommending, approving, or advising others to quit the service of the receivers of the Northern Pacific Railroad Company on January 1, 1894, or at any other time, and from ordering, recommending, approving, or advising by communication or instruction or otherwise, the employés of said receivers, or any of them, or of said Northern Pacific Railroad Company, to join in a strike on said January 1, 1894, or at any other time, and from ordering, recommending, or advising any committee or committees, or class or classes of employés of said receivers to strike or join in a strike on January 1, 1894, or at any other time, until the further order of this court.[32]

On February 15 (six weeks after the strike was supposed to have begun) the brotherhoods moved the court to strike from its writs of injunction the parts italicized above. Argument was heard, and on April 6 the court rendered its opinion.

Judge Jenkins' first statement in his opinion was a denial that the court had any intention of taking part in the conflict between capital and labor, a noteworthy comment in the light of the background and development of the case. If the danger from that conflict required additional laws, Jenkins continued, that was for the legislature to determine. "But it is the duty of the court," the Judge felt bound to point out, "to restrain those warring factions, so far as their action may infringe the declared law of the land, that society may not be disrupted, or its peace invaded, and that individual and corporate rights may not be infringed." [33]

Jenkins only briefly discussed the power of the court to issue a writ of injunction generally in the case—threatened irreparable injury to the property, inadequacy of compensation at law, multi-

[32] *Ibid.*, p. 812.   [33] *Ibid.*, p. 804.

plicity of suits, and great public privation—and quickly turned
his attention to the particular paragraphs in dispute. "It is contended," he took note, "that the restraint imposed . . . [in the
original injunction] . . . is in derogation of common right, and
an unlawful restraint upon the individual to work for whomsoever he may choose, to determine the conditions upon which he
will labor, and to abandon such employment whenever he may
desire." But that interpretation, explained Judge Jenkins, was
based upon

a lamentable misapprehension of the terms "liberty" and "right." . . .
Rights are not absolute but relative. Rights grow out of duty and
are limited by duty. One has not the right arbitrarily to quit service
without regard to the necessities of that service. His right of aban-
donment is limited by the assumption of that service, and the conditions and exigencies attaching thereto.

And the Judge offered this example in point: "It would be mon-
strous if a surgeon, upon demand and refusal of larger compensation, could lawfully abandon an operation partially performed,
leaving his knife in the bleeding body of his patient." Unable to
agree with counsel that this illustration was weakened because
human life was involved, Jenkins said: "Whether the effect be the
destruction of life or the destruction of property, the principle
is the same." [34]

But the most strongly worded part of Jenkins' opinion dealt
with his supplemental writ where he had enjoined the calling of
a strike per se, without any qualification as to intent "to cripple
the property" or "to embarrass the operation of the railroad."
As Jenkins himself phrased the issue, it was nothing less than
"whether a strike is lawful," any strike, that is. But first, what
was a strike? Counsel for the brotherhoods had proposed this
definition of the term:

A strike is a concerted cessation of or refusal to work until or unless
certain conditions which obtain or are incident to the terms of the

[34] *Ibid.*, p. 812.

employment are changed. The employé declines to longer work, knowing full well that the employer may immediately employ another to fill his place, also knowing that he may or may not be reemployed or returned to service. The employer has the option of acceding to the demand and returning the old employés to service, or of employing new men, or of forcing conditions under which the old men are glad to return to service under the old conditions.

To which Judge Jenkins made the following reply:

I doubt, if in the light of the history of strikes, the child would be recognized by this baptismal name. One who has read the history of the strike at Homestead, with its cruel murders and barbarous torture; . . . one who has read of the not infrequent summoning of the militia by the authorities of the state to put down riot and turbulence,—the universal concomitants of a strike,—would hardly yield assent to the definition suggested as even faintly conveying the true idea of a strike, as known of all men. . . .

To my thinking, a much more exact definition of a strike is this: A combined effort among workmen to compel the master to the concession of a certain demand, by preventing the conduct of his business until compliance with the demand. The concerted cessation of work is but one of, and the least effective of, the means to the end; the intimidation of others from engaging in the service, the interference with, and the disabling and destruction of, property, and resort to actual force and violence, when requisite to the accomplishment of the end, being the other, and more effective, means employed. It is idle to talk of a peaceable strike. None such has ever occurred. The suggestion is an impeachment of intelligence. . . . All combinations to interfere with perfect freedom in the proper management and control of one's lawful business, to dictate the terms upon which such business shall be conducted, by means of threats or by interference with property or traffic or with the lawful employment of others, are within the condemnation of the law.[35]

Inserting here a long quotation from Justice Brewer's New York State Bar Association speech of 1893, wherein Brewer had

[35] *Ibid.*, pp. 820–821.

also characterized the strike as essentially coercive and unlawful,[36] Jenkins concluded:

The strike has become a serious evil, destructive to property, destructive to individual right, injurious to the conspirators themselves, and subversive of republican institutions. Certainly no court should give encouragement to any combination thus destructive of the very fabric of our government, tending to the disruption of society, and the obliteration of legal and natural rights. Whatever other doctrine may be asserted by reckless agitators, it must ever remain the duty of the courts, in the protection of society, and in the execution of the laws of the land, to condemn, prevent, and punish all such unlawful conspiracies and combinations.[37]

In the first year of this important series of federal cases, 1893, professional reactions to the new uses of the injunction were few, and generally favorable. Surprisingly too, they crossed over the broad divisions of opinion between conservative and progressive that otherwise marked legal attitudes. Thus, the May–June, 1893,

---

[36] See *supra*, ch. v, n. 3. Jenkins' quotation from Brewer, almost a full page of small type in the Federal Reporter, was the lengthiest excerpt of any bar association speech in a judicial opinion seen by this writer.

[37] 60 Fed. 822–823. Jenkins' general denial of the brotherhoods' motion (he granted it in a minor particular) was reversed in part in October, 1894, by Supreme Court Justice Harlan, speaking for the 7th Circuit Court of Appeals, in an important opinion (*Arthur* v. *Oakes*, 63 Fed. 310), which finally arrested the spreading scope of the labor injunction at the threshold of compulsory labor. Striking down key sections of Jenkins' original and amended writs as "an invasion of one's natural liberty" and establishing "a condition of involuntary servitude," Harlan stated: "We are not prepared, in the absence of evidence, to hold, as matter of law, that a combination among employés, having for its object their orderly withdrawal in large numbers or in a body from the service of their employers, on account simply of a reduction in their wages, is not a 'strike,' within the meaning of the term as commonly used. Such a withdrawal, although amounting to a strike, is not . . . either illegal or criminal." The injunctions should have been more specifically drawn, he concluded, to indicate that the restraints were meant to apply only to strikes unlawfully conducted or lawfully conducted for an unlawful purpose.

number of the *American Law Review,* under the editorship of
the progressive Seymour D. Thompson, ended a long note describing the Ann Arbor injunctions of Judges Taft and Ricks
with this paragraph:

It is to be remarked, in conclusion, that this is a new and most
interesting phase of the struggle between labor and capital. The
spectacle of the action of the Federal judges above referred to is
simply that of a new, independent, fearless, conservative force entering the arena. . . . The action of the Federal judges seems to have
been applauded by the best portion of the public press without
distinction of party, and there is hardly any doubt that their action
is largely supported by the conservative public opinion of the
country.[38]

The labor injunction also received approbation at the 1893
meeting of the American Bar Association in the course of a
broader discussion of capital and labor by U. M. Rose, a prominent attorney of Little Rock, Arkansas.[39] Speaking on the topic,
"The Law of Trusts and Strikes," Rose was on the whole not unsympathetic to labor and to labor unions. He pointed out that the
strike, though often having disastrous effects upon the strikers
themselves, had benefited labor in important ways: as an influence
contributing to the long-term upward trend of wages; as a potent
threat inducing concessions not otherwise attainable; and as a
demonstration that "laboring men have rights as well as employers, rights which they are able and willing to defend." Rose also
deplored the tendency of political economists to regard labor
"as a mere commodity": labor was indeed a commodity, but a
commodity of a "peculiar kind," the laborer transferring not

[38] *American Law Review,* 27 (May–June, 1893), 409–410. See also the
Minnesota Law Journal, 1 (May, 1893), 17–19, supporting the "aggressive" opinions of Judges Ricks and Taft.

[39] U. M. Rose, "The Law of Trusts and Strikes," *Report of the Sixteenth Annual Meeting of the American Bar Association* (1893), pp. 287–
321. Rose was one of Arkansas' most distinguished lawyers of the late
1890's and 1900's, becoming president of the Arkansas Bar Association
and the American Bar Association.

only his labor but also a part of his personal liberty. In making this transaction, Rose explained, the individual laborer suffered from many inequalities vis-à-vis the capitalist, and from this derived the necessity for trade unions and for laws protecting laborers from the "oppression of employers"—in order to improve labor's bargaining position.

Nevertheless, when Rose turned to the question of how to prevent strikes and their injurious consequences, he commended with great favor "the very able and instructive opinions" of Taft and Ricks in the *Ann Arbor* case, quoting long excerpts therefrom. Those decisions, said Rose, were "among the most important . . . that have been rendered for many years. It opens a new perspective of practical utility to be attained through the preventive process of courts of equity." [40]

Apparently then, in these early evaluations of the labor injunction, the lawyer's concern for public order and the well-regulated society, common alike to every segment of professional opinion, had been sufficient to override other considerations. It remained for Oliver Wendell Holmes, still a Judge of the Massachusetts Supreme Court, to clarify the nature of the judicial process in injunction cases. Exploring the frontiers of the law of torts, Holmes's masterly paper in the *Harvard Law Review* of April, 1894, "Privilege, Malice, and Intent," [41] revealed to lawyers that in any borderline case, the judicial determination of liability or unlawfulness was essentially a judgment on policy. By the law of torts, not all inflictions of injury, no matter if intentional, were liable for damages; under certain circumstances, the claim of privilege might be invoked to outweigh the harm inflicted.

What were those circumstances? Examining various categories

[40] *Ibid.*, p. 314. Rose also sharply attacked the trusts, criticizing in particular their monopolistic concept of "overproduction," and urging vigorous enforcement of the Sherman Act "in the spirit in which it was enacted."

[41] Oliver W. Holmes, Jr., "Privilege, Malice, and Intent," *Harvard Law Review*, 8 (April, 1894), 1–14.

of cases, Holmes directed special attention to the business world, where the intentional doing of harm to competitors had become privileged on the ground that free competition was a valued public policy the worth of which outweighed its costs. A similar balancing of values, Holmes contended, took place when the acts of trade unions in labor disputes were brought within the judicial purview. In any specific case, said Holmes,

the ground of decision really comes down to a proposition of policy of rather a delicate nature concerning the merit of the particular benefit to themselves intended by the defendants [the trade unionists], and suggests a doubt whether judges with different economic sympathies might not decide such a case differently when brought face to face with the issue.[42]

Holmes was careful to point out that he was not criticizing the judges for having to decide questions primarily legislative in character—this was unavoidable where no statutory guide existed; nor was he attempting to instruct them as to correct public policy. As Holmes put it, his purpose was to awaken judges to

the danger . . . that such considerations should have their weight in an inarticulate form as unconscious prejudice or half conscious inclination. To measure them justly needs not only the highest powers of a judge and a training which the practice of law does not insure, but also a freedom from prepossessions which is very hard to obtain. It seems to me desirable that the work should be done with express recognition of its nature.[43]

Judge Holmes's contention that the judicial decision in injunction cases depended ultimately upon the attitudes of the judge, rather than any imperative dictates of legal right, seemed borne out by the Jenkins injunctions in the *Northern Pacific* case. For the first time a movement of opinion against the labor injunction, at least in its latest uses, was evident in the profession. William Draper Lewis, associate editor of the *American Law Register*, who had been highly critical of labor after the Homestead riot,[44] reproved the Jenkins injunctions for having treated the employees of the railroad "as if they were members of the United States army and had surrendered their will into the hands of the Federal judiciary."[45] Seymour D. Thompson, writing in the *American Law Review*, though supporting the labor injunction when used to restrain strikers from disabling property, interfering with other employees, or engaging in certain types of boycotts, attacked the Jenkins injunctions as clearly beyond those bounds.[46] To prevent, under the threat of contempt, the mere going out on strike was "tantamount," he charged,

> to decreeing a specific performance of a contract of service, which results in a state of *slavery*. . . . As they [the workers] have no contract on which they can claim a continuation of their employment, upon what principle can it be claimed that their master has a contract on which he can seize them in the iron vise of a Federal injunction, and hold them to their employment indefinitely?[47]

But the most searching examination of the Jenkins decision, with implications for the labor injunction generally, came from the Far Western Territory of Utah, in a paper read by Walter Murphy of Salt Lake City before the first annual meeting of the Territorial Bar Association of Utah, held in June, 1894.[48] Seeking to delineate the radical nature of the Northern Pacific injunctions, Murphy's first task was to establish the traditional limitations of equity. He agreed that "a legal remedy, like wine, ought to improve with age." Still, when any medicine was made a panacea, there was the risk that "the remedy might itself become a disease," and Murphy pointed out that Congress was already finding it necessary to consider a statutory cure[49] for "the in-

[44] *American Law Register*, n.s., 31 (Oct., 1892), 691–700.
[45] *Ibid.*, 33 (Jan., 1894), 81–82.
[46] *American Law Review*, 28 (March–April, 1894), 268–269.
[47] *Ibid.*, pp. 271–272 (italics in source).
[48] "The Use of the Writ of Injunction to Prevent Strikes," *Report of the First Annual Meeting of the Territorial Bar Association of Utah* (1894), pp. 30–54.
[49] The House Committee that investigated the Jenkins injunctions

junction habit, a habit that had begun to assume the proportions of a national epidemic and to ravage some of our most valued courts." Summing up his argument that equity was not expansible at mere will, Murphy said:

Although, in other words, equity jurisprudence had its *origin* in the actual making of new law by the chancellors according to their untrammeled individual notions of justice and expedience, without regard to any body of fixed rules or principles, nevertheless courts of equity have for generations ceased to be parts of the law-making power, for generations the individual "conscience" of the chancellor has ceased to govern the decision of his case, for generations equity jurisprudence has been a crystallized mass of well-defined rules and principles.[50]

Murphy then went directly to his principal question, on what grounds, if any, equity could enjoin a strike. "But what is a strike?" asked Murphy. Judge Jenkins in the *Northern Pacific* case, he noted, after having "laugh[ed] . . . to scorn" the definition advanced by counsel for the employees, had attempted his own definition. Quoting substantial excerpts from the Jenkins opinion on the nature of a strike, Murphy was quite outspoken in his comments:

So far is it from being true, as said by Judge Jenkins, that the suggestion that a strike may be a peaceable affair is "an impeachment of intelligence," that on the contrary His Honor's assertion that all strikes are crimes or necessarily or even in most cases attended by the perpetration of criminal acts is an impeachment of the learned Judge's candor and truthfulness.[51]

After a lengthy analysis and criticism of the Jenkins opinion in the light of traditional uses of equity, Murphy concluded his paper with this farseeing perception into the broader issues at stake:

---

recommended a limitation of the power to punish for contempt (*Receivership of the Northern Pacific Railroad Company*, p. 18).

[50] *Op. cit.*, p. 32 (italics in source).   [51] *Ibid.*, p. 38.

The subject touched upon in this paper has wider aspects than such as are merely legal or constitutional. We are here brought into the great domain of economics and sociology. . . . Not strikes alone but violent and bloody strikes are beyond all question increasing as time goes on. . . . However ardent his desire to maintain the majesty of the law, every thoughtful man feels the certainty that neither legislatures nor courts can permanently control the phenomena of a broadening and deepening social and industrial evolution, that any statute or any course of judicial decision which runs counter to the great tendencies of the times may create an eddy in the stream of events, but cannot either stop or divert it. If modern industrial warfare is to be stopped, it can be stopped only by an alteration of the conditions which produce it.[52]

The conditions producing industrial warfare were indeed becoming steadily more serious in 1894. The financial panic that broke upon the country in May, 1893, when the gold reserve in the Treasury fell below $100,000,000 precipitating a general flight of capital and a collapse of business values, had resulted by the end of the year in 2,000,000 or more unemployed out of a total nonagricultural labor force of some 15,000,000.[53] The distress of the unemployed combined with the fiat-money beliefs of Jacob S. Coxey to produce the "industrial armies" of the spring of 1894, "petitions on boots" which with courageous, if pathetic, optimism proposed to march on Washington and persuade Congress to adopt inflationary road-building programs—this, forty years before the New Deal.[54] Although the various Coxey armies

[52] *Ibid.*, p. 54.

[53] On unemployment, see Samuel Rezneck, "Unemployment, Unrest, and Relief in the United States during the Depression of 1893–1897," *Journal of Political Economy*, 61 (Aug., 1953), 327; Donald L. McMurry, *Coxey's Army* (Boston, 1929), p. 9. The labor force figure is an approximation obtained by interpolation from the Bureau of Census figures for 1890 and 1900 (U.S. Bureau of the Census, *Historical Statistics of the United States*, 1789–1945 [Washington, 1949], p. 63).

[54] McMurry's monograph cited above is the standard work on all phases of the Coxey movement, including its more amusing and bizarre

seldom numbered more than five to ten thousand at any one time, and although the main marches from Ohio and California were generally disciplined and law-abiding, there was enough excitement and train-stealing, particularly in the Northwest,[55] to confirm the alarms of many conservatives. Conservatives were particularly alarmed—and incensed—at the enthusiastic receptions the marchers received where Populist governors were in office, in Oregon, Colorado, and Kansas.[56] "What goes on to-day may be little more than a farce, but those who tolerate and encourage it," the eminent Judge Thomas M. Cooley admonished, "should bear in mind, that success achieved in ways which defy the laws is incipient revolution, and may possibly grow in time to proportions that threaten if they do not precipitate civil war." [57]

---

as well as serious aspects. Coxey and his leading associates were arrested for trespassing on the Capitol grounds, and their demands were ignored by Congress.

[55] Most of the railroads in the Northwest were in the hands of court-appointed receivers, and the United States District Courts in the area refused to permit the "borrowing" of trains. Attorney General Olney directed United States attorneys to obtain injunctions to prevent interference with the trains and to enforce the injunctions with federal marshals and, when necessary, with units of the regular army (McMurry, *op. cit.,* pp. 197–226).

[56] As the "industrials" passed through these states, often accompanied by a large retinue of reporters, Governors Pennoyer, Waite, and Lewelling found numerous opportunities to broadcast widely their denunciations of "the money power" and "Wall Street." For the anticapitalist attitudes of Colorado Populism and its leader, Governor Davis H. Waite, see Leon W. Fuller, *"Colorado's Revolt against Capitalism," Mississippi Valley Historical Review,* 21 (Dec., 1934), 343–360.

[57] "Fundamentals of American Liberty," *Michigan Law Journal,* 3 (June, 1894), 149–156. Cooley criticized the plans for mass petitions in person as "unknown to our political system" and a threat to the distinction between "representative" and "democratic" government. The *American Law Review,* which reacted with marked disfavor to the direct-action methods of labor protest in 1894, characterized the men of Coxey's armies as the "least deserving of the community" and their demands for a public works program as a "new advance in State socialism." Dwelling at length on the seizure of trains and the "terrorizing" of com-

Even stronger provocation to rising conservative fears was a major resurgence of labor militancy. A turn to industrial unionism had begun shortly after the great defeats of organized labor in the strikes of 1892, at Homestead, Coeur d'Alene, and Buffalo.[58] The two largest industrial unions of the 1890's, the Western Federation of Miners and the American Railway Union, were both organized in 1893 and grew rapidly in the next year. In 1894, as wages were cut sharply, over 700,000 workers became involved in strikes,[59] surpassing the record of 1886. The miners strike in Ohio, which began at the end of April and ended in defeat three months later, pulled out 125,000 miners though the union membership numbered only 20,000. And on May 11 began the famous strike at Pullman, Illinois; with the entrance into the fray on June 26 of the 150,000 men of the American Railway Union, organized for aggressive action and determined to make the strike a major test of labor solidarity, the conflict of the 1890's between capital and labor came to its climax. An already gravely disturbed legal conservatism was thrown into a state of acute tension, while both judiciary and executive became closely involved with the course of the strike.

---

munities, editor Seymour D. Thompson urged Congress to pass a national vagrancy act: "Interstate tramping is interstate commerce, and as such is subject to regulation by Congress" (28 [May–June, 1894], 420).

[58] Commons and Associates, *History of Labour in the United States*, II, 495–499.

[59] The number of strikers is stated in Commons as "nearly 750,000," *ibid.*, p. 501, and this figure is followed by Rezneck, *op. cit.*, pp. 334–335. The figure of the Commissioner of Labor, as given in *Historical Statistics of the United States*, p. 73, is 690,000. The same publication calculates this as 8.3 per cent of the total employed wage earners. Comparable figures for 1893: 288,000 and 3.2 per cent.

VII

The "Debs Rebellion" and Legal Conservatism

THE conservative crisis of the mid-nineties developed in three main phases. The first phase in 1894 was the immediate consequence of the depression and involved direct-action methods of lower-class protest, culminating in the great Chicago railroad strike. In meeting this phase of the crisis, the Executive and the Judiciary, employing principally the army and the injunction, worked hand in hand, with the Legislature in a passive role. The second phase, the most significant of the three from the constitutional point of view, witnessed the climax in the first half of 1895 of the decade-long struggle between legislative majorities and judicial review. The income tax case was now the decisive factor; and here the Judiciary, standing alone among the arms of government in defending conservative interests, and with the legal profession itself sharply divided, struck down the income tax by a narrow margin. Out of these two phases developed the third phase in the second half of 1895 and in 1896, a major revolt within the profession against judicial supremacy, capped by the political challenge of the Bryan campaign with its free-silver and anticourt planks. In this period the Judiciary was on the defensive, and when it had successfully withstood this attack, the conservative crisis of the 1890's was over.

The Chicago railroad strike of 1894, or as it was often called at the time, the "Debs rebellion," ranks among the major landmarks in the history of American labor. The largest union of the mid-nineties challenged the most powerful of capitalist concentrations; and as the interstate commerce and transportation of almost half the nation were caught in the stranglehold of the strike, the public attention was riveted on the struggle. Both sides laid claim to public virtue: labor fought for the solidarity of the union but declared that the principle of arbitration was at stake; capital fought for the prerogatives of management but asserted it was defending law and order. What finally determined the outcome of the strike, however, was neither capital nor labor, but rather the crisis psychology of the 1890's. For as the strike spread, assuming more and more the aspects of class warfare, an alarmed legal conservatism, unfavorable to the strike to begin with, intervened in strength and broke the strike.

The background and development of the strike are worth reviewing in some detail.[1] The strike had its origin in the action

[1] The most comprehensive study of the strike, written from a prolabor point of view, is Almont Lindsey's monograph, *The Pullman Strike* (Chicago, 1942). Also valuable are Ray Ginger, *The Bending Cross: A Biography of Eugene Victor Debs* (New Brunswick, 1949), pp. 108–151; Harry Barnard, *Eagle Forgotten: The Life of John Peter Altgeld* (Indianapolis, 1938), pp. 280–317; and Allan Nevins, *Grover Cleveland: A Study in Courage* (New York, 1932), pp. 611–628. All are biographies containing interesting material on various aspects of the strike, and all are largely sympathetic to labor. The conservative viewpoint may be examined in Henry James's *Richard Olney and His Public Service* (Boston, 1923), pp. 42–59 and 201–207, which contains important material on Olney; an Amherst College lecture by Willard L. King, reprinted in *The Pullman Boycott of 1894: The Problem of Federal Intervention*, Colston E. Warne, ed. (Boston, 1955), pp. 85–97; and a recent biography by George Shiras, 3rd, *Justice George Shiras, Jr., of Pittsburgh* (Pittsburgh, 1953), pp. 149–153, drawing largely on King's paper. For primary sources, invaluable materials are in the report of the special commission

of the Pullman Palace Car Company in reducing wages at its manufacturing plants some 25 per cent between September, 1893, and May, 1894. The company claimed this was necessary to meet a decline in its construction orders, although the company's stocks paid the usual 8 per cent dividend in fiscal 1893 and 1894. At the same time the company refused to reduce its rents in the so-called model town of Pullman, a company-owned residential area south of Chicago—rents which averaged 25 per cent higher than in similar communities. By the spring of 1894 conditions had become intolerable in the town. Enduring in many cases hunger and privation, and resentful over long-standing abuses associated with Pullman paternalism, the Pullman workers turned in large numbers to the newly organized and aggressive American Railway Union. So rapidly did organization take place that by the beginning of May the workers felt strong enough to demand of the company an adjustment of grievances. The president of the company, George M. Pullman, refused, however, to make any concessions in wages or rents, though stating he was willing to investigate shop abuses. On May 10 three members of the grievance committee were dismissed from employment (though the company claimed afterward their dismissal was for other reasons), and the next day 3,000 workers went out on strike. The company dismissed the remaining 300 workers and closed its plants.

One month later the first annual convention of the American Railway Union opened in Chicago. The American Railway Union had been organized in June, 1893, under the leadership of Eugene V. Debs. For many years a leading official of the Brotherhood of Locomotive Firemen, Debs had become dis-

---

appointed by President Cleveland to investigate the causes of the strike (U.S. Strike Commission, *Report on the Chicago Strike of June–July, 1894*, 53d Cong., 3d sess., Sen. Ex. Doc. 7 [1895]). Grover Cleveland's *The Government in the Chicago Strike of 1894* (Princeton, 1913), offers only the bare outline of federal policies. My review of the strike proper relies upon the sources above, supplemented for the legal aspects by the same categories of material used throughout this study.

satisfied with the conservative policies of the brotherhoods, and in 1892 he had resigned his offices in the B.L.F. to be free to form one big union for all railroad employees, skilled and unskilled. The American Railway Union, the fruit of his efforts, grew rapidly, especially in the Midwest and West, and reached the surprising total of 150,000 members by June of 1894. Membership in the union was open only to railroad employees, but the union made room for the Pullman workers on the basis of a few miles of private track maintained by Pullman and because most of the Pullman workers were said to be former railroad men.[2]

The main order of business at the Chicago convention turned out to be the Pullman strike. Debs and other leaders of the union, well aware of the depression conditions throughout the nation, had vainly cautioned the Pullman workers against a strike. The union leaders realized that in the event of a deadlock at Pullman the whole union might find itself involved in behalf of the Pullman locals, and the times were unpropitious for any major action. The depression had left many railroad men unemployed in the East who could be used for strikebreaking; the old brotherhoods were still hostile and might work actively against the new union; and the American Railway Union itself, though zealous and large numerically, was young, inexperienced, and possessed of very little in the way of strike funds. Nevertheless, the Pullman workers had struck; and when their delegation appeared at the union convention with tales of the injustices suffered under Pullman and pleaded for help from their fellow unionists, the convention was aroused to great emotion. The other convention delegates were themselves smarting under a variety of grievances occasioned by depression wage cuts and discrimination against the union, and it was easy to feel that the

[2] As the Strike Commission rightly pointed out, the incorporation into the American Railway Union of nonrailroad workers "so alien to its natural membership as the Pullman employees" was a major weakness in the union and ultimately entailed its destruction (*Report on the Chicago Strike*, p. xxvii).

common interest demanded a united stand against the arbitrary power of corporate capital. Besides, the prestige of the union was now at stake; to see the strikers at Pullman defeated without a real struggle would seriously weaken the morale of the membership and hurt the union's chances for future expansion.

The convention determined to intervene. With Debs urging patience, one committee and then another tried to persuade the Pullman Company to arbitrate; but the company's attitude was entirely negative. The Pullman workers, said Vice-President Wickes, now stood to the company "in the same position as the man on the sidewalk." On June 22 a special committee proposed that if Pullman refused to arbitrate within four days, the American Railway Union should strike the company's two small repair shops and declare a general boycott of all Pullman cars, the major source of the company's revenue. As planned by Debs, the union would demand of the individual railroads that they cut out their Pullman cars. If a railroad refused, the union switchmen would refuse to switch Pullman cars; the switchmen would undoubtedly be discharged, and then the whole membership of the union on the road involved would go on strike. The convention accepted the report; the company's position remained unyielding; and on June 26 the great Chicago strike commenced.

In undertaking a general boycott of Pullman cars, the American Railway Union came into direct conflict with the General Managers Association, a close-knit organization representing twenty-four railroads having terminals in Chicago. First formed in 1886 to deal with strike situations on various roads, the association had developed by 1893 a number of techniques for handling common labor problems, including such matters as uniform wage schedules, recruitment of strikebreakers, apportionment of revenue losses resulting from strikes, and the handling of relations with county and city officials.[3] It was partly

[3] Chairman St. John, addressing a meeting in August, 1893, claimed the members of the association were protected against strikes "to an extent that can hardly admit defeat" (quoted in Donald L. McMurry, "Labor

to meet this formidable nexus of power that Debs had advocated one strong railway union, and the two opposing organizations, union and management association, had always been on hostile terms.

The announcement of the boycott afforded the general managers an opportunity to crush the American Railway Union. All the railroads comprising the association had strict contracts with the Pullman Company, obliging them to carry Pullman cars on regular schedules, and had the railroads acceded to the union's boycott and cut out their Pullman cars, they would have been subject to civil suit by Pullman for breach of contract. The general managers were thus in a very strong position vis-à-vis the strikers, both legally and for the purpose of appealing to public opinion. The American Railway Union, with no overt grievance of its own against the railroads, was demanding nevertheless that the railroads violate their contracts with the Pullman Company, and in support of these conceivably unlawful demands was prepared to go the length of tying up interstate commerce in vast areas of the nation, obstructing the passage of the United States mails, and bringing distress and ruin to large numbers of innocent persons. To the conservative mind of the 1890's, subject to growing fears of unruly majorities and class conflict, the decision of the American Railway Union to press ahead with a boycott and strike, despite all considerations of contractual and property rights and the public necessity, smacked of the most irresponsible radicalism, of "anarchy" and "communism." 4 Under these circumstances, all that the General Managers Association had to do was stand on a policy of noncompliance with the union's demands, pleading its contracts with Pullman and the

---

Policies of the General Managers' Association of Chicago, 1886–1894," *Journal of Economic History*, 13 [Spring, 1953], 160–178).

4 It was also known that there were more than 100,000 unemployed in the Chicago area, and many observers feared that any spark, such as a major strike centering at Chicago, would ignite a dangerous conflagration among these men.

public needs, and wait for public pressure to bring about government intervention and the breaking of the strike.

The course of the strike moved rapidly. All railroads affiliated
with the General Managers Association rejected demands of the
union to operate without Pullman cars; and when union switchmen refused to switch Pullmans, they were summarily dismissed.
The A.R.U. men then struck on one road after another, successfully hampering the movement of freight trains in particular. By
July 1, despite the nonco-operation of the old brotherhoods with
the American Railway Union, freight traffic in and out of
Chicago was almost at a standstill, with a similar condition prevailing at other key points of the twenty-seven Western states
and territories where the strike extended. Meanwhile the sen-
sationalism and misrepresentation of the press aided the General
Managers Association by playing up isolated instances of violence during the first few days as mob rule and anarchy. The
way was thus opened for government intervention, which was
soon forthcoming through the office of the Attorney General.

In the person of Attorney General Richard Olney, former
railroad lawyer and corporation executive, the railroads had an
excellent ally. For Olney, partly no doubt because of his pro-
railroad associations, but perhaps more decisively because of his
conservative repugnance to the direct-action techniques of lower-
class radicalism, saw eye to eye with the General Managers Association on the necessity of crushing both the strike and the
American Railway Union, and he was prepared to take the
strongest steps to accomplish these ends.[5]

[5] Olney's attitude toward organized labor, like that of many legal
conservatives, was ambiguous. He was not unfriendly to unions per se.
Commenting in his annual report on Judge Billings' application of the
Sherman Act to labor in 1893, Olney criticized Billings' ruling as "strikingly illustrating the perversion of a law from the real purpose of its
authors." In refusing to use the Sherman Act in a later case, Olney said
he opposed putting "the whole power of the federal government on one
side of a civil controversy, of doubtful merits, between the employers of
labor on one hand and the employed on the other" (Cummings and Mc-
Farland, *Federal Justice*, p. 438). In 1895 Olney intervened in behalf of

As early as June 28 Olney had instructed United States attorneys throughout the West to secure warrants and take other steps necessary to prevent any obstructions of the mails—and according to an interpretation of the Department of Justice, obstruction of any part of a mail train, i.e., of a Pullman car, was obstruction of the mails. On June 30, at the suggestion of the General Managers Association, Olney appointed Edwin Walker, counsel for the Chicago, Milwaukee and St. Paul Railroad, as special United States attorney at Chicago; and in his instructions to Walker the same day, Olney advised the procurement of court injunctions and indicated that federal troops would probably be necessary to enforce them.[6]

Thus far, although the boycott was effective, there had been little violence. On July 1, however, in the village of Blue Island on the outskirts of Chicago, a riotous mob of strike sympathizers, ignoring the United States Marshal and his deputies, interfered with the passage of trains. This was enough for the Attorney General's office, and on the morning of July 2, Special Counsel

---

the brotherhoods in an unsuccessful attempt to enjoin the receivers from discharging workers for joining labor unions (*Platt* v. *Philadelphia & Reading R.R. Co.*, 65 Fed. 660 [E.D. Pa.]). He then helped draft the Erdman Act of 1898 which recognized labor unions as proper parties to mediation and arbitration in railroad disputes, and in 1908 criticized the *Adair* decision (208 U.S. 161) striking down the anti-"yellow dog" provisions of the Erdman Act ("Discrimination against Union Labor—Legal?" *American Law Review*, 42 [March–April, 1908], 161–167). But like most of the profession, Olney reacted angrily to the mass action that accompanied industrial unrest in 1894. Olney was relentless in obtaining court injunctions against the Coxey marchers and enforcing them with federal marshals and army units. Olney also approved Judge Jenkins' injunctions in the *Northern Pacific* case and criticized Justice Harlan's reversal in part of Jenkins' opinion (Cummings and McFarland, pp. 438–439; see also Lindsey, *op. cit.*, pp. 157–158). Olney's intervention against Debs and his union fell clearly within this pattern.

[6] The Olney papers revealed later that Olney would have preferred to use troops at the onset of the strike, but knew that President Cleveland would not act until judicial process had been established (James, *op. cit.*, p. 203; Nevins, *op. cit.*, p. 616).

Walker and the regular United States attorney at Chicago,
Thomas E. Milchrist, petitioned the United States District Court
in Chicago for a restraining order against Debs and others.
Circuit Judge William A. Woods and District Judge Peter S.
Grosscup, after suggesting revisions in the petition, granted the
order ex parte.[7]

The Debs injunction, later to be known as the "omnibus injunction," occasioned surprise at the time for its breadth and
scope and has been considered by many historians as unprecedented. As a matter of fact, the groundwork for the Debs injunction had been laid in the new departures in equity jurisprudence in the early 1890's, and the injunction of July 2 was the
culmination of these new trends.[8] Its chief significance from the
long-term point of view was to dramatize the injunction as a
major new weapon in labor disputes and fasten its use in the
federal jurisdiction. Developed in an age of tension, and crystallized in crisis, the labor injunction became the principal legal
instrument for governing industrial conflict and a major obstacle
to unionism for the next four decades.

Judges Grosscup and Woods asserted jurisdiction to issue the
injunction under the Sherman Act and the interest of the United
States government in the mails. Directed against Eugene V. Debs
and other named officers of the American Railway Union as well
as the American Railway Union itself, all persons combining and
conspiring with them, and "all other persons whomsoever," the
injunction commanded and enjoined its recipients absolutely to

[7] The text of the injunction is printed as an appendix to Frankfurter
and Greene, *The Labor Injunction*. The important sections of the injunction may also be found in the reports of the Debs contempt case (64
Fed. 726–727 [N.D. Ill.], and 158 U.S. 570–572).

[8] Injunctions were already being obtained by the railroads some days
before July 2. In *Southern California Ry. Co. v. Rutherford*, 62 Fed. 796
(S.D. Cal.), reported June 30, District Judge Ross issued an injunction
restraining the employees of the company, so long as they continued at
work, from refusing to handle any trains because Pullman cars might be
attached thereto.

desist and refrain from, among other things, interfering with the business of any of twenty-two named railroads; interfering with any mail trains or other trains engaged in interstate commerce; compelling or inducing "by threats, intimidation, persuasion, force, or violence" any of the employees of said railroads not to perform any of their duties; compelling or inducing "by threats, intimidation, force, or violence" any of the employees to leave the service of said railroads; doing any act whatever in furtherance of any conspiracy to interfere with the free and unhindered transportation of interstate commerce; and "ordering, directing, aiding, assisting, or abetting, in any manner whatsoever, any person or persons to commit any or either of the acts aforesaid."

The injunction did not, as is sometimes asserted, prohibit the right to strike or prohibit peaceful persuasion to strike. But it did prohibit persuasion not to perform the duties of the job, i.e., persuasion not to handle Pullman cars. In any event, the net effect of the several provisions of the injunction, and of similar injunctions secured from United States District Courts throughout the Midwest and West, would likely have been sufficient to isolate the leadership and break the strike.

Debs and the other strike leaders, who had been repeatedly cautioning the strikers against any form of violence or intimidation, maintained that their actions were in no way illegal, and they determined to ignore the injunction. On July 2, however, further rioting occurred in Blue Island, the newspaper headlines became even more sensational, and on July 3 Olney was able to persuade President Cleveland that the situation was serious enough to warrant the use of the United States Army. Thus far, the city of Chicago had been relatively quiet, and no appeal had been made by police officials or by the railroads for state militia. Nevertheless, federal troops took up stations in Chicago in the early morning of July 4, under orders to protect interstate commerce and the United States mails and to enforce the orders of the courts. Governor Altgeld had not been informed of the

President's action,[9] and he protested in two forceful communications, but the President made only cursory replies.[10]

It was only after the entry of United States troops that violence and disorder mounted to major proportions, reaching its high point on July 7, when rioting left four dead and twenty wounded. Meanwhile the food and fuel situation was become grave, with perishable commodities immobilized and spoiling all over the West. On July 8 the President issued a proclamation ordering all unlawful assemblages to disperse and serving notice that federal troops would act promptly and energetically. The next step would have been martial law; but the strike was already passing its peak. Three factors were operating to break the strike: the recruitment by the railroads of thousands of unemployed railroad men in the East; the effect of the injunction, which confused and demoralized many of the normally law abiding rank and file; and the presence of the troops, which by July 8 was overawing the mobs of strike sympathizers, at least enough to permit the new men to resume the movement of trains.

Two days later, July 10, Debs and other strike leaders were arrested for conspiring to obstruct the mails and interfere with interstate commerce. Although Debs was immediately released on bail, the cause by this time was lost. Help expected from the

[9] Conservatives were suspicious of Altgeld because in June, 1893, he had pardoned the three anarchists still imprisoned from the Haymarket trial of 1886. See Barnard, *op. cit.*, pp. 236–249; David, *Haymarket Affair*, pp. 479–503; and Ray Ginger's recently published *Altgeld's America: The Lincoln Ideal versus Changing Realities* (New York, 1958), pp. 74–88. What particularly infuriated legal conservatives was Altgeld's attack upon the judicial proceedings as biased and improper and his accusations of prejudice against Trial Judge Gary. See *Green Bag*, 5 (Oct., 1893), 470–473, and *American Law Review*, 28 (Jan.–Feb., 1894), 66. The railroads would have been reluctant to call upon Altgeld in any case, for his prolabor sympathies were well known.

[10] Substantial excerpts from the Altgeld-Cleveland correspondence are printed in Barnard, *op. cit.*, pp. 295–307. The constitutional controversy as to whether Cleveland's intervention invaded the rights of the states need not concern us here. It is enough to note that the action was unusual if not unprecedented.

Chicago trade-unionists failed to materialize, and the American Federation of Labor also refused to intervene. By July 13 trains were moving freely in Chicago, and one week later the strike collapsed in all areas. Debs was arrested again on July 17, charged with contempt of court, and, for a time refusing bail, remained in jail while the case was continued to the twenty-second. The strikers at Pullman, whose plight had been the precipitant of the futile struggle, were forced to return to work on the old terms, and then only after promising not to join a labor union. The American Railway Union was wrecked, losing most of its membership, and thousands of strikers were black-listed throughout the country by the victorious General Managers Association. Labor had suffered one of its most crushing defeats.

To the legal profession, the complete failure of the strike and the collapse of the American Railway Union were highly gratifying. Divided on many other issues, almost all segments of the profession united in condemning the Debs rebellion. The boycott was illegal and unjustified from the beginning, ran the argument, and inevitably it had led to turbulence and riot. Debs himself was a reckless agitator, who completely disregarded private rights and the public interest. And only the effective intervention of the federal government had saved the day.[11]

The most publicized statement of the position of legal conservatism was made by Thomas M. Cooley, the famous author of the *Constitutional Limitations,* in the course of his presidential address at the August, 1894, meeting of the American Bar As-

11 *West Virginia Bar,* 1 (July, 1894), 124; *Legal Advisor* (Chicago), 34 (July 7, 1894), 222; S. R. Harris, "President's Address," *Ohio State Bar Association Reports, Vol. XV* (1894), pp. 105–119. Harris was particularly virulent, denouncing the "seditious demagogues . . . [who] arouse the dormant passions and stupidity of the laborer." The extremely embittered, in part violent, comments of Judge Taft in letters to his sister are quoted in Henry F. Pringle, *The Life and Times of William Howard Taft* (New York, 1939), I, 128–129.

sociation.[12] Reviewing what he termed the "leading peculiarities" of the Chicago strike, Cooley emphasized two factors: that the only way the railroads could influence the Pullman Company, as desired by the strikers, was to discriminate against Pullman cars, which would violate valid prior contracts and be illegal under the Interstate Commerce Act; and that, whatever the real intentions of the strikers, the great burden of the strike was bound to fall upon the general public through the disruption of train services and the economic losses to producers and shippers. As for the violence, while Cooley did not charge the strike leaders with direct responsibility, he contended that Debs and his associates should have recognized its inevitability in view of the large numbers of unemployed and the easily aroused passions of the mob. The strike leaders had failed to show good faith, concluded Cooley, in having thus ignored the interests of innocent third parties.[13]

Legal opinion was also aroused by the Altgeld-Cleveland controversy and sided overwhelmingly with Cleveland. Cooley was particularly peremptory on this score, dismissing Altgeld's states' rights position as not even plausible, as "unwarranted" and "revolutionary." [14] The more moderate William Draper Lewis declared the President could act without having to wait "until an irreparable amount of damage" had been done, if in his opinion the local authorities were unable to maintain peace and preserve property.[15] Richard C. McMurtrie, similarly defending Cleveland's actions, asserted caustically that all were "glad to be relieved from the government of a mob even at the expense of

[12] "Address of the President," *Report of the Seventeenth Annual Meeting of the American Bar Association* (1894), pp. 181–243.

[13] This assignment of culpability to the strike leaders for not having sufficiently considered the social context of their actions was quite common. See for example William P. Aiken, "Legal Restraint of Labor Strikes," *Yale Law Journal*, 4 (Oct., 1894), 13.

[14] Cooley, *op. cit.*, p. 233.

[15] *American Law Register*, n.s., 33 (July, 1894), 542.

an usurpation." But besides this, he continued, obstructions to interstate commerce and the carrying of the mails were matters "exclusively federal," and the President had the right and duty to use as much force as was necessary to execute the law.[16]

That legal conservatives of every degree should have little sympathy for Debs and the strikers and should support the federal intervention was not perhaps surprising. Less to be expected, however, were the fierce denunciations of the railroad strike appearing in the pages of the *American Law Review*, whose senior editor, Seymour D. Thompson, could generally be counted on the progressive side of public issues. The *Review*, to be sure, had given tentative support to the early uses of the labor injunction, especially in the *Ann Arbor* case, and had also been highly critical of the Coxeyites; [17] but nothing could better illustrate the depth and pervasiveness of the social tension produced by the events of 1894 than the excited declamations of Seymour D. Thompson in July of that year.

The attack of the *American Law Review* upon the Chicago strike began with an editorial note entitled "President Cleveland and 'President Debs,' " [18] which reminded Debs that it had been settled thirty years ago "amid the thunder of cannon that this country was not large enough for two flags or two presidents." Characterizing as "editorial drivel" the argument that Cleveland had infringed the rights of the states, the *Review* described Altgeld's protests as "a tissue of falsehoods from beginning to end." The note concluded: "Conservative and patriotic opinion everywhere approves the action of the president and rejoices that, at an unusual crisis, we had a president possessing the nerve to take the responsibility, just as General Grant would have done."

Thompson's attitudes toward the Chicago strike were made

[16] *Pennsylvania Law Series*, 1 (Nov., 1894), 4–18. See also the comments of James J. H. Hamilton of Scranton, Pa., *Albany Law Journal*, 50 (Aug. 4, 1894), 77–79.

[17] See *supra*, p. 123, and ch. vi, n. 57.

[18] *American Law Review*, 28 (July–Aug., 1894), 591–592.

even more explicit in the course of a long book review, written
July 7:

Failing to persuade him [George M. Pullman] to submit to arbitration where there was nothing to arbitrate except the manner in
which he should conduct his own business . . . the striking employees appealed to the adventurer Debs, as the head of the vast
trades union which he had organized. . . .

A submission to the demand of their employees . . . would have
been a breach of their contracts with the Pullman Company and
would have laid them liable to damages. . . .

The corporations, and especially the railway corporations, have
often been in the wrong. . . . But in this instance they were in the
right. They entered upon a struggle with an unknown and appalling
force, which threatened to revolutionize the very foundations of
society and to reverse all the processes by which our splendid industrial system has been built up. In the stand which they took,
they represented the right of every man to manage his own business and to keep his own contracts without dictation from third
persons.[19]

Having thus defended Pullman and the railroads on the
grounds of managerial prerogative and the sanctity of contracts,
Thompson continued with a philippic against Debs:

Meantime, the fellow Debs, reeling with the intoxication which
springs from the possession of almost unlimited power, busied himself for days in launching telegrams in every direction ordering this
or that railway to be "tied up." . . . The commerce of great cities
lay at the feet of this irresponsible vagabond. Their supplies ran
out and in some cases it became a question whether their inhabitants
would not starve. . . . The groans produced by these widespread
calamities served only to increase the insane hilarity of the fiend
who had produced them. . . .

If this were the mere problem [the character of the strike], the
answer would be from a million throats that it is an insurrection;
that it is in the nature of a servile insurrection; that it is an attempt

[19] *Ibid.*, pp. 630–633.

to put the bottom on top; to put the intelligent under the ignorant; to wrest from intelligent and capable men the property which they have acquired, and to put it into the hands of the unintelligent and ignorant. And the further response would be that this cannot be done without fighting; that men who have earned property and acquired rights are not going to surrender that property and those rights peaceably.[20]

Seymour D. Thompson too, eloquent and fearless spokesman for legal progressivism though he was, had succumbed to the conservative fear of July, 1894.

Although all elements of the profession, conservative and progressive, were critical of Debs and the boycott and were laudatory of Cleveland's use of the military, the role of the courts in granting the omnibus injunctions was not so universally approved. For with the issuance of the Debs injunctions, the new departures in equity jurisprudence that had been building up since the late 1880's were brought to the attention of the profession in a manner sensational enough to cause serious concern among those legal conservatives chiefly interested in the preservation of the traditional procedures and principles of law.

The most enlightening examination of the injunction problem took place at the August meeting of the American Bar Association—the same meeting where Cooley delivered his presidential address referred to earlier—when Charles Claflin Allen of St. Louis, a member of the association's special committee on federal code of criminal procedure, read a scholarly paper entitled "Injunction and Organized Labor." [21] Allen's paper, which provoked a lively discussion among his audience, sharply crit-

---

[20] *Ibid.*, pp. 633-634, 637. For further comment by Thompson in this period, including a demand that the Western Union Telegraph Company be held an accomplice of Debs for having transmitted Debs' many messages to his lieutenants, see *ibid.* (Sept.–Oct., 1894), 764-765.

[21] Charles C. Allen, "Injunction and Organized Labor," *Report of the Seventeenth Annual Meeting of the American Bar Association* (1894), pp. 299-331. Allen was active in St. Louis politics, serving as a member of the Missouri House of Representatives and then as Associate City Counselor (1895-1901).

icized the new uses of the injunction, including its application in the Debs strike, as constituting dangerous innovations upon ancient legal procedures. Among the most prominent of these innovations, said Allen, was the new "Public Rights" concept, as evidenced in the Northern Pacific and Debs injunctions. But the essential idea of equity jurisprudence, argued Allen, had always been the protection of the private rights of suitors, and not "the preservation of public rights, or the punishment of public wrongs." [22]

Allen then questioned such startling features of the Debs injunction as its issuance against "ten thousand strikers and all the world besides," its novel method of service by posting copies on the sides of freight cars and railroad terminals, and the apparent anticipation of the lawyers and judges concerned that enforcement by the military would be necessary. If all this meant that the injunction was intended as a mere executive proclamation to keep the peace, as a device to act *in terrorem* over the strikers, and failing that, as a basis for invoking the military, it was, said Allen, "a degradation of the judicial process."

Refusing to accept this interpretation,[23] Allen saw as the primary reason for the injunction the power behind it to punish for contempt. Since the acts which the injunction forbade were crimes at law, the injunction had thus become a means of administering criminal law without trial by jury. But in such a use of equity power, warned Allen, there lay the gravest dangers to civil liberties. Punishment for contempt, though a power absolutely essential to courts of justice, was "the most summary and arbitrary exercise of authority" known to English and American law. After delineating the several arbitrary aspects of contempt proceedings, Allen summarized:

[22] *Ibid.*, p. 308.

[23] This was, of course, as later evidence revealed, the correct interpretation of the motives behind the use of the injunction, at least insofar as the Attorney General was concerned (*supra*, n. 6).

In short, a party to a suit may go to jail for contempt of a preliminary injunction, issued *ex parte*, without notice to defendant, which is subsequently—and after the defendant has served his term of imprisonment—held to be without equity,—that is, void. There is a tremendous power to place in the hands of one man; for from his judgment there is no appeal.[24]

Allen agreed that the nation was passing through a period of social crisis. The mere fact of a nationwide sympathy strike, he felt, was "incredible except upon a theory of wide-spread discontent." The theory was confirmed, he continued, by the constant increase in labor organization—which was perfectly natural, in view of the prior organization of capital: "Power breeds tyranny, which in turn brings rebellion and opposition, then counter-forces produce a new tyranny." [25] But did this mean that age-old standards of jurisprudence were to be suddenly swept aside? Allen made clear that he was not opposing Cleveland's use of the troops as such; they might have been employed, if necessary, simply to aid the marshals in enforcing federal law and protecting federal property. But when troops were used as part of a process to punish for contempt, and thereby imprison for crime without benefit of trial by jury or other safeguards of the criminal law, then the question at issue, said Allen, went "deeper than any mere conflict of classes"; for it now involved the fundamental constitutional rights of civil liberty. It was for the bar and bench to decide, concluded Allen, whether the decree of injunction would become "on the one hand an instrument of tyranny, or, on the other hand, a mere *brutum fulmen*." [26]

But Allen's earnest appeal to the older conservatism of legal tradition apparently had little effect upon his auditors, who seemed more impressed with the threatening nature of the attacks upon property and public order than with questions of civil liberty. Thirteen speakers participated in the discussion of Allen's paper, and all thirteen admitted that the new uses of the

[24] Allen, *op. cit.*, pp. 318–319.   [25] *Ibid.*, p. 323.   [26] *Ibid.*, p. 325.

injunction were, to some degree at least, unprecedented.[27] But only three of the thirteen indicated any support of Allen's criticisms, and from two of these three the support was on the most limited grounds.[28]

The excitement of the Chicago strike and the controversy over the injunction gave rise to a broader assessment by the legal profession of the problems of capital and labor. A trend toward moderation was definitely noticeable, as thoughtful lawyers and judges, now reassured by prompt intervention of government in behalf of social order, began to realize that if the experiences of July were not to be repeated (including the abuses of equity), the root causes of the disorders would have to be sought out.

An exceptionally temperate and balanced analysis of the labor-capital issue was presented as early as July 26 at the annual meeting of the Texas Bar Association by Judge B. D. Tarlton, Chief Justice of the Court of Civil Appeals at Fort Worth.[29] Judge Tarlton opened his address by noting that an air of "gloomy prophecy" prevailed in the country, based on the assumptions "that the industrial world is divided into hostile camps, and that society is on the verge of an 'irrepressible conflict' between

[27] *Report of the Seventeenth Annual Meeting of the American Bar Association* (1894), pp. 15–51.

[28] One of these two was Woodrow Wilson, who had just joined the association. Wilson's point was that in the eyes of public opinion, the injunctions had only weakened the position of the President. Public opinion supported Cleveland because the public recognized "the intrinsic power in the Government to defend itself"; but by going to the courts "the impression has been created that the courts were put in a panic by the strike and that they therefore used an extraordinary process to meet a situation which would have been met in the ordinary way if it had not been for . . . the character of the Governor of the State of Illinois" (*ibid.*, pp. 42–44).

[29] "Some Reflections on the Relations of Capital and Labor," *Proceedings of the Thirteenth Annual Session of the Texas Bar Association* (1894), pp. 51–66. The same meeting also heard an extremely conservative and antipopularist address by Judge Edwin Hobby of the Houston Bar (*ibid.*, pp. 81–92).

capital and labor." The concentration of capital and the restlessness of labor were indeed serious situations, agreed Judge Tarlton, but he perceived no ground for despair. The period of
present tensions, said the Judge, with far-ranging perspective,
"will be found to be a transition period in our history, from
which the common sense conservatism of our people will evolve
renewed life and prosperity by the application of established
principles of government to new conditions." [30]

Labor organizations, asserted Judge Tarlton, were the laborer's
inevitable and necessary defenses against corporate organizations.
The so-called freedom of contract, insisted the Judge, was non-
existent in the industrial world, where the employer was generally in a position "to coerce an acceptance of the terms, how
hard so ever they may be." The contrast between the laborer's
industrial inequality, continued Tarlton, and his newly gained
political equality must increase discontent. Universal education
and the spread of the democratic philosophy were making the
laborer aware "that in the race of life he is entitled to the same
opportunities with the capitalist, unhampered by . . . inequi-
table conditions. . . . Political freedom and intellectual enlightenment may not co-exist with economic servitude." [31]

Turning to possible remedies for labor's grievances, Judge
Tarlton thought strikes and boycotts "futile," because they often
alienated public sympathy and hurt the workers' cause. He recommended instead that labor leaders concentrate on the courts
and the legislature, placing their trust in the power of public
opinion. Public opinion, exclaimed Tarlton in ringing language,
had "struck the shackles from the arms of four millions of
domestic slaves; it can, and properly aroused, it will strike them
from the arms of millions of industrial slaves." [32]

As an example of legal remedies, Tarlton advocated destruction of the trust with its "unreasonable depression of wages" and
urged the courts to issue injunctions against capital, as was done
in the *Northern Pacific* case against labor, "to prevent combina-

[30] *Op. cit.*, pp. 51–52.   [31] *Ibid.*, pp. 55, 56.   [32] *Ibid.*, p. 61.

tion or conspiracy to depress wages." But more important than
legal process, said the Judge, was an expansion of the scope of
legislation. Speaking with fine insight into the changing role of
government, Judge Tarlton took up the charge of paternalism:

"Paternalism" has been rightly described as "a word to conjure
with." And wherever it can be properly applied to legislative action,
such action should be condemned, for the end of government is
public protection, not private nourishment.

For reasons above indicated, however, legislation which would,
under conditions prevailing in the time of Thomas Jefferson, have
been properly regarded as government usurpation, might, under
present conditions, be oftentimes viewed as reasonable protection. . . .

Must all considerations yield to the behests of "individualism"
. . . under economic conditions in which the identity of the individual is wholly absorbed by corporate existence—in which, indeed,
whether under corporate management he orders or obeys, he is
become to all intents and purposes as insensate and mechanized as
the different parts of the machine which he may guide or operate? [33]

Judge Tarlton proposed no specific legislation, but closed with
an expression of faith in the justness of whatever solution the
American people should arrive at. Regard would be had alike,
he said, "for capital and for labor, for the wife of the millionaire
and for the sad-eyed widow who in patience plies her needle for
a living."

Judge Tarlton then, with social tension near its highest level,
was advancing a plea for an enlightened and humane conservatism, for a pragmatic response to the challenge of the times. The
values of the past, he was making clear, could be preserved
only by meliorating the institutions of the present; and tradition
could be reconciled with progress only by solidly constructive
effort.

Although few spokesmen approached Judge Tarlton in breadth
of view, the reaction away from extremism in the evaluation of

[33] *Ibid.,* pp. 65–66.

labor questions continued, with some exceptions,[34] through the late summer and fall of 1894. The *Albany Law Journal,* which would soon be in the forefront of the conservative crisis over the income tax, commented favorably on an article in the *Annals* criticizing the recent use of the injunction and thought it certainly strange that, while corporations could combine to control the labor market, employees who organized in defense were liable to prosecution.[35] The *Chicago Legal News* reprinted in part an article by the prominent Judge Reuben M. Benjamin of Bloomington, Illinois, blaming the cause of strikes upon "starvation" wages and proposing a constitutional amendment authorizing Congress to regulate wages of coal miners and railroad employees.[36] A paper read to the Tennessee Bar Association by Lee Thornton of Memphis, explaining that labor organizations so long as not unlawfully coercive were legal, urged that the law "reach by summary remedy the calm, cool, calculating combination of capital, as it reaches the turbulent, impulsive one of labor." [37] Other commentators were particularly unhappy over the implications of the recent injunctions.[38]

[34] Ardemus Stewart, "The Legal Side of the Strike Question," *American Law Register,* n.s. 33 (Sept., 1894), 609–622, denounced the strike as a menace to legal rights, and advocated "repressive legislation, the more stringent the better."

[35] *Albany Law Journal,* 50 (Aug. 4, 1894), 69.

[36] *Chicago Legal News,* 26 (Aug. 11, 1894), 406. Judge Benjamin was an influential member of the Illinois Constitutional Convention of 1869–1870, which framed the articles regulating railroads and grain elevators, and later was special counsel defending the "Granger" laws before the Illinois Supreme Court (Fairman, "The So-called Granger Cases," 592–620; Chester M. Destler, *American Radicalism, 1865–1901* [New London, 1946], p. 11).

[37] Lee Thornton, "Strikes," *Proceedings of the Thirteenth Annual Meeting of the Bar Association of Tennessee* (1894), pp. 67–71.

[38] The *West Virginia Bar,* 1 (Sept., 1894), 173, held the injunction "not an ideal remedy to the American mind"; the *Minnesota Law Journal,* 2 (Dec., 1894), 307, favorably reviewed Allen's paper at the American Bar Association meeting; and the *Chicago Law Journal,* 6 (Jan., 1895), 79, urged legislative restriction of *"Judicial Misfits,* yclept injunctions."

Toward the end of the year two developments again focused public attention on the Chicago strike. The United States Strike Commission, which had been appointed by President Cleveland on July 26 to investigate the causes of the strike under the terms of the Arbitration Act of 1888, reported in November on the results of its study. The report was unexpectedly favorable to labor, absolving the strikers of culpability for the major part of the violence and assigning considerable responsibility for the struggle to the Pullman Company and the General Managers Association, particularly for their refusal to consider mediation or arbitration.[39] While many conservative publications criticized the report,[40] the revelation that there was more to the strike than simply its surface manifestations seemed to have had a sobering effect.[41]

Then on December 14, Circuit Judge Woods, after some ten weeks' deliberation, sentenced Eugene V. Debs to six months' imprisonment for contempt of court, with several associates of Debs receiving three months each.[42] Counsel for defense had entered no demurrer to the scope of the injunction nor very much evidence as to whether or not defendants had in fact violated its provisions. Instead defense counsel had relied on these three points: that the court had no jurisdiction to issue the injunction in the first place; that sentence for contempt would be the equivalent of punishment for crime without trial by jury; and that in any event defendants had done no more than advise a peaceable strike.[43]

[39] U.S. Strike Commission, *Report on the Chicago Strike*, esp. pp. xxvii, xxxi, xxxix, xlv–xlvi.

[40] Excerpts of the criticisms are in Lindsey, *op. cit.*, pp. 357–358, and *The Forum*, 18 (Jan., 1895), 523–531.

[41] See the *Albany Law Journal*, 51 (Feb. 2, 1895), 66. Cooley in his August address had praised President Cleveland's appointments to the Commission as "admirable selections," men of "wisdom, prudence and . . . integrity" (*Report of the Seventeenth Annual Meeting of the American Bar Association* [1894], p. 238).

[42] *United States* v. *Debs*, 64 Fed. 724 (N.D. Ill.).

[43] Lindsey, *op. cit.*, pp. 288–289; Shiras, *op. cit.*, p. 234, n. 35.

Judge Woods's opinion rejected all three defense contentions. Jurisdiction to issue the injunction he sustained on the basis of the Sherman Act, holding the strike a conspiracy in restraint of interstate commerce.[44] As for the question of criminal law, equity could intervene by injunction to prevent irreparable harm to property even though the acts enjoined might also be crimes. But the principal justification for the injunction, he asserted, lay in the "threats, violence, and other unlawful means of interference" that accompanied the strike. Accusing Debs and others of insincerity in pleading that they advocated only peaceful means, Judge Woods laid the blame for the violence directly on the strike leadership, thereby disregarding the Strike Commission's report and going beyond even Cooley's position of August. Said Woods:

Strikes by railroad employees have been attended generally, if not in every instance, with some form of intimidation or force. . . . Under conditions of last summer, when there were many idle men seeking employment, it was impossible that a strike which aimed at a general cessation of business upon the railroads of the country should succeed without violence; and it is not to be believed that the defendants entered upon the execution of their scheme without apprehending the fact, and without having determined how to deal with it.[45]

Thus the fact of the strike itself was indicative of planned violence, and Debs had been guilty of contempt of court by continuing the strike along the same lines after the injunction as before it.

Woods's opinion received a comparatively mild reaction from the profession. The *American Law Review* praised the opinion

[44] For other litigation developing out of the Chicago strike which also held the Sherman Act applicable to labor, see *United States* v. *Elliott*, 62 Fed. 801 (E.D. Mo.); *Thomas* v. *Cincinnati, N. O. & T. P. Ry. Co.*, 62 Fed. 803 (S.D. Ohio); and *United States* v. *Agler*, 62 Fed. 824 (D. Ind.).

[45] 62 Fed. 757.

and commended the federal judiciary for its "conservative" role during the "anarchy" of the previous July; but it subjected the Judge's views to a long legal analysis and concluded that final settlement of the question would have to await the verdict of the Supreme Court.[46] The *American Law Register*, on the other hand, disapproved of Debs' prison sentence as a deprivation of the right of trial by jury. Conceding that the officials of the American Railway Union had been guilty of actions amounting to "public nuisances of the most serious and alarming sort," the *Register* denied that this was any reason to strain the principles of civil liberty and set a dangerous precedent.[47]

The settled position of legal conservatism on the great Chicago strike and its implications for the problems of capital and labor, after all the facts were apparently in and the law all but finally decided,[48] may be seen in two interesting statements of January, 1895. Edgar A. Bancroft, a Chicago corporation lawyer, read a lengthy paper on the strike at the annual meeting of the Illinois State Bar Association.[49] He gave a comprehensive history of the background and development of the strike, including such often-overlooked matters as the intolerable conditions at Pullman and the history of tension between the American Railway Union and the General Managers Association. Nevertheless, Bancroft severely criticized Debs and the leadership for calling such a widespread work stoppage during a time of depression, with the in-

[46] *American Law Review*, 29 (Jan.–Feb., 1895), 138–140. See also *ibid.* (Mar.–Apr., 1895), 282 and (May–June, 1895), 473–474, defending, on limited grounds, "government by injunction" as "better than no government at all."

[47] *American Law Register*, n.s., 33 (Dec., 1894), 879–883.

[48] The complete story of the strike, at least as regards the role of the Attorney General's office, was not made known until a number of years later when the Olney papers were opened. As for legal process, the Supreme Court had yet to rule on the appeal from Judge Woods's decision.

[49] "The Chicago Strike of 1894," *Proceedings of the Illinois State Bar Association at Its Eighteenth Annual Meeting* (1895), pp. 274–292. Bancroft's paper was published in book form in 1895. Bancroft was counsel for many large corporations in the 1890's and 1900's, and was Ambassador to Japan in the 1920's.

evitable violence and damage to the interests of management, labor, and the public. Although expressing understanding and support for the original strike against Pullman, Bancroft maintained that the boycott and sympathetic strike were both illegal, part of "a gigantic conspiracy under which no act . . . could be lawful." [50] He praised the President for his intervention to protect interstate commerce and the mails and defended the controversial injunctions as necessary and proper.

Despite these condemnations of the strike, Bancroft's paper was on the whole judiciously phrased and moderate in tone. He admitted the gross inequality of bargaining power between employer and employee and defended strong railway unions as a means of developing that "equilibrium of forces" which held the best hope of industrial peace and fair play. Legislation of some kind was also a probable necessity of the times, to help remedy the unfortunate situation of workingmen facing hostile combinations of capital.

But these problems, he declared, could not be settled by unlawful violations of private and public rights. It was not in the spirit of American institutions to act hastily and irresponsibly when faced with social crisis; the issues of the day were to be resolved only along the traditional lines of "established law," through the judgments of calm deliberation. "Social and moral questions," he concluded righteously, "cannot be discussed with violators of law. Conciliation ends where lawlessness begins." [51]

In the same month of January, a new publication, *Case and Comment*,[52] printed its first editorial on the Chicago strike and revealed a position at once conservative as regards legal processes and constructive as regards the role of government.[53] The editorial first launched into a vigorous condemnation of the "epidemic of mobs" in July and denounced the "pusillanimous and imbecile

[50] *Ibid.*, p. 288.   [51] *Ibid.*, p. 291.

[52] *Case and Comment*, a Rochester publication still being published, was designed as an informal monthly supplement to the highly technical *Lawyers Reports Annotated*.

[53] *Case and Comment*, 1 (Jan., 1895), 1.

conduct of public authorities" for failing to enforce law and order at the first signs of mob violence. Citizens had to be protected in their rights and property, including the right of any man "to earn bread for his family without permission of a union."

But then with peace restored, the editorial continued, it was the duty of legislators "to get a grip on living questions of the public welfare." Abuses did exist, remedies were available, and it was the business of the state to fit the latter to the former. *Case and Comment* offered two specific suggestions: that all corporations, at the least all quasi-public corporations, be required to arbitrate differences with employees; and that the hours of labor for employees of corporations be limited by law. Dismissing the argument of freedom of contract, the editorial maintained that the legislative power surely embraced the regulation of hours of labor that proved "degrading and brutalizing." Nor could the editor see any virtue in the "favorite cry of some well-fed people . . . against legislative interference with their business." Concluded this outspoken editorial:

The fangs of anarchy may now need violent extraction, but the food of anarchy must be destroyed. . . .

The bitter charge made now with too large a grain of truth, that this government "of the people" is a government of the rich, needs to be made untrue by honest, intelligent consideration of the welfare of the poor. Demagogues are sure to grasp the opportunity and abuse it. The brainiest and best of our legislators must take hold of the problem in earnest.[54]

The first phase of the conservative crisis of the mid-nineties had thus passed. Direct-action movements of mass protest, whether of unemployed industrial "armies" or of striking workingmen, had been decisively repulsed. Then, with the conflict between capital and labor temporarily stabilized—on capital's terms—moderate conservatism had indicated willingness to consider remedies for the more obvious evils in industrial society.

[54] *Ibid.*

But the initial responses of the legal profession to the labor unrest of 1894 bore significant implication for the crisis phases still to come. For in applying so widely in 1894 the very newest and still unexplored developments of the labor injunction, legal conservatism had revealed the radicalism of method to which bar and bench would resort when necessary to effect a conservative end.

VIII

Development of the

Income Tax Crisis

THE second phase of the conservative crisis of the mid-nineties was already developing even as the excitement over the Debs rebellion was quieting down. The easing of conservative tension as regards capital and labor in late 1894 could not long obscure the basic problem confronting American conservatism in the 1890's: how to restrain discontented majorities from riding rough-shod over the rights and property of the individual and threatening in the process the foundations of the ordered society. To have kept within bounds marches of unemployed and depredations by strike sympathizers could be accounted no very marvelous achievements; all the forces of law and order had been mobilized in conservatism's behalf. But to overcome the political threat of determined legislative majorities was a far more demanding task. Many of the Federalists of 1787 had feared the possible downfall of American republicanism on just this basis: that in a time of crisis, with classes polarized in conflict, majority rule would press around and through every constitutional barrier in its assault upon accumulated property.[1] Against this peril, the only sure

[1] A recent study of Federalist pessimism on the long-term prospects

protection, believed the legal neo-Federalists of the 1890's, was a firm judiciary, wielding boldly the power of judicial review. It was in this context that the income tax case assumed such momentous significance to the conservative mind: not only was the tax itself a dangerous first installment of lower-class leveling movements; but at least equally important, as the judicial process of the case unfolded, it became increasingly clear that the conflict of the 1890's between majority rule and judicial interposition had reached its decisive issue.

The income tax of 1894 owed its immediate origin to Democratic attempts at tariff reform.[2] Grover Cleveland's election to the Presidency in 1892 and the Democratic sweep in House and Senate were commonly regarded as protests against the high McKinley tariff of 1890, and tariff reform was to be of first importance in the new Congress. But lower tariffs, it was assumed, would mean lower revenue, and with the government already incurring deficits from the excessive expenditures of the Harrison administration, new sources of revenue were deemed essential. The specific choice of the income tax, however, had deeper roots.

---

for republican government is Douglass Adair's "The Founding Fathers and History: The Historical Pessimism of Alexander Hamilton," a paper read at the December, 1955, meeting of the American Historical Association and shown this writer in manuscript form. Professor Adair cites Madison's prediction that by 1929–1930 the pressure of population on available land would make inevitable major constitutional change away from republicanism.

[2] My discussion of the legislative background of the tax relies principally on the following sources: Knoles, *The Presidential Campaign and Election of 1892*, pp. 231–234, 246; Nevins, *Grover Cleveland*, pp. 666–671; Sidney Ratner, *American Taxation: Its History as a Social Force in Democracy* (New York, 1942), chs. v, vii, viii, and ix; Edwin R. A. Seligman, *The Income Tax* (2d ed.; New York, 1914), pp. 493–530; Paul Studenski and Herman C. Kroos, *Financial History of the United States* (New York, 1952), pp. 221–224; Roy G. Blakey and Gladys Blakey, *The Federal Income Tax* (New York, 1940), pp. 1–17; and George Tunell, "Legislative History of the Second Income Tax Law," *Journal of Political Economy*, 3 (June, 1895), 311–337.

Income taxes had been first levied by the federal government during the Civil War, and they included graduated rates, amounting by 1865 to 5 per cent on income from $600 to $5,000 and 10 per cent on income over $5,000. Although the rates were lowered in the Reconstruction period and the graduated principle abandoned, an income tax remained in force till 1872, when a revenue surplus enabled opponents of the tax to prevent its renewal. Since the Civil War inheritance tax had been eliminated in 1870, this meant that after 1872 the revenue needs of the federal government, including payment of the public debt, were met principally by taxes on consumption, i.e., the tariff and internal taxes on such commodities as whiskey and tobacco.

This essentially regressive tax structure of the 1870's and 1880's, which coincided with the great increase in large fortunes and the widening gap between rich and poor, was subject to continued criticism from various agrarian and reform elements. Sixty-eight bills seeking to restore the income tax were submitted between 1874 and 1894,[3] but congressional leaders of the two major parties managed to sidetrack all of them. The rise of the Populist party, however, with its demand for a graduated income tax, and the growing radicalism in the West and South gave added impetus to the movement for tax reform. The expected revenue shortage of 1894 was thus enough wedge to open wide the door for the reentrance of the income tax issue.

The House Ways and Means Committee in the Fifty-Third Congress, under the control of southern and western Democrats led by Benton McMillin of Tennessee and William Jennings Bryan of Nebraska, voted late in 1893 to submit an income tax bill along with the new tariff proposals. After a series of complicated parliamentary maneuverings on the floor of the House, McMillin and Bryan succeeded in attaching the income tax to the tariff bill, thus making the tax a party measure.[4] In the Senate

[3] See the table with years and geographical origins of the sixty-eight different income tax proposals, Blakey and Blakey, *op. cit.*, p. 9.
[4] Bryan's outstanding work for the income tax, both as floor tactician

the proposed lower tariff duties suffered disaster, as more than six hundred protectionist amendments ruined Cleveland's hopes of tariff reform. But the income tax provisions withstood all assaults from Republicans and conservative Democrats. The tax passed the House 182-48, with 122 not voting (mostly Republicans), and the Senate 40-24. On August 28 the combined tax and tariff bill, often designated the Wilson Act, became law without the President's signature.[5]

The income tax of 1894 provided for a 2 per cent tax on all incomes over $4,000. The net profits of corporations were also taxed at 2 per cent with no minimum exemptions. So-called double taxation on income from corporate stocks was avoided by individuals deducting prior taxes paid on their income. Gifts and inheritances were treated as income and subject to the same 2 per cent tax rate. Although the law contained a number of serious weaknesses,[6] the income tax of 1894 was the first important step toward rectifying the unbalanced tax structure of post-Reconstruction finance. The income tax was easily the most popular part of the truncated tariff bill and appeared to be in great favor with the poorer classes everywhere.[7]

During the legislative progress of the income tax, the debates proceeded largely along class lines, exposing to full view, and exacerbating further, the social tension of the times. Democratic

---

and eloquent orator, has been overlooked by some historians who have arrived at unsympathetic estimations of Bryan: e.g., Richard Hofstadter, *The American Political Tradition and the Men Who Made It* (New York, 1951), pp. 192–193.

[5] Cleveland had no objection to the income tax as finally incorporated in the tariff bill, though he had suggested only a small tax on corporations in his annual message. The President was highly indignant, of course, over the bill's rebuff to his low-tariff plans and for this reason refused to sign it.

[6] See Ratner, *op. cit.*, pp. 191–192; Seligman, *op. cit.*, pp. 522–530.

[7] "No other part of the [tariff reform] bill received on the one hand such unstinted praise and on the other such wholesale condemnation" (Tunell, *op. cit.*, p. 328).

proponents of the tax, including the highly respected William
L. Wilson of West Virginia, charged repeatedly in Congress that
the rich had failed to carry their just proportion of the federal
tax load, that the tariff and the internal taxes on consumption
had discriminated against the poor, and that the income tax would
only partially re-establish a fair balance of tax burdens. A smaller
group of Populists and radical Democrats went farther, proclaimed with vigor that the top-heavy concentration of wealth
fostered by corporate capital in the past thirty years was a
menace to the liberties and opportunities of the masses, and asserted that the 2 per cent tax on incomes would be but the
beginning of an advancing scale of graduated taxation.

On the conservative side, Republicans and eastern Democrats
in Congress, led by Senator David B. Hill of New York, attacked the tax as an attempt to penalize thrift and industry, as
socialistic, as inspired by sectional and class antagonism. The
conservative press was more denunciatory, labeling the tax "the
spirit of communism," "class legislation on a tremendous scale." [8]
What gave these charges considerable plausibility even to more
dispassionately inclined observers were, first, the high exemption
of $4,000, which seemed to emphasize the class discrimination of
the tax, and, second, the retention of the tax in the tariff bill
despite the Senate restoration of high duties, which made a budget
deficit unlikely.[9] Insistence upon an income tax, therefore, coming in the very midst of the tensions stemming from the Coxey
armies and the Chicago railway strike, reinforced the alarms of
those conservatives most alive to the dangers of popular radical-

[8] For a general survey of conservative attitudes toward the income tax,
with emphasis on the press and Congress, see Elmer Ellis, "Public Opinion
and the Income Tax 1860–1900," *Mississippi Valley Historical Review*,
27 (Sept., 1940), 225–242.

[9] The income tax, said one academician, was the fruit of that "radical
democracy" which demanded a new distribution of income and property
(A. C. Miller, "National Finance and the Income Tax," *Journal of Political Economy* [June, 1895], 276).

ism.[10] In the words of John F. Dillon, eminent spokesman for traditional legal conservatism, taxation levied not for revenue but as

a forced contribution from the rich for the benefit of the poor, and as a means of distributing the rich man's property among the rest of the community . . . is class legislation of the most pronounced and vicious type . . . violative of the constitutional rights of the property owner, subversive of the existing social polity, and essentially revolutionary.[11]

When opponents of the income tax, defeated in the legislature, looked to the judiciary for relief, they confronted the most unpromising prospects. The federal power of taxation, to begin with, was a plenary one, since Congress under the broad sweep of Article I, Section 8, of the Constitution had the power: "To lay and collect taxes, duties, imposts and excises, to pay the debts and provide for the common defense and general welfare of the United States." The government under the Articles of Confederation had suffered from a grievous lack of taxing power, and the Convention of 1787, determined to rectify the inadequacy, had gone all the way in the other direction, the sole limitation on the subjects of taxation being the prohibition of an export tax.

In the exercise of this plenary power, it was true, Congress was not equally unrestricted. Two broad categories of taxation had been set out in the Constitution, and certain conditions as to their

[10] Not all conservatives, even from the Northeast, opposed the income tax, many cautious-minded men regarding it merely as a long-overdue reform of an inefficient and inequable fiscal system. Thus, Simeon E. Baldwin, whose moderate and optimistic view in 1889 of the growth of American republicanism has been noted *supra*, pp. 35–38, expressed strong approval of the income tax bill in January, 1894. Baldwin was a Judge of the Connecticut Supreme Court at the time (Jackson, *Simeon Eben Baldwin*, p. 144).

[11] John F. Dillon, "Property—Its Rights and Duties in Our Legal and Social Systems," *Proceedings of the New York State Bar Association—Eighteenth Annual Meeeting* (1895), pp. 33–64 at 46.

use attached to each. Thus, in the very same paragraph that granted the tax power, it was ordered that "all duties, imposts and excises" be uniform throughout the United States; and back in Section 2 of Article I, it was stated that "direct taxes" and representatives in the House were to be apportioned among the states according to population.[12]

But other than the qualifications above, no limitations on the taxing power of Congress appeared in the Constitution. An attack upon the constitutionality of the income tax of 1894, therefore, had to be confined to one or both of two approaches: that the income tax was a direct tax as understood in the Constitution, and therefore could not be levied unless apportioned among the states according to population; or, if not a direct tax, that the tax of 1894, because carrying the $4,000 exemption and because of other discriminations, violated the requirement of uniformity imposed upon all forms of taxation other than direct taxes. To both of these approaches, however, the road seemed firmly barred in the fall of 1894.

The first issue, that of direct taxes, depended on the meaning of the term as used in the Constitution.[13] But apparently there had been no consensus of opinion at the Convention, and in the course of discussion the term was employed in several ways. When Rufus King asked during the final days' debates what was "the precise meaning" of direct taxation, Madison's *Journal* records: "No one answered." [14] Agreement was general that the term did include capitation or poll taxes and taxes on land [15] and did not include import and export duties, but other than this

[12] The apportionment requirement also appears in Sec. 9 of Art. I: "No capitation, or other direct tax, shall be laid, unless in proportion to the census or enumeration hereinbefore directed to be taken."

[13] The most authoritative analysis is in Seligman, *op. cit.*, pp. 540–571. See also Corwin, *Court over Constitution*, pp. 181–185.

[14] Cited in 157 U.S. 563.

[15] The term direct tax was first employed in consistent manner by the French physiocrats of the 18th century who believed that land was the only productive factor, and that therefore the only *direct* tax was a tax on land.

nothing was settled. The economic distinction of shiftability developed by the classical economists, i.e., that a direct tax was a tax the incidence of which could not be shifted away from the taxpayer, was not generally current until the nineteenth century, and apparently was not mentioned at the Convention. As for an income tax proper or an inheritance tax, neither was in use in 1787 [16] and were probably not envisaged by the Founding Fathers.

With the Constitution and the records of the Convention so unspecific, the Supreme Court, in ruling on disputed taxes, had adopted the broad premise that, since Congress had been granted a plenary power over taxation, direct taxes were only those taxes that could as a matter of practicality be apportioned according to population. Put another way, if by presuming a tax to be direct, the constitutional requirement of apportionment would result in such manifest injustice as to preclude the tax from ever being levied at all, then the tax in question was not a direct tax within the meaning of the Constitution.

The first occasion for the Supreme Court to develop and apply this doctrine was in 1796 in the case of *Hylton* v. *United States*.[17] The *Hylton* case involved a tax on carriages held for use or for hire. Congress had not specified the Constitutional denominative of the tax, but had simply levied it on a straight per carriage basis, thus in effect considering the tax as "indirect." Eminent counsel opposing the tax, including the Attorneys General of Virginia and other states, claimed that the tax was a direct tax and must be levied according to population. Chief counsel for the government was Alexander Hamilton, who as Secretary of the Treasury had

---

[16] The closest relative to the income tax in 1787 was the "faculty" tax levied in some of the states upon the "profits" of various trades, professions, and occupations. The faculty tax corresponded more to franchise or occupation taxes, however, than to the true income tax, since assessments were seldom made in proportion to income or gains. The faculty tax soon passed into disuse (Seligman, *op. cit.*, pp. 383–387).

[17] 3 Dal. 171.

sponsored the tax. Hamilton argued that since the Constitution was indecisive as to the meaning of direct tax, the "boundary" between direct and indirect "must be settled by a species of arbitration, and ought to be such as will involve neither absurdity nor inconvenience." [18] By this standard, he said, only capitation taxes, land taxes, and general assessments on the whole property of individuals were direct taxes.

The Court accepted Hamilton's thesis and ruled unanimously that the federal carriage tax was not a direct tax, but, within the terminology of the Constitution, a "duty." Of the four Justices who seriatim rendered the decision, two, James Wilson and William Paterson, had been prominent members of the Constitutional Convention, and the two others, James Iredell and Samuel Chase, members of state ratifying conventions. All the Justices emphasized the plenary grant of taxing power and all deduced therefrom a limited application of the direct tax clause. Their opinions in this case formed the basis for one hundred years of judicial decision, until reversed in 1895, and are worth some quotation.

Justice Chase declared:

The Constitution evidently contemplated no taxes as direct taxes, but only such as Congress could lay in proportion to the census. The rule of apportionment is only to be adopted in such cases where it can reasonably apply, and the subject taxed must ever determine the application of the rule.[19]

Since a tax on carriages could not be levied fairly by apportionment according to population,[20] it could not be a direct tax but was a duty, the most comprehensive term after tax. The

[18] Quoted by Corwin, *Court over Constitution*, p. 184, from the Hamilton *Works*. See also Seligman, *op. cit.*, p. 572.

[19] 3 Dal. 174.

[20] Chase gave this example: "Suppose two States, equal in census, to pay 80,000 dollars each by a tax on carriages, of 8 dollars on every carriage; and in one State there are 100 carriages and in the other 1,000. The owners of carriages in one State would pay ten times the tax of owners in the other" (*ibid.*).

Justice added he was "inclined to think" that the direct taxes contemplated by the Constitution were only two, a capitation tax and a tax on land.

Justice Paterson stated:

The Constitution has been considered as an accommodating system; it was the effect of mutual sacrifices and concessions; it was the work of compromise. The rule of apportionment is of this nature; it is radically wrong; it cannot be supported by any solid reasoning. . . . The rule, therefore, should not be extended by construction.[21]

He had "never entertained a doubt," continued Paterson, "that the principal, I will not say, the only, objects, that the framers of the Constitution contemplated as falling within the rule of apportionment, were a capitation tax and a tax on land."

Justice Iredell put it most flatly:

As all direct taxes must be apportioned, it is evident that the Constitution contemplated none as direct, but such as could be apportioned.

If this cannot be apportioned, it is, therefore, not a direct tax in the sense of the Constitution.

That this tax cannot be apportioned is evident.[22]

Iredell concluded that, while he saw no difficulties in stating that only a land tax and a poll tax were direct taxes, he could not say for certain how some new tax in the future might be regarded—but to be a direct tax it would need be "something capable of apportionment under all such circumstances."

Justice Wilson, whose words would have been of the greatest importance, delivered his judgment in the circuit court, where it was not recorded. Having approved the tax, he merely stated, after Iredell, that there was no need to add anything more to the opinions of the other three Justices.

In subsequent cases the rule of the *Hylton* case was invariably followed, the Court sustaining a variety of taxes as indirect and not requiring apportionment. In 1869 in *Pacific Insurance Co.* v.

[21] *Ibid.*, pp. 177–178.   [22] *Ibid.*, p. 181.

Soule [23] a unanimous Court upheld that part of the Civil War income tax which taxed the revenue from premiums and assessments of insurance companies. Noting the comprehensiveness of the federal taxing power and standing on the *Hylton* case, the Court called attention to the unfairness of attempting an apportionment of the disputed tax, and concluded: "It cannot be supposed that the framers of the Constitution intended that any tax should be apportioned, the collection of which on that principle would be attended with such results. The consequences are fatal to the proposition." [24] One year later, 1870, in *Veazie Bank* v. *Fenno* [25] a Court unanimous on the direct tax issue upheld as indirect a federal tax on state bank notes, Chief Justice Salmon P. Chase observing that by the "practical construction of the Constitution" direct taxes had been limited to land taxes and poll taxes. Next, in 1874 in *Scholey* v. *Rew* [26] the Court unanimously declared an inheritance tax on real estate an indirect tax on the ground that it had been "expressly decided that the term [direct tax] does not include the tax on income, which cannot be distinguished in principle from a succession [inheritance] tax." [27]

Then, in 1881, as if writing *finis* to the sequence, the Court decided the case of *Springer* v. *United States*,[28] holding very specifically this time that a tax upon the income of individuals was not a direct tax within the meaning of the Constitution. Justice Noah H. Swayne, speaking for the unanimous Court, reviewed the *Hylton* case and declared that the views there expressed as to the unjustness of apportionment applied "with even greater force to the tax in question in this case. Where the population is large and the incomes are few and small it would be intolerably oppressive." After citing the other direct tax cases since 1796, Swayne concluded with this authoritative statement:

All these cases are indistinguishable in principle from the case now before us, and they are decisive against the plaintiff in error.

The question, what is a direct tax, is one exclusively in American

[23] 7 Wall. 433.   [24] *Ibid.*, p. 446.   [25] 8 Wall. 533.
[26] 23 Wall. 331.   [27] *Ibid.*, pp. 347–348.   [28] 102 U.S. 586.

jurisprudence. The text-writers of the country are in entire accord upon the subject. . . .

Our conclusions are, that direct taxes, within the meaning of the Constitution, are only capitation taxes, as expressed in that instrument, and taxes on real estate; and that the tax of which the plaintiff in error complains is within the category of an excise or duty.[29]

Beyond this, as Professor E. R. A. Seligman put it, "it would seem impossible to go." [30] With this remark most observers in the fall of 1894 would doubtless have concurred. One hundred years of firmly settled precedent, approved by all the authorities,[31] was not to be taken lightly. The legal principle of *stare decisis*, from which the law took both its certainty and its continuity, was among the most fundamental tenets of traditional legal conservatism, one of the great bastions of Anglo-Saxon jurisprudence. While the doctrine of *stare decisis* never carried as much weight in constitutional law, with its unavoidable political and policy-making implications, as in other fields of law, still, the impressive series of decisions that constituted the judicial interpretation of direct tax would have seemed impregnable; the income tax of 1894 could not be successfully challenged on the ground that it was a direct tax that could be levied only if apportioned among the states.

But what of the other possible approach, that the tax, because of the $4,000 exemption and other classifications, violated the requirement of uniformity? While the question of uniformity had never been considered in connection with an income tax, the outlook here was hardly more promising to opponents of the tax. The rule of uniformity as adopted by the Convention had been associated with the grant to Congress of the commerce

[29] *Ibid.*, p. 602.   [30] Seligman, *op. cit.*, p. 576.

[31] As Justice Swayne had pointed out in the *Springer* case, all the text writers at that time, including Kent, Story, and Cooley, had endorsed the Hylton rule of feasibility as the guide to the meaning of direct tax. Following the *Springer* case, opinion was even more affirmative (Justice Samuel F. Miller, *Lectures on the Constitution of the United States* [New York, 1891], pp. 237, 238).

power and was a safeguard that, when Congress regulated or taxed commerce, it would not discriminate between one state or section and another.[32] The very wording of the clause "all duties, imposts and excises shall be uniform throughout the United States" connoted specifically geographical uniformity. And so the Court had held in the well-known *Head Money Cases* of 1884,[33] the Court describing the rule of uniformity as having "reference to the various localities in which the tax is intended to operate. . . . The tax is uniform when it operates with the same force and effect in every place where the subject is to be found." [34] Joseph Story's *Commentaries* had also given this interpretation of the clause, explaining its origin in the desire "to cut off all undue preferences of one State over another in the regulation of subjects affecting their common interests." [35] Furthermore, from another point of view the mere fact of classification was a commonplace in tax laws, both state and federal, and had never been denied by judicial opinion. As a vehicle for judicial interposition, then, the issue of uniformity would seem to have offered little more to the opponents of the income tax than the direct tax issue.

Beyond all these considerations of *stare decisis* and settled constitutional construction was the fact that no national tax law had ever been declared unconstitutional. The power of taxation was at the very heart of the governing process, and the courts had usually been extremely reluctant to interfere with this singularly political power.[36] Given even the most flexible interpretation of Chief Justice Marshall's rule that the issue of repugnancy to the Constitution was "at all times a question of much delicacy,

[32] See Seligman, *op. cit.*, p. 547. See also *Knowlton* v. *Moore*, 178 U.S. 41 (1900), at 95–106.

[33] 112 U.S. 580.   [34] *Ibid.*, p. 594.

[35] *Commentaries on the Constitution of the United States* (5th ed.; Boston, 1891), I, 706–707 (Sec. 957).

[36] On the city and state levels, however, a number of courts had developed in the 1870's and 1880's the doctrine of "public purpose," by which the legislature was restricted from taxing or spending for the benefit of private groups (particularly railroads) or for unusual types of government enterprise (Jacobs, *Law Writers and the Courts*, pp. 98–159).

which ought seldom, if ever, to be decided in the affirmative, in a doubtful case," [37] the constitutional inviolability of the income tax of 1894 seemed well assured.

Despite the apparent weakness of a charge of unconstitutionality, opponents of the tax decided to go ahead with a major effort at securing judicial intervention.[38] And on December 18, 1894, the New York *Sun* reported that the eminent attorneys Joseph H. Choate and Clarence A. Seward "regard the new income tax as unconstitutional" and were representing "a large body of public-spirited New York merchants and business men" in a court test of the tax.[39]

Before the plans of Choate and Seward could get well under way, however, another case against the income tax had begun, the initial outcome of which held small comfort to opponents of the tax. This was a suit at equity filed on December 22 by one John G. Moore in the Supreme Court of the District of Columbia to enjoin the Commissioner of Internal Revenue from collecting the income tax. Chief counsel for Moore was former Senator George F. Edmunds of Vermont, who was widely reputed an authority on constitutional law. Edmunds made no argument on the direct tax issue, conceding that the *Springer* and *Pacific Insurance Co.* cases were conclusive on this point. He claimed, however, that the tax violated the rule of uniformity, and he also presented a number of minor objections.

[37] *Fletcher* v. *Peck*, 6 Cr. 128 (1810).

[38] The debates in Congress had assumed constitutionality, except for one interchange when Senator Hill of New York had expressed his hope "that with the Supreme Court as now constituted this income tax will be declared unconstitutional. . . . The times are changing, the courts are changing." Hill's statement was sharply attacked by Senator Allen of Nebraska: "Are we to understand that the Supreme Court of the United States is packed upon this question?" (quoted in Carl B. Swisher, *American Constitutional Development* [2d ed.; Boston, 1954], pp. 444–445).

[39] Cited in Robert T. Swaine, *The Cravath Firm and Its Predecessors*, 1819–1947 (New York, 1946), I, 518.

The Court delivered its opinion on January 23, 1895, rejecting all of Edmunds' contentions.[40] On the major issue of uniformity, after citing the *Head Money Cases* and quoting Story, the Court ruled that counsel for the United States was correct in representing the required uniformity as "rather geographical in its character, inasmuch as it was designed only to inhibit different rates of duty or tax upon the same subject in the different States."[41] The Court also pointed out, somewhat gratuitously, that in any event the exemption of $4,000 did not discriminate against anybody, since everyone regardless of income had the first $4,000 exempt, and that such exemptions were commonplace in the state property taxes. Finally, the Court held that the suit was improper because precluded by Section 3224 of the *United States Revised Statutes*, which provided that "no suit for the purpose of restraining the assessment or collection of any tax shall be maintained in any court."

Edmunds and associated counsel made plans to appeal at once. Meanwhile, the more broadly based case of the New York counsel had gotten under way. William D. Guthrie, thirty-five-year-old partner of the well-known Seward law firm,[42] had devised a means of circumventing Section 3224 by having stockholders in two trust companies bring suits against the companies to prevent their paying an unlawful tax; *Hyde* v. *Continental Trust Co.* was filed in the Circuit Court on January 11 and *Pollock* v. *Farmers' Loan and Trust Co.* on January 19. Guthrie then persuaded Solicitor General Lawrence Maxwell to consent

---

[40] The full text of this opinion is in *Moore* v. *Miller*, 5 App. D.C. 413, which is the Appellate Court's affirmation of the decision.

[41] *Ibid.*, p. 421.

[42] For a number of interesting sidelights on Guthrie's role in managing the *Pollock* case, see Swaine, *op. cit.*, pp. 518–536. Still largely unknown at the time, Guthrie's success in the handling of the tax cases immediately elevated him to the front rank of the legal profession. He was soon known as a most dedicated ultraconservative (Twiss, *Lawyers and the Constitution*, pp. 214–217). For Guthrie's hatred of labor unions, see Swaine, p. 483.

to *pro forma* proceedings in the lower courts, thereby expediting the cases directly to the Supreme Court.[43] And on January 28, 1895, the Supreme Court agreed to consolidate all three of the income tax cases and hear them together at an early date.[44] The focus of the conservative crisis of the 1890's was thus shifted squarely to the Supreme Court.

Even before the January 28 agreement to hear the income tax cases, the Supreme Court was deep in social and political controversy. For just one week previously the Court had handed down its decision in the famous *E. C. Knight* case, severely narrowing the Sherman Anti-Trust Act, and eight months before had rendered two important decisions affecting legislative regulation of corporate enterprise in the *Brass* and *Reagan* cases.

We last left the Supreme Court in February, 1892, sustaining *Munn* v. *Illinois* with its decision in the *Budd* case, but with Justice Brewer and two other Justices lamenting the rise of "odious" paternalism.[45] For the next two years no important case affecting the growth of the new judicialism was decided by the Court. Nor was the Court an active factor in the depression stresses of 1893 and 1894, since the evolving labor injunction and the mass strikes of the time had as yet brought no legal process

[43] The Solicitor General merely filed demurrers to the suits, the demurrers were sustained without opinion, and appeals were taken immediately. This rapid-fire procedure proved harmful to the government's cause, for it deprived the government "of the very important advantage of a rehearsal in the lower court," as Assistant Attorney General Edward B. Whitney complained in an article some years later: "The Income Tax and the Constitution," *Harvard Law Review*, 20 (Feb., 1907), 280–296. Solicitor General Maxwell had made the arrangements with Guthrie without consulting his superiors. Both Olney and President Cleveland were furious with Maxwell's high-handed methods, and he was forced to resign a few days later (Swaine, pp. 521–522).

[44] For a critique of the Supreme Court's acceptance of these cases, despite the collusive nature of the *Hyde* and *Pollock* cases and the obvious indirection for avoiding the restrictions of a federal statute, see Corwin, *Court over Constitution*, pp. 177–181.

[45] See *supra*, p. 74.

before the Court. Then in May, 1894, the Court decided the *Brass* and *Reagan* cases.

The first of these, *Brass* v. *North Dakota*,[46] a 5-4 decision, involved a North Dakota act of 1891 regulating grain elevators and establishing maximum prices. The act was similar in most respects to the Illinois and New York acts sustained in the *Munn* and *Budd* cases. The Illinois and New York acts, however, applied only to the strategic geographic centers of the two states, such as Chicago in Illinois and Buffalo and the Erie Canal territory in New York, crossroads of commerce where combinations could, in truth, "take toll from all who pass";[47] the North Dakota act on the other hand was state-wide in its application, affecting some six hundred grain elevators in dozens of small towns spread out along the state's several railroad lines. And the contention was pressed that the differing circumstances in North Dakota negated the claim of "virtual monopoly" upon which the *Munn* and *Budd* opinions appeared to have so largely relied and made of the act, therefore, an unconstitutional invasion of private rights.

Justice George Shiras, reading the majority opinion, made short work of plaintiff's argument. Stating flatly that "the facts rehearsed are matters for those who make, not for those who interpret the laws," Shiras declared that once admitted that it was within the legislative power to regulate the grain storage business, then the circumstances presumed to warrant the regulations were no longer matters of judicial inquiry.[48] As for the emphasis in the *Munn* case on virtual monopoly, said Shiras, that went to the propriety of the law, and was in the way of dicta not pertinent to the decision. Most important, repeated Shiras, was that the subject matter of the enactment "fall within the legislative power."

The Court's opinion in *Brass* v. *North Dakota* was potentially

[46] 153 U.S. 391.
[47] Chief Justice Waite's phrase in *Munn* v. *Illinois*, 94 U.S. 113 at 132.
[48] 153 U.S. 403.

of great significance. By discarding the requirement of virtual monopoly, the door might have been opened to a wide extension of state regulatory powers.[49] The 5-4 majority, however, a closer vote than in either the *Munn* or *Budd* decisions,[50] indicated that the Court's forbearance of the legislative will might soon be reversed. Certainly, Justice David J. Brewer's dissent, proclaiming that by such decisions the country was "rapidly travelling the road which leads to that point where all freedom of contract and conduct will be lost," [51] gave notice that the advocates of judicial guardianship had no intention of abandoning their cause.

The second important case of May, 1894, was *Reagan* v. *Farmers' Loan and Trust Co.*,[52] a decisive advance in the evolution of the Court's power of superintendence over the reasonableness of legislative rate-setting. In the *Chicago, Milwaukee* case of 1890, it will be recalled, the Court had declared that the reasonableness of railroad rates was a judicial question, "requiring due process of law for its determination," and that by due process of law was meant the forms and machinery traditional to courts of law. And the Minnesota act in question, which established a railroad commission with powers to set rates, had been held invalid because it did not permit judicial review of the commission's conclusions.[53] Mindful of this decision, the Texas legislature in 1891 had established a railroad commission with the same powers as in Minnesota, but requiring notice and hearing as a matter of right (the Minnesota commission had allowed these as a matter

[49] For a discussion of the effect of the *Brass* decision on the development of the public interest doctrine, see Breck P. McAllister, "Lord Hale and Business Affected with a Public Interest," *Harvard Law Review*, 43 (March, 1930), 770–775.

[50] The only changed position among Justices still sitting from 1892 was Justice Brown's; Brown had been with Brewer and Field on the *Budd* dissent, but now voted with the majority to sustain the legislative discretion. Besides Brewer and Field, the other two dissenters in the *Brass* case were Jackson and White, two new appointees of moderate conservative leanings.

[51] 153 U.S. 410.   [52] 154 U.S. 362.

[53] 134 U.S. 418. See *supra*, pp. 39–40.

of course), and providing for appeal to any court of competent jurisdiction. Until "finally found otherwise," the commission's schedules were to be considered "conclusive."

John F. Dillon, appearing for the trustees of the railroad, attacked the existing schedule of rates as unreasonable and asserted that the section of the Texas act declaring the commission's rate conclusive until finally found otherwise, was a deprivation of due process of law and invalidated the whole act. Dillon argued that the conclusiveness clause forced the railroads to carry out the commission's schedules until all legal proceedings had been completed; and then, even after a legal decision in the railroad's favor, there was nothing to prevent the commission from setting a new schedule of rates only slightly different from the previous one, again putting the railroad to loss and expense.[54]

The Supreme Court, speaking unanimously through Justice Brewer, rejected Dillon's contention that the whole act was invalid, Brewer declaring it was not to be assumed the commission would deliberately set out to destroy the railroads. The federal courts were competent to give relief in all proper cases, the word "conclusive" being no bar thereto and no valid reason for preventing the commission doing its duty. But the Court agreed, after a twelve-page analysis, that the commission's schedules were unreasonable and ordered them set aside. Justice Brewer then amplified the holding of the *Chicago, Milwaukee* case in this key paragraph:

It is doubtless true, as a general proposition, that the formation of a tariff of charges for . . . a common carrier . . . is a legislative or administrative rather than a judicial function. . . . The courts are not authorized to revise or change the body of rates imposed by a legislature or a commission; . . . they do not engage in any mere

---

[54] Dillon's argument had convinced the Circuit Court to the extent of the Court invalidating the existing rates and issuing a permanent injunction prohibiting the Commission from establishing any other schedule of rates—in effect, reducing the Commission to the status of a fact-finding body. See 154 U.S. 370.

administrative work; but still there can be no doubt of their power and duty to inquire whether a body of rates prescribed by a legislature or a commission is unjust and unreasonable, . . . and if found so to be, to restrain its operation.[55]

The Court had defined its powers more precisely. It would not interfere with the intermediate steps of the administrative process; but in the final determination of appeals, the judiciary could invalidate a given schedule of rates as unreasonable—and this whether set by a commission after notice and hearing or by a legislature directly on the basis of committee reports.[56] Chief Justice Waite's assertion of 1877 that for protection against the abuses of legislative regulation "the people must resort to the polls, not to the courts" had been effectively rejected.

The *Brass* and *Reagan* decisions failed to attract much notice in the law journals,[57] professional attention being drawn mainly toward rising labor tension. By the time the *E. C. Knight* case was decided, however, on January 21, 1895, the near panic created by the labor movements of 1894, which affected legal conservatives and progressives alike, had largely subsided, and the dissident elements in the profession were prepared to reassert themselves. And *United States v. E. C. Knight Co.*[58] was an ideal instrument for awakening protestants.

[55] 154 U.S. 397.

[56] The power asserted in the *Reagan* case was first exercised in regard to direct legislative rate-setting in 1898 in the well-known case of *Smyth v. Ames*, 169 U.S. 466, striking down rate schedules of the Nebraska legislature.

[57] On the *Brass* case, see the *Central Law Journal*, 39 (Aug. 24, 1894), 157, warning of the socialistic implications of the decision. On the *Reagan* case, see the *American Law Review*, 28 (Sept.–Oct., 1894), 787–792, praising Brewer's "clear, strong, just and well-balanced opinion," and expressing satisfaction that the decision would restore public confidence in American railroad securities, so badly shaken by current financial and labor disturbances. The *American Law Review*, as noted *supra*, ch. vii, had moved toward a more approving position in 1894 on the question of judicial power.

[58] 156 U.S. 1.

The case involved a suit by the government asking the dissolution under the Sherman Act of the American Sugar Refining Company on the ground that it had acquired by purchase of stock in competing companies a monopoly of more than 90 per cent of the sugar-refining capacity of the United States. The suit had been instituted by President Harrison's Attorney General, William H. H. Miller, but Miller was succeeded in 1893 by Richard Olney. Olney had opposed the passage of the Sherman Act and had then worked for its repeal. He had advocated a narrow interpretation of the act (except in July, 1894, at the height of the Pullman strike), and during his two years in office no new suits were brought under the act.[59] Under these circumstances it would have been surprising had the government's side in the sugar trust case received a very thorough or a very vigorous prosecution. The American Sugar Refining Company, on the other hand, was exceptionally well represented by John Edward Parsons, a leader of the New York bar who had helped organize the company in 1891, and by John C. Johnson of Philadelphia, for fifteen years one of the foremost practitioners before the Supreme Court and attorney for many of the great corporations of the nation.[60]

Whether influenced by superior argument of company counsel or deciding on its own reading of the case, the Court threw out the government's suit in an opinion that seemed to leave little left of the Sherman Act. Chief Justice Melville W. Fuller for the Court agreed at the outset that the existence of the monopoly might be conceded. But the monopoly, he said, was a monopoly of manufacture, and manufacture was not commerce:

Doubtless the power to control the manufacture of a given thing involves in a certain sense the control of its disposition, but this is a secondary and not the primary sense; and although the exercise of

---

[59] Cummings and McFarland, *Federal Justice*, pp. 321–323; Nevins, *op. cit.*, p. 671.

[60] Twiss, *op. cit.*, pp. 201–213, has an interesting chapter on Parsons and Johnson and their work on the *E. C. Knight* case.

that power may result in bringing the operation of commerce into play it does not control it, and affects it only incidentally and indirectly. Commerce succeeds to manufacture, and is not a part of it.[61]

For protection from monopolies in manufacturing, continued Fuller, or other forms of production, the people would have to look to the individual states. Congress could repress a monopoly only when the monopoly was a monopoly of commerce. To permit otherwise, said Fuller, would interfere with the residual power of the states to control their internal affairs and thus weaken the federal structure of American government.

The Chief Justice admitted that combinations in manufacturing might restrain interstate commerce, but such restraint, he said, "would be an indirect result, however inevitable and whatever its extent." Although the bill alleged that the products of the sugar refining combination were sold and distributed among the several states, and that all the companies of the combination were engaged in interstate trade or commerce, "this was no more than to say that trade and commerce served manufacture to fulfill its function." There was nothing in the proofs, concluded Fuller, "to indicate any intention to put a restraint upon trade or commerce, and the fact, as we have seen, that trade or commerce might be indirectly affected was not enough to entitle complainants to a decree." [62]

Justice John M. Harlan, in an opinion establishing his position as the Court's leading sympathizer with the progressive point of view,[63] filed a long and vigorous dissent. Recurring repeatedly

---

[61] 156 U.S. 12.   [62] *Ibid.*, p. 17.

[63] Justice Harlan was described by Justice Brown as "a strong Federalist, with a leaning toward the popular side of cases and a frequent dissenter from the more conservative opinions of his brethren" (Kent, *Memoir*, p. 31). The wide extent of Harlan's dissidence from the court of the 1890's is well surveyed by Loren P. Beth, "Justice Harlan and the Uses of Dissent," *American Political Science Review*, 49 (Dec., 1955), 1085–1104. See also the *Kentucky Law Journal*, 46 (Spring, 1958), 321–474, an interesting symposium of four articles on various phases of Harlan's life and judicial career.

to Chief Justice Marshall's great opinion in the case of *Gibbons*
v. *Ogden*,[64] which first laid down the plenary power of Congress
over interstate commerce, Harlan attacked the Court's majority
opinion as destructive of the Marshall doctrine and of the federal
commerce power. The national power was intended to be sufficient for national objects, and an unlawful restraint on the free
course of trade which affected the people of all the states was
properly a matter for national and not state regulation. The reserved powers of the states could not be considered a bar to
national regulation, for the will of the nation was supreme within
its spheres. By the Court's decision in the present case, declared
Justice Harlan, the public was left

> entirely at the mercy of combinations which arbitrarily control the
> prices of articles purchased to be transported from one State to
> another State. . . . In my judgment, the general government is not
> placed by the Constitution in such a condition of helplessness that it
> must fold its arms and remain inactive while capital combines . . .
> to destroy competition, not in one State only, but throughout the
> entire country, in the buying and selling of articles—especially the
> necessaries of life—that go into commerce among the States.[65]

The decision in the *E. C. Knight* case was a great victory for
laissez-faire conservatism. The long-term implications of the
case, with its artificial categorizing of "indirect" and "direct"
effects, and the consequent fracturing of the federal commerce
power in an age of business nationalization, need not concern us
here.[66] It is enough to take note of what was apparent to all observers at the time, that corporate combination in all forms of
production could proceed unrestrained by federal interference
under the Sherman Act. The Court's opinion was also a victory

[64] 9 Wheat. 1 (1824).   [65] 156 U.S. 43.

[66] Numerous scholarly books and articles have been written on the
E. C. Knight case and its deleterious influence on American constitutional
history until the late 1930's. See especially Edward S. Corwin's suggestive
interpretations in his *Twilight of the Supreme Court*, ch. i, and *The
Commerce Power versus States Rights* (Princeton, 1936), pp. 151–156
and 189–209.

for states' rights advocates, and the line-up of Justices [67] re-
flected this dual nature of the decision. Voting together with
ultraconservatives like Fuller, Brewer, and Field were moderate
conservatives who were also states' righters like Shiras and Edward D. White. The presence on the majority side of Horace
Gray, a moderate conservative and nationalist, and Brown, probably the least conservative Justice after Harlan, needs further
explanation: the answer here may be perhaps the government's
weak presentation, which left enough loopholes on the technical
side of its case to allow the conservative pressures of the time full
play.[68]

The *E. C. Knight* case brought an uproar from the legal
progressives. Ardemus Stewart, associate editor of the *American
Law Register* in charge of recent decisions, castigated the Court's
opinion for "studiously ignoring the facts." The Constitution was
not a "cast-iron frame," affirmed Stewart, but was designed for
adaptation to changing conditions. "It is enough to say," he concluded bitterly,

that if this decision stands, and it is true that the national government is powerless to protect the people against such combinations as
this, which the states are both unwilling to assail and powerless to
overthrow, then this government is a failure, and the sooner the

[67] The division of the Justices was 7-1, Justice Jackson not voting
because of illness.

[68] The contracts placed in evidence by the government related solely
to the purchase of stock and made no mention of trade or commerce.
It has been suggested that Olney should have offered direct proofs of
interstate control of sales and prices (Nevins, *op. cit.*, p. 671; Cummings
and McFarland, *op. cit.*, p. 323; Shiras, *George Shiras, Jr.*, p. 147). It is
true that this failure on the government's part, however explicable
(according to Twiss, pp. 210–212, the case was expected to turn on def-
initions of restraint of trade), left the door open for Fuller and the
majority. But as Justice Harlan cogently queried in his dissent, "Was it
necessary that formal proof be made that the persons engaged in this
combination admitted, in words, that they intended to restrain trade or
commerce? . . . Why, it is conceded that the object of this combination
was to obtain control of the business of making and selling refined sugar
throughout the entire country" (156 U.S. 43).

social and political revolution which many far-sighted men can see already darkening the horizon overtakes us, the better.[69]

In the *American Law Review* Seymour D. Thompson, who had been deterred somewhat from his reformist stance by the labor unrest of 1894, once again turned his fire on the corporation-protecting federal judiciary. Writing under "Notes of Recent Decisions," [70] Thompson characterized Fuller's opinion as "weak, specious, and obviously unsound"; Harlan's dissent on the other hand was "strong, clear, vigorous, and entitled to the greatest respect." Thompson then subjected the Court's opinion to a long and caustic review, which he summarized with this resounding blast:

The Sherman "Anti-Trust Law" has at last been vetoed by the third House of Congress and sponged out of existence, except for the purpose of enabling the Federal courts to enjoin railway strikes, as effectually as though it had never been enacted. This has been done by the only non-elective branch of our government. The decision is the most deplorable one that has been rendered in favor of incorporated power and greed, and against popular right, since the Dartmouth College case. What are the American people going to do about it? That is the question! [71]

But Thompson had not said his last on the *E. C. Knight* case. Noting that Judge Dillon had stated in his address to the New York State Bar Association that socialism in America was unnecessary because the state already possessed sufficient power to regulate harmful combinations,[72] Thompson wondered what Dillon would say now in view of the *E. C. Knight* case. Continued Thompson, with mounting anger:

If that decision is to stand, the American people are helpless in the face of every monopoly engrossing all their markets in any article of prime necessity. . . . Such, we are told, is the constitution which

[69] *American Law Register*, n.s., 34 (Feb., 1895), 89–90.
[70] *American Law Review*, 29 (March–April, 1895), 293–306.
[71] *Ibid.*, p. 306.   [72] *Supra*, note 11.

our fathers made for us. They conquered political liberty for us through seven years of blood and privation, and then gave us a constitution under which we are handed over, helpless, bound hand-and-foot, to industrial and commercial slavery.

Although the "usury States" of the Northeast might prevent amendment to the Constitution, the Supreme Court itself, Thompson gave grim notice, could be amended—"even by as drastic a measure as the amendment of the House of Lords by the creation of new peers." Disclaiming any intent "to create alarm," the *Review*'s senior editor closed, nevertheless, with this burst of rhetoric: "The American people are not yet ready to have the eagle on their coat of arms removed and its place taken by a fool's cap-and-bells and a pointless spear." [73]

The stage had thus been well set for the income tax cases. The left wing of the legal profession, aroused by the *E. C. Knight* case from its cautiousness of 1894, was in loud protest against the judicial interventionism of the Supreme Court; while the right wing, determined to bar the door to lower-class reformism, mobilized resources [74] for its greatest effort, the struggle to secure a judicial veto on the critical question of graduated taxation. On the center would depend the issue: on the hierarchy of values and the social attitudes of the moderate center of traditional legal conservatism would hinge the outcome of the tax cases—and, in a larger sense, of the whole conflict of the 1890's between popular majorities and the power of the judiciary.

[73] *American Law Review, op. cit.,* pp. 288–289.
[74] Guthrie, as manager of the tax case for the Seward firm, sent letters to leading law firms throughout the country soliciting contributions in the common interest (Swaine, *op. cit.,* I, 520).

IX

The Pollock *Case and the*

Triumph of the New Judicialism

ARGUMENT before the Supreme Court on the consolidated income tax cases, reported as *Pollock* v. *Farmers' Loan and Trust Company*,[1] began on March 7. The great significance of the case and the eminence of counsel on both sides contributed to unusual public interest in the hearings. Although counsel had already submitted voluminous briefs to the Court, the oral arguments were expected to be decisive, and press and public followed closely the rising tempo of debate.[2]

The opening statements to the Court were dry and legalistic. William D. Guthrie, managing the case for appellants, argued on the uniformity question, charging that the constitutional requirement that "all duties, imposts and excises shall be uniform

[1] 157 U.S. 429.

[2] Robert T. Swaine, chronicling the history of the Cravath law firm of New York City, the contemporary descendant of the Seward firm which handled the tax cases, writes that the *Pollock* case "attracted as much attention in the press of the entire country as any case in the history of the Court. The briefs were described with considerable detail by most of the papers in the larger cities and each day's argument was reported at great length" (*The Cravath Firm*, I, 522).

throughout the United States" had been violated by the various exemptions in the income tax enactment of 1894. The exemption of the first $4,000 income of individuals was particularly unequal in its effects, he declared, because it discriminated on the one hand against corporations, which had no exemptions, and on the other hand against persons with incomes over $4,000, who bore the whole burden of the tax though constituting only 2 per cent of the population. The congressional power of classification must show "some principle of public policy," said Guthrie, or else it was merely arbitrary and capricious. Rejecting as "without merit" the government's contention in its briefs that the uniformity clause was limited to a strictly geographical meaning, Guthrie insisted that uniformity meant also equality of burden. But irrespective of the specific limitation of Article I, Section 8, continued Guthrie, moving on to a wondrously latitudinarian constitutionalism, "the requirement of approximate equality inheres in the very nature of the power to tax, and it exists whether declared or not in the written Constitution." The due process and just compensation clauses of the Fifth Amendment embodied this restriction, he concluded, and made the exemptions of the income tax unconstitutional.[3]

Guthrie was followed by Clarence A. Seward, senior partner of the Seward law firm, who concentrated on the direct tax issue, that is, whether an income tax was a direct tax as understood in Article I, Section 2, and therefore could not be levied unless apportioned among the states according to population. Although until then the question had been thought so firmly settled in the negative that argument on the point would probably be futile,[4]

---

[3] 157 U.S. 442–452.

[4] *Moore* v. *Miller,* 5 App. D.C. 413; *Albany Law Journal,* 50 (Dec. 29, 1894), 416–421; 51 (Jan. 12, 1895), 19–22; (Feb. 2, 1895), 65–66. In all these references opponents of the tax acknowledged the hopelessness of a new ruling on direct taxes. After the direction of the Seward firm's case became known, however, opinion began to change, though uncertainly: Carman F. Randolph, a writer of legal texts, taking a position

Seward asked the Court to re-examine the whole matter.[5] He purported to show that the definition of direct taxes was well known at the Convention of 1787 and that taxes on incomes were included in that definition. Seward maintained that the Convention's major objective in requiring apportionment of direct taxes was to make unlikely their use by the federal government and thus reserve to the states a concurrent power over this type of tax. To exempt the income tax from this rule, he concluded, would weaken the relative position of the states in the federal system and defeat the purposes of the framers.[6]

On the government side, the Assistant Attorney General, Edward B. Whitney, replied to Guthrie and Seward. On direct taxation, Whitney simply recited the previous decisions, expressing his confidence that the Court would not now reopen this long-settled question. On uniformity, he insisted that the term as used in the Constitution meant only geographical uniformity. But even if a broader meaning were allowed, he continued, the

---

similar to Seward's in the *Albany Law Journal*, 51 (Feb. 16, 1895), 104–108, admitted this was the "radical" side of the tax litigation.

[5] Seward dismissed the precedents almost casually: the *Hylton* case, he said, had been predicated solely on the "presumption" of Hamilton and was mostly dicta anyway; and the *Pacific Insurance Co.* and *Springer* cases involved the wartime income tax and were therefore not conclusive for a later period. The wartime origin of the previous income taxes was not, of course, constitutionally relevant.

[6] 157 U.S. 452–469. Seward's assertions were surprising indeed. The meaning of direct taxes in 1787, far from being well known, was fluctuating and unsettled (*supra*, pp. 165–166). As for the origin of the direct tax clause, this stemmed principally from the problem of the slave states and was associated with the three-fifths compromise. To reassure the Southern states against overtaxation (per acre on their land or per head on their slaves—both direct taxes), the South was guaranteed an apportionment according to population, three-fifths of the slaves to be counted. The three-fifths clause was also the device for the compromise about representation, and accordingly, direct taxes and representation had been conjoined in Article I, Section 2. See Seligman's lucid analysis of the Convention debates (*The Income Tax*, pp. 548–555), and Justice Paterson's explanation in the *Hylton* case, 3 Dal. 177.

$4,000 exemption, although admittedly discriminating against the rich, was defensible as a counterweight to the consumption taxes which had weighed most heavily on the poor. Whitney also attempted to answer the argument in the appellants' brief that the part of the income tax which fell on rental from land was equivalent to a tax on the land and therefore a direct tax. A tax on rentals was not the same as a tax on land values, Whitney argued, and in any event the income tax was not a tax on rentals. The income from rentals was taxed only after having been lumped together with other incomes and after permissible deductions from the whole.[7]

The fireworks really began on March 11 with the appearance of former Senator George F. Edmunds, an orator in true Senatorial style. As counsel for appellant in the original *Moore* case, it may be recalled, Edmunds had conceded back in December that the precedents were conclusive on the direct tax issue. Now, three months later, having associated his case with the Seward firm's cases, the Senator declared it "beyond cavil or doubt" that the income tax was a direct tax requiring apportionment among the states. The main intent of the direct tax clause, Edmunds argued, in a significant variation of Seward's argument, was to prevent "the mere majority of the voters" from throwing on a few the whole burden of government. The income tax of 1894, he declared, was "intentionally and tyrannically and monstrously unequal," violating not only the direct tax clause and the uniformity clause but the Fourteenth Amendment as well, by inference applicable to Congress as well as the states. If the Supreme Court failed to bring Congress back to the true sense of its powers, warned Edmunds, "one evil step will lead to another . . . until by and by we will have revolution, then anarchy and then a tyrant to rule us." [8]

Edmunds' oratory had changed the tenor of the hearings, and on March 12 and 13 the three leading counselors in the case, Olney, Carter, and Choate, each contributed to the growing

[7] 157 U.S. 469–482.   [8] *Ibid.*, pp. 482–499.

excitement. First of the three was the Attorney General himself, the suave and urbane Richard Olney. A former railroad lawyer, who had opposed the Sherman Act and then as Attorney General had by his own admission neglected to enforce it,[9] an impeccable conservative who had relentlessly harassed the Coxey marchers and the Debs railway strikers, Olney now turned out a smoothly reasoned, even brilliant defense of the income tax.[10] Like Whitney, Olney also insisted that the direct tax question had been absolutely settled by the previous judicial opinions of the Court. Even were the error of those opinions "ever so certain," Olney continued, the Court dare not now reconsider:

A constitutional exposition practically coeval with the Constitution itself, that has been acted upon ever since as occasion required . . . deserves to be considered as immutable as if incorporated into the text of the Constitution itself. To reject it after a century's duration is to set a hurtful precedent and would go far to prove that government by written constitution is not a thing of stable principles, but of the fluctuating views and wishes of the particular period and the particular judges when and from whom its interpretation happens to be called for.[11]

Moving on from this profoundly *conservative* position, Olney gave some time to the question of the tax on rentals, presumed to be a subsidiary question, and then turned to the appellants' charge of inequality, "*the* constitutional objection" as Olney put it. Pure equality of taxation was impossible, he pointed out, and therefore the incidence of taxation was "an uncommonly practical affair." The congressional power to classify, to exempt and except, was

[9] Olney wrote to a friend after the decision in the *E. C. Knight* case: "You will have observed that the government has been defeated in the Supreme Court on the trust question. I always supposed it would be and have taken the responsibility of not prosecuting under a law I believe to be no good" (cited in Nevins, *Grover Cleveland*, p. 671, from the Olney papers).

[10] But see Ratner, *American Taxation*, p. 199, n. 24, for a qualification of Olney's interest in the tax case.

[11] 157 U.S. 502.

thus virtually unlimited so long as some relation to public policy could be shown. In the matter of the $4,000 exemption, the principle involved was ability to pay. As for the differential treatment of corporations—"a class which the plaintiffs' counsel dwell upon at great length and with exceeding unction"—this was referable to the "plain and notorious" business advantages enjoyed by corporations.

The Attorney General concluded with a sharp reminder to the Court of the inherent limitations of its own powers. The plea of the plaintiffs, he declared, was in essence

nothing but a call upon the judicial department of the government to supplant the political in the exercise of the taxing power; to substitute its discretion for that of Congress. . . . It is inevitably predestined to failure unless this court shall, for the first time in its history, overlook and overstep the bounds which separate the judicial from the legislative power—bounds, the scrupulous observance of which it has so often declared to be absolutely essential to the integrity of our constitutional system of government.[12]

Even stronger than Olney's argument, and more outspoken, was the defense of the tax by James C. Carter, a past president of the American Bar Association and one of the most distinguished lawyers of the day.[13] Carter plunged at once into a social justification of the tax that accepted the appellants' premise of "equality of burden" but drew from it a startling conclusion. Real equality of taxation, said Carter, meant but one thing: apportionment of the burden where it could most easily be borne. But real equality had seldom been obtained. The reason?—control of the state by

[12] *Ibid.*, p. 513.

[13] Carter was appearing on the record for the Continental Trust Co., in accordance with Guthrie's procedure for circumventing Sec. 3223 (see *supra*, p. 173). In selecting Carter the company—or Guthrie—showed good faith. Carter was known to have favored the tax for some time, and his reputation as a successful advocate of important causes was equal to any. Carter was also a leading scholar and legal theorist. See Twiss, *Lawyers and the Constitution*, pp. 174–179, for a discussion of Carter's legal philosophy and role in the New York bar.

the upper classes, with the consequence "that in every country and in every age the principal burdens of taxation have been borne by the poor." [14]

The same injustice, he continued, had long prevailed in the United States, where all federal revenue had been secured from taxes on consumable commodities. If the appellants complained that 2 per cent of the population would now pay the whole of the income tax, they might reflect that this same 2 per cent, receiving "probably more than fifty per cent" of the national income, had long been paying only a trifle more than 2 per cent of the nation's tax bill. The people had connected this up with the "growing concentration of large masses of wealth in an ever diminishing number of persons" and had finally determined to devise a remedy. The purpose of the income tax was therefore "plain upon its face"—to redress the "flagrant inequality" of the existing tax system. The income tax was indeed "class legislation." But class legislation had always been the case—now at last no longer "in the wrong direction." [15]

Having taken his stand on this essentially *radical* position, Carter's purely legal arguments may have seemed almost afterthoughts to the Court. As a matter of fact, Carter was very thorough. On the direct tax issue, not content to rest on *stare decisis* like Olney and Whitney, Carter made a point-by-point rebuttal to all of Seward's contentions. Emphasizing the indefiniteness of the line between direct and indirect taxes in 1787, Carter commended the Court for having developed the practical rule that those taxes not able to be apportioned with at least some show of equity should not be regarded as direct taxes. On uniformity, Carter presented a detailed defense of the various exemptions in the law, all justifiable, he asserted, on the grounds of well-understood public policy.

Carter's closing peroration built up to a fine climax. Like the Attorney General, Carter reminded the Court that it too had limits to its power, limits "already transgressed when it finds it-

[14] 157 U.S. 516.   [15] *Ibid.,* p. 518.

self even considering whether this or that point of view of a
question of political economy, or of the wisdom of taxation, is
a sound one." But Carter added something more, a bold warning
to the Court that infuriated the conservative opposition:

Nothing could be more unwise and dangerous—nothing more foreign to the spirit of the Constitution—than an attempt to baffle and
defeat a popular determination by a judgment in a lawsuit. When
the opposing forces of sixty millions of people have become arrayed
in hostile political ranks upon a question which all men feel is not
a question of law, but of legislation, the only path of safety is to
accept the voice of the majority as final.[16]

The echoes of Carter's formidable challenge to judicial interventionism had barely waned when the last and most dexterous
of counsel, Joseph H. Choate, rose to speak.[17] By general repute
the most skillful orator at the bat, celebrated for his spectacular
jury trials, Choate had been retained as chief counsel for the appellants; and Choate fully justified his fame and the confidence
of the Seward firm as he delivered an exceptionally persuasive
address.[18] Not unexpectedly, in view of the nature of Carter's
argument just concluded, Choate opened with a blast against the
policy of the income tax and in particular the character of its
defense by counsel. "The Act . . . is communistic in its purposes and tendencies, and is defended here upon principles as
communistic, socialistic—what shall I call them—populistic as
ever have been addressed to any political assembly in the

[16] 157 U.S. 531–532. Swaine, *op. cit.*, I, 528, contains excerpts from the
uproar in the conservative press over Carter's argument.

[17] Carter finished late in the afternoon, and Choate followed him immediately. For Choate's illustrious career, see Edward S. Martin, *The
Life of Joseph Hodges Choate* (New York, 1920), 2 vols.

[18] For a eulogistic description of Choate's address by a correspondent
of a newspaper (*New York World*) which favored the income tax, see
ibid., II, 7–15. The full text of Choate's argument is printed in Frederick
C. Hicks, ed., *Arguments and Addresses of Joseph Hodges Choate* (St.
Paul, 1926), pp. 419–472.

world." [19] If the Court approved the present law, "and this communistic march goes on," the Court would then be helpless.
"There is protection now or never," he charged the Court in an
eloquent passage:

You cannot hereafter exercise any check if you now say that Congress is untrammelled and uncontrollable. My friend says you cannot enforce any limit. He says no matter what Congress does . . .
this Court will have nothing to say about it. I agree that it will have
nothing to say about it if it now lets go its hold upon this law. . . .

I have thought that one of the fundamental objects of all civilized
government was the preservation of the rights of private property.
I have thought that it was the very keystone of the arch upon which
all civilized government rests, and that this once abandoned, everything was in danger. . . . According to the doctrines that have
been propounded here this morning, even that great fundamental
principle has been scattered to the winds.[20]

With the conservative stake in a negative decision thus firmly
established, Choate proceeded to the constitutional question
proper.[21] Admitting candidly that it was unlikely the Court
would overrule its previous adjudications and call a tax on incomes of any and every source a direct tax, he contended nevertheless that there was a narrower ground on which the direct
tax clause could be applied, a "safe and practicable alternative,"
not inconsistent with any case yet decided. What was this
alternative, this indirection which would accomplish the conservative end and yet escape the stringency of *stare decisis?*

[19] 157 U.S. 532. This passage is frequently cited in accounts of the
income tax case as illustrating the "exaggerated shadow of radicalism"
called forth by defense counsel (quoted from Studenski and Kroos,
Financial History of the United States, pp. 233–234). In justice to
Choate, however, it should be noted that he was the last of seven counsel,
at least three of whom had also appealed to the social tension of the times
to sustain their positions. Exaggeration was endemic to the times.

[20] 157 U.S. 533–534.

[21] Choate's argument on the constitutional aspects was based on a brief
by his retired partner, Charles F. Southmayd (Martin, *op. cit.,* pp. 15–17).

Basically, what Choate now offered the Court was a simple, an almost ingenuously simple, set of analogies. It was admitted by all that a tax on real property was a direct tax, one of *the* two direct taxes specifically categorized as such ever since the *Hylton* case. If so, then inescapably, said Choate, a tax on the income from real property, i.e., on rents, was also a direct tax— "For what is the land but the profits thereof?" [22] But Choate went further. A tax on personal property, he insisted, was in no important way different from a tax on real property—"Is a tax upon the house one kind of a tax and a tax upon the proceeds of the house another? It cannot be; it is impossible." Well then, since a tax on the income from *real* property has just been shown in effect a direct tax on the property, then a tax on the income from *personal* property—say, dividends from stocks and bonds— was also in effect a direct tax on the property. Thus, in Choate's hands, the universally subscribed-to and supposedly restricted ruling that a tax on lands was a direct tax had become the hinge for the far-reaching proposition that a tax applying to incomes derived from property in general was a direct tax.

Equally telling points were Choate's razor-edge distinctions between the present case and the precedents. In neither the *Pacific Insurance Co.* nor the *Springer* cases, affirming Civil War income taxes, had the possession of income-bearing property, real or personal, been specifically considered in the opinions. And the *Hylton* case, involving a tax principally on the *use* of carriages, had nothing to do with an income tax. Choate's message was now complete: the Court could accept these arguments, drastically emasculate the income tax, and still render formal obeisance to the niceties of precedent.

[22] 157 U.S. 540, quoting Coke on a common law question. A reading of the context of this line from Coke (given *ibid.*, p. 580) adopted by Chief Justice Fuller and made an important hinge of his opinion, discloses no discernible relevancy to the questions under consideration. See the excoriating comments of Professor Corwin, *Court over Constitution*, p. 189, and of Francis R. Jones, "Pollock v. Farmers' Loan and Trust Company," *Harvard Law Review*, 9 (Oct. 25, 1895), 205.

Choate ended his address with a final appeal to the stern duty of the Justices in this hour of crisis:

I do not believe that any member of this Court has ever sat or ever will sit to hear and decide a case the consequences of which will be so far-reaching as this. . . . If it be true, as my friend said in closing, that the passions of the people are aroused on this subject, if it be true that a mighty army of sixty million citizens is likely to be incensed by this decision, it is the more vital to the future welfare of this country that this court again resolutely and courageously declare, as Marshall did, that it *has* the power to set aside an act of Congress violative of the Constitution, and that it will not hesitate in executing that power, no matter what the threatened consequences of popular or populistic wrath may be.[23]

The closing arguments before the Supreme Court, which emphasized so forcefully the theme of conflict between majority rule and the power of the judiciary, affected sharply the attitudes of legal conservatives. The moderates were split down the middle, the long-term drift to the right gaining momentum, while many traditional conservatives still shied away from so radical an application of judicial review.

The growing tension on the right was typified by the *Albany Law Journal*, the leading weekly law review of the East. On most social and constitutional questions of the 1890's the *Journal* had taken a moderately conservative position, supporting a limited version of freedom of contract for example, but sympathizing with the problems of labor and questioning the widespread use of the injunction.[24] For some time the *Journal* had indicated a desire for a judicial annulment of the income tax; however, its views had been expressed without especial rancor and apparently without much hope of success.[25] But immediately following the close of counsel's arguments, the *Journal's* edi-

[23] 157 U.S. 553 (italics in source).
[24] *Albany Law Journal*, 45 (June 24, 1892), 528; 47 (April 4, 1893), 161–162; 50 (Aug. 4, 1894), 69.
[25] *Ibid.*, 51 (Jan. 12, 1895), 19–22; (Feb. 2, 1892), 65.

torials demonstrated a new shrillness. In its issue of March 16, lavishing unstinted praise on the "patriotic utterances" of counsel opposing the tax, the *Journal* declared its fervent belief

that the rights of citizenship are to be preserved against the tyranny of unjust legislation, the theories of agitators and the forerunners of socialism and that the historical guarantee of no taxation without representation shall be forever kept sacred from the attacks of fanatics, anarchists and the scum which has overflowed from Europe.[26]

And in an editorial of April 6, just two days before the decision of the Court was due, the *Albany Law Journal* submitted this opinion:

that if Congress has the power to divide the persons taxed into two classes, viz., those with $4,000 income and those with less . . . that it may at any time contend that it has the power to divide the country into many classes taking from one a greater or less proportion of their property, and accepting little or none from the others . . . thus encouraging anarchists and socialists, recognizing the vast body of communists and those who believe in confiscating enough from the rich to properly support their shiftless and useless existences.[27]

A contrasting reaction to the oral arguments was represented by William Draper Lewis, whom we have seen frequently as among the most temperate of legal conservatives. Commenting in the *American Law Register* on the "battle royal" before the Supreme Court, Lewis made plain his personal opposition to an income tax "at the present time," but maintained that the taxing power of Congress should not be curtailed by judicial interpretation.[28] Lewis deplored particularly the argument of "the extreme case" put forth by opponents of the tax law. The present tax was exceedingly moderate, he pointed out, and in no sense confiscatory. Should it become so in the future, it would be time enough then to consider judicial intervention.

[26] *Ibid.*, (March 16, 1895), 161.   [27] *Ibid.*, (April 6, 1895), 209.
[28] *American Law Register*, n.s., 34 (March, 1895), 189.

Some traditional legal conservatives, perhaps subject to various pressures, chose to avoid commitment. Waitman T. Willey, highly respected editor of the *West Virginia Bar*, was an example.[29] The *West Virginia Bar*, a new monthly begun in 1894, at first had derided the critics of the income tax. "The *New York Sun* has been amusing itself," said an editorial of December, 1894, "by the re-publication of a very interesting and profound essay . . . upon the unconstitutionality of the income tax." But the old argument on the direct tax question, the editorial continued, had been finally settled by the Supreme Court in the *Springer* case, and "the *Sun* must be regarded as talking through its hat." [30] Subsequent issues of the *West Virginia Bar*, however, gave no notice to the income tax case except for the quotation, without comment, of Choate's opening statements to the Court.

We should also note the comment of the *Central Law Journal*, a solidly conservative weekly published in St. Louis and given to restrained understatement of its views. The *Central Law Journal* had supported all the freedom-of-contract decisions of the state courts during the past few years,[31] while by the same standard of protection for economic liberty and property rights, it had criticized the Supreme Court for extending the police power too far in its *Munn, Budd,* and *Brass* opinions.[32] On the income tax case, however, though printing substantial excerpts from the arguments of counsel, the *Journal* merely noted laconically that the "attentive reader . . . would undoubtedly be impressed by the fact that the arguments against the constitutional-

[29] Willey may be recalled for his prediction in 1887 of a coming social crisis (*supra*, pp. 21–22). Willey was Professor of Law at West Virginia University in 1895. The *West Virginia Bar* was the organ of the West Virginia Bar Association, and Willey was responsible to an executive council for his editorial policies.

[30] *West Virginia Bar*, 1 (Dec., 1894), 244.

[31] *Central Law Journal*, 30 (May 16, 1890), 405; 34 (Jan. 22, 1892), 69; (April 15, 1892), 315.

[32] *Ibid.*, 30 (April 4, 1890), 277; 34 (April 29, 1892), 363; 39 (Aug. 24, 1894), 157.

ity of the law have been less weighty than those against its
policy." [33]

On April 8 the Supreme Court announced its decision in the
Pollock case.[34] The decision, delivered by Chief Justice Fuller,
was a partial one. By a majority of six to two, Justice Jackson
having been ill and not having heard the case, the Court declared unconstitutional that part of the income tax imposing a
tax on the income or rents of real estate, on the ground that
this was a direct tax and must be apportioned among the states
according to population. The Court also decided unanimously
that the application of the tax to income from state and municipal
bonds was unconstitutional because it burdened improperly the
borrowing power of the states and their instrumentalities. On
each of three other major issues—(1) whether the voiding of
the tax on rents and income from real estate invalidated the
whole income tax; (2) whether that part of the income tax falling on income from personal property was also a direct tax; and
(3) whether any part of the income tax was invalid for want
of uniformity—the Justices were equally divided, 4-4, and the
Court expressed no opinion.

Chief Justice Fuller's opinion on the issues decided was a
skillful blend of appellant counsels' arguments. Fundamental
to the opinion were certain assumptions that Fuller made concerning the origins of the direct tax clause: that to form a more
perfect union the states were prepared to surrender their taxing
powers over commerce and imports and grant concurrent taxing
power over persons and property; that in return for this self-
denial and to obtain protection for their diverse and often conflicting interests, the states insisted upon apportionment according to population, thereby guaranteeing that any federal tax on
property would fall "upon the immediate constituents of those
who imposed it." As Fuller summarized this view in the final

[33] *Ibid.*, 40 (March 22, 1895), 226.
[34] *Pollock* v. *Farmers' Loan and Trust Co.*, 157 U.S. 429, 553–586.

part of his opinion, "nothing can be clearer than that what the Constitution intended to guard against was the exercise by the general government of the power of directly taxing persons and property within any State through a majority made up from the other States." Although the requirement of apportionment necessitated in certain instances an inequality of burden,

this inequality must be held to have been contemplated, and was manifestly designed to operate to restrain the exercise of direct taxation to extraordinary emergencies, and to prevent an attack upon accumulated property by mere force of numbers.[35]

The significance of this theory of the direct tax clause was tremendous. In all the previous cases, the guiding question had always been whether by calling a tax a direct tax and requiring its apportionment, such inequality would result that the tax could not justly be collected as a direct tax and must therefore be considered indirect. Now, the guiding question must be no longer the practicability of apportionment but whether, if the tax were levied without apportionment, the consequence would be "an attack upon accumulated property by mere force of numbers" and therefore a defeat of the intentions of the framers of the Constitution.

Having already shifted the grounds for decision of the case, Fuller then very neatly put the burden of proof upon the law— and he did this not in one but in two respects. He stated first that the economic view of direct tax, which included taxes on income, was the ordinary view, *"prima facie* correct." Fuller thus made the law suspect, since the tax was there treated as indirect, contrary to the ordinary view—the *"prima facie* correct"

[35] *Ibid.*, pp. 582–583. The high priority given to this type of argument by Court and counsel in the *Pollock* case was reflective of a broader approach previously noted in this study: the tendency of conservative spokesmen, in their attempts to hold the line judicially against majoritarian protest, to insist that the Constitution-makers themselves were great antimajoritarians and that to be true to the Constitution, the judiciary had no alternative but to apply antimajoritarian interpretations.

view. It was true, however, Fuller agreed, that "the Constitution may bear a different meaning, and . . . must be recognized." [36] The presumption of constitutionality was beautifully reversed; instead of the law being assumed at the outset constitutional, as postulated by the theory of judicial review, the law was now unconstitutional at the outset, to be granted constitutionality only on a positive showing that the constitutional meaning of direct tax was other than the ordinary view.

Fuller managed the same thing again a dozen pages later. Recalling his premise that direct taxation was to be resorted to only in emergency situations, he noted ominously that such had been the case "down to August 15, 1894. . . . The act of that date was passed in a time of profound peace, and . . . that fact furnishes an additional reason for circumspection and care in disposing of the case." [37]

Meanwhile Fuller inquired into the constitutional meaning of direct taxes, and, after reviewing a variety of quotations from the debates over ratification, concluded: first, that the meaning of direct taxes was well understood at the time of the Constitutional Convention; second, that direct taxes were taxes "directly levied under the systems of the States"; and, third, that by those state systems "all taxes on real estate or personal property or the rents or income thereof were regarded as direct taxes." [38] The constitutional meaning thus matched the "ordinary" meaning: direct taxes included income taxes, at least insofar as property or its returns were concerned. Lifted almost bodily without qualification from Seward's argument, Fuller's conclusions suffered from the defects previously noted.[39]

Thus far Fuller's analysis had given no indication that the Court was divided on major issues and had been able to assemble a majority against the tax on only two questions, income from rents and the relatively minor problem of income from state and municipal bonds. But the Chief Justice still had to overcome

---

[36] 157 U.S. 558.   [37] *Ibid.*, p. 574.   [38] *Ibid.*, pp. 568, 572–574.
[39] *Supra*, n. 6.

the obstacle of *stare decisis,* that formidable line of previous decisions all holding that direct taxes as used in the Constitution had a very special and limited meaning, which meaning did not include income taxes. It was in confronting this hurdle that Fuller's opinion began to disclose the precise scope of the Court's rulings. "Doubtless," said Chief Justice Fuller, "the doctrine of *stare decisis* is a salutary one, and to be adhered to on all proper occasions, but it only arises in respect of decisions directly upon the points at issue." And the duty of the Court required it "not to extend any decision upon a constitutional question if it is convinced that error in principle might supervene." [40] Fuller's approach was now clear: the prior cases would not be overruled directly, even with benefit of the Court's new conclusions on the meaning of direct tax, but they would be given the narrowest possible interpretation.

From here on, Fuller followed closely the lawyer Choate's guide lines for disentanglement from *stare decisis,* with the difference that Fuller's analysis was primarily in terms of rents from real property whereas Choate had aimed at refining out at once both real and personal property. Fuller's main distinction was that in none of the previous cases, principally *Hylton, Pacific Insurance Co.,* and *Springer,* had income from real property been involved, and therefore anything said in those cases concerning the meaning of direct taxes or the status of an income tax was mere dicta as it affected the matter of rents. Fuller hinted that this analysis was correct for personal property too: that though the original record in the *Springer* case showed that Springer's earnings were partly from government bonds (personal property), this need not be considered binding because the opinion of the Court had made no reference to the specific source of the man's income. Unable to command a majority on personal property, however, Fuller drove home the argument on real property. A tax on the income from land was like a tax on the land itself, conceded by all to be a direct tax. " 'For what is

[40] 157 U.S. 574, 576.

the land but the profits thereof?' . . . The name of the tax is unimportant. . . . It is the substance and not the form which controls." [41]

The rule of apportionment, concluded the Chief Justice,

> was one of the Compromises which made the adoption of the Constitution possible. . . . If, by calling a tax indirect when it is essentially direct, the rule of protection could be frittered away, one of the great landmarks defining the boundary between the Nation and the States . . . would have disappeared, and with it one of the bulwarks of private rights and private property.[42]

This opinion, considering the difficulties that faced the Chief Justice, may well have been, as his biographer insists, his "greatest." [43] Professor Corwin's critical analysis, in his *Court over Constitution*, of the many defects in Fuller's position is also no doubt valid.[44] But granted the intention of Fuller and the Court

[41] *Ibid.*, pp. 580–581.   [42] *Ibid.*, p. 583.

[43] Willard L. King, *Melville Weston Fuller* (New York, 1950), p. 204. King commends Fuller for his "daring" in not supinely following the precedents and the text writers (p. 221). King's defense of the *Pollock* case is important for its fresh approach to certain problems—i.e., Justice Jackson's return for the second hearing, and the question of the "vacillating jurist" (infra, notes 58, 80). King's analysis, however, should be regarded with considerable reservations, the author's great affection for the kindly Chief Justice having evidently inspired Herculean efforts to explain away all possible blemishes on the Fuller Court's record. To be viewed less sympathetically is an apparent attempt by King to impugn the motives of the *Pollock* case critics—to the extent of including Professors Corwin and Ratner among the so-called "not entirely disinterested." See pp. 193, 196, 218, 220–221.

[44] In Corwin's chapter entitled "The Court Makes a Misstep—The Pollock Case," pp. 177–209. An extended critique of the *Pollock* case is also made by Louis B. Boudin, *Government by Judiciary* (New York, 1932), II, 206–261. Boudin's work, though comprehensive and in some respects penetrating, is marred by too-evident heat against the Court's conservatism and an argumentative approach that prejudices his whole review. He unfairly disparages Fuller's two opinions as "a confused mass of unrelated and partly contradictory arguments" (p. 224).

majority to debilitate the tax, despite seemingly insuperable obstacles, Fuller's opinion quite likely was as acceptable an explanation as could be offered in the circumstances. Particularly effective was his smooth conjoining of states' rights and private rights as in the paragraph just quoted.[45] Fuller's central thesis, that the direct tax clause was specifically intended by the Fathers as a bulwark for the wealthier states against "an attack upon accumulated property by mere force of numbers," had little support in the historical evidence to be sure—the weight of the evidence indicating very firmly that the direct tax clause was intended principally as a bridge between the free and the slave states over the question of representation.[46] And yet from another point of view there may well have been an inner core of truth to Fuller's contention. For it is not impossible that had the conservative framers of the Constitution been able to foresee a situation wherein a popular majority, operating through universal suffrage, could so levy a tax as to bear heaviest, if not solely, on the wealthy few of the states, they, the framers, would have labored to qualify this prospect. Of course, as Justice White pointed out in his dissent, the whole question of intention and effect was irrelevant and no proper business of the Court's; the *right* to tax was the sole judicial question before the Court, and not whether an otherwise lawful exercise of the taxing right

[45] Fuller's solicitude for states' rights here, and in the *E. C. Knight* case too, may be compared with his dissenting opinion, joined by Brewer and Field, in *Plumely* v. *Massachusetts,* 155 U.S. 461 (decided Dec. 10, 1894, at the same term of the Court), which upheld the state's right to prohibit the sale of oleomargarine colored in imitation of butter. Justice Harlan, the strongest nationalist on the Court, held the law an exercise of the state police power to prevent deception in the sale of a much-desired article, and no intrusion on the federal commerce power (the main contention of the Illinois petitioner). But the Chief Justice held differently: "I deny that a State may exclude from commerce legitimate subjects of commercial dealings because of the possibility that their appearance may deceive purchasers in regard to their qualities" (*ibid.,* p. 481).

[46] Seligman, *op. cit.,* pp. 548–555; 3 Dal. 177.

should be limited because, in the eyes of the Justices, the exercise contemplated might effect indirectly a result not intended by the framers.[47] Fuller's opinion was in this procedural sense bad constitutional law; but it was, from the point of view of neo-Federalist conservatism, good constitutional judicialism, an updated reading of the Fathers in the light of the conservative needs of the 1890's.

Justice Field filed a separate opinion, not only supporting the Court's view on the issues decided, but leveling a fierce attack upon the whole income tax on the grounds of uniformity.[48] Justice Field's opinion was as remarkable in many ways as was the man. Although seventy-nine years of age at the time and reportedly showing signs of failing strength,[49] the temperamental and acidulous Field seemed to have lost none of his forcefulness, none of his self-righteousness, and certainly none of his ultra-conservatism. The operation of the legislative power had been "arbitrary and capricious and sometimes merely fanciful." The only proper system of taxation, he instructed the Congress, was for every citizen to contribute his proportion. "That there should be any question or any doubt on the subject surpasses my imagination." Field's closing pronouncement was widely quoted:

If the provisions of the Constitution can be set aside by an act of Congress, where is the course of usurpation to end? The present assault upon capital is but the beginning. It will be but the stepping-stone to others, larger and more sweeping, till our political contests

[47] White makes this point at 157 U.S. 643. His dissent is discussed infra.

[48] 157 U.S. 586–608. Swisher, *Stephen J. Field*, pp. 376–412, discusses Field's role in the tax case and reviews his opinion. Boudin, *op. cit.*, II, 228–234, subjects Field's opinion to a scathing attack, dripping with heavy irony and sarcasm. Boudin's criticisms are largely valid, but he has let his hostility run away with him, even to the palpable error of stating that Field was the only Justice holding the tax violative of the uniformity rule.

[49] Charles Evans Hughes, *The Supreme Court of the United States* (New York, 1928), pp. 75–76; Swisher, *op. cit.*, pp. 403, 442–444; Charles Fairman, "The Retirement of Federal Judges," *Harvard Law Review*, 51 (Jan., 1938), 427. Field resigned in 1897, after thirty-four years on the Court.

will become a war of the poor against the rich; a war constantly growing in intensity and bitterness.[50]

The dissenting opinion of Justice White, in which Harlan concurred with a brief note, was a work of closely knit logic. White, a states' righter from Louisiana and a moderate conservative just beginning his second year on the Court, might perhaps have been expected to choose the easy way out and follow the other moderates on the income-from-rents issue. But White, who was to prove one of the most pertinacious intellects on the High Court,[51] refused to be compromised. Resisting Choate's rationales, the future Chief Justice stood fast by precedent and constitutional traditionalism. White's opinion throughout was a soundly conservative one, upholding the income tax solely on the basis of settled construction and adjudicated cases and eschewing all references to public policy or social justification.

White's acuteness was particularly impressive on the question of income from lands, which the majority, separating it out from the income tax as a whole, had declared unconstitutional. "Can there be serious doubt," asked Justice White, "that the question of the validity of an income tax, in which the rentals of real estate are included, is covered by the decisions which say that an income tax is generically indirect, and that therefore it is valid without apportionment?" Reminding the Court that the issue at stake was not the congressional power to tax land—its power here was plenary—but only whether it was reaching the land directly or indirectly, White inquired again: "In other

[50] 157 U.S. 607. The intensity of Field's emotionalism on the tax case may be gathered from dissenting Justice Harlan's statement in a letter to his sons that Field had "acted often like a mad man during the whole of this contest about the income tax" (quoted by David G. Farrelly, "Harlan's Dissent in the Pollock Case," *Southern California Law Review*, 24 [Feb., 1951], 179).

[51] For evidence of White's strength of intellect and persistency of will, see the references to his influence on the commerce power in Corwin's *Commerce Power versus States Rights*, pp. 38–46, 159–164, 257–258.

words, does that which reaches an income, and thereby reaches rentals indirectly, and reaches the land by a double indirection, amount to a direct levy on the land itself?" [52]

White's summation was a strong one. The present decision, he warned, was "fraught with danger to the court, to each and every citizen, and to the republic." If the great issues of the day were to be decided differently with changes in personnel, then the Court must become "inevitably a theatre of political strife" and the Constitution itself no longer a source of stability but "a most dangerous instrument to the rights and liberties of the people." [53]

The partial decision of April 8 satisfied no one, certainly not the conservative opposition. The *Albany Law Journal*, leading off its main editorial with the Field peroration, hurled bitter recrimination at the Court majority, who had refused "to boldly assert their position and protect their country from the insidious evils of a nefarious statute." There was no reason, the *Journal* insisted, "why a learned jurist should quibble with the right and duty of the Supreme Court of the United States, by declaring, that the power of the tribunal of passing on the constitutionality of acts of Congress, should be discreetly and carefully exercised." The *Journal* concluded:

At a critical time, when the eyes of the whole country were watching the conflict, when broad minded men hoped for a crushing defeat of the pet schemes of the scum of Europe, there was a voice heard, lamentation and weeping, Rachel weeping for her children and would not be comforted because they are not (hers).[54]

The *Legal Advisor* of Chicago, an advocate of extreme *laissez faire*,[55] denounced the Court majority for having failed to go

---

[52] 157 U.S. 639, 641.   [53] *Ibid.*, pp. 651, 652.
[54] *Albany Law Journal*, 51 (April 13, 1895), 225–226.
[55] The *Legal Advisor* characterized legislatures which passed labor laws as "foolish papa-and-moma legislatures," "cheap legislative assemblies"; maximum-hours legislation for women was "socialism," "a step backward

all the way in annulling "agrarianism." "Never since civilized
man first planted foot on this continent," said the *Advisor*, "has
any legislative body enacted a statute more threatening to human
liberty than the income tax act of the late Congress." And the
editorial pointed to Field's warning that the income tax would
prove but a first step in the "assault upon capital." [56]

In this atmosphere counsel against the tax filed a petition on
April 15 for rehearing of the questions not decided. The Attorney General then filed a counterpetition requesting that if a
rehearing were granted it cover all questions, including those
decided. The Court granted both the petitions, limited the number of counsel to two on each side, and set May 6 for the oral
arguments.[57] The date of May 6 had been selected after correspondence between Chief Justice Fuller and the ailing Justice
Howell E. Jackson, Jackson assuring the Chief Justice that he
would be well enough to leave his Tennessee home and arrive
in Washington by the sixth.[58] The full Court of nine Justices
would now hear the case, and it was expected that Justice Jackson's vote would break the 4-4 deadlock on the key issues. Press
and public excitement rose to a new high.

Appearing for opponents of the tax at the May 6 rehearing
were William D. Guthrie and Joseph H. Choate. Defending the
tax for the government were Richard Olney and the Assistant
Attorney General, Edward B. Whitney. James C. Carter, who
had defended the tax on behalf of the trust companies, was

---

toward barbarism," "reactionary and vicious" (34 [June 13, 1894], 188;
35 [March 20, 1895], 178).

[56] *Ibid.*, (April 10, 1895), 225–226.

[57] The texts of the petitions and the Court's orders are in 158 U.S.
602–607.

[58] See King, *op. cit.*, pp. 207–212, for texts of the correspondence. King
asserts that "pressure" was put on Jackson to participate in the rehearing.
Jackson, like Harlan and White, was a Southerner, and his residence was
Nashville, the home town of Congressman Benton McMillin, chief spon-
sor of the income tax in the House. According to King, the local press
put Jackson in the position of having to choose between resigning (and

dropped for the rehearing, his effective advocacy apparently being more than the companies had bargained for.[59]

Counsel opposing the tax used their partial victory in the first decision as the lever to overthrow the whole structure. Choate argued that there was no significant difference between income from real property and income from personal property, and, if a tax on the one source of income was a direct tax, so was a tax on the other source. Even if *stare decisis* should appear to indicate otherwise, he continued, the Court should not hesitate to act in the light of the true and correct meaning now disclosed. Finally, he pointed out smoothly, the exemption of rents and municipal bonds had left free much of the accumulated wealth at which the tax law had aimed. To allow the rest of the tax to stay would be incongruous, turning a law directed at capital into a law falling mainly on labor.[60]

The government counsel concentrated their arguments on Fuller's April 8 opinion. For the first time the government elaborated fully the direct tax question, submitting voluminous briefs on the matter.[61] Olney's argument was chiefly concerned with getting "the rents back into the law." Criticizing Fuller's contention that the tax on rentals was in reality a tax on land, and that "what cannot be done directly cannot be done indirectly," Olney replied: "This is undoubtedly true when correctly interpreted. It cannot mean in a broad sense that whatever is taxed directly cannot be taxed indirectly, because the very distinction under consideration is one between direct and indirect taxation." Besides, he pointed out, the tax which fell on income from rentals was not a tax on rentals at all. "It is not a

---

allowing a protax Justice to be appointed in his stead) and making the effort to attend the rehearing.

[59] Ratner, *op. cit.*, p. 205, citing the Olney papers.

[60] The oral arguments at the rehearing were not printed in the *Reports*, but brief summaries are in Ratner, *op. cit.*, pp. 206–208, and Swaine, *op. cit.*, I, 533–535. The full text of Choate's argument is in F. C. Hicks, *op. cit.*, pp. 473–526.

[61] 158 U.S. 613–617 contains excerpts from these materials.

tax measured by anything present. It is measured simply by the taxpayer's ability to pay as indicated by his income from the previous year. The rentals have become moneys inextricably mingled with the other funds of the taxpayer." [62]

On May 20 before another packed courtroom, the Supreme Court by a vote of 5-4 ruled the entire income tax unconstitutional.[63] The Court's opinion, again delivered by Chief Justice Fuller, was considerably less imposing intellectually than the original opinion. Repeating substantially the assumptions and arguments of the first decision, and emphasizing again the view that the purpose of the apportionment requirement was the prevention of discriminatory taxation by power of mere majorities, the Court reaffirmed its position that a tax falling on income from rentals on land was a direct tax and must be apportioned.

The next step was the extension of this ruling to income from personal property. In reaching its conclusion on rentals in the first opinion, however, the Court had escaped some of the pressure of *stare decisis* by underlining the distinction between real and personal property, Fuller having pointed out that taxes on real property had always been considered direct taxes, and then having simply asserted that for tax purposes the land and the income thereof were as one. But now the Court proceeded to blur this distinction by noting that there was nothing in the Constitution which prohibited Congress from levying direct taxes on personal property as well as on real property; and this being so, then a tax on the income from personal property, as on the income from real property, was also a direct tax. The fact that Congress in its four prior instances of admitted direct

[62] *Ibid.*, p. 617.
[63] *Pollock* v. *Farmers' Loan and Trust Co.* (*Rehearing*), 158 U.S. 601, 617–637. For a vivid re-creation of the atmosphere and dramatic sequence of events of the May 20 decision day, see the address of Henry H. Ingersoll, "The Revolution of 20th May, 1895," *Proceedings of the Fourteenth Annual Meeting of the Bar Association of Tennessee* (1895), pp. 161–180. See also Shiras, *George Shiras, Jr.*, pp. 167–168.

taxation had never included personal property Fuller dismissed with the observation that the Constitution could not "become weakened by a particular course of inaction under it." [64]

Thus the Court had granted Congress an unexpected and unwanted power, to levy direct taxes on personal property, in order to insist that taxes on income from personal property must also be considered direct, and therefore collectible only by apportionment—something manifestly impracticable if not impossible.[65] The *Hylton* case, which involved a tax on carriages—personal property—Fuller explained away as based solely on a definition of the term "excises" and not pertinent to more general considerations. *Pacific Insurance Co.* v. *Soule* and *Springer* v. *United States* were nowhere mentioned in the Chief Justice's opinion.

With the tax on income from property of any genre invalidated, the final denouement followed quickly. The Court did agree that the part of the tax which bore upon income from business, professions, or employment was not a direct tax but in the nature of an excise. With so much of the tax already voided, however, the remainder must fall too—else, paraphrasing Choate, "what was intended as a tax on capital would remain in substance a tax on occupations and labor." [66]

At last the dreaded income tax had been struck down by the Supreme Court, judicial conservatism's most arresting intervention of the 1890's. In the triumphant words of the *Albany Law Journal*,

Well, indeed, may the people place their confidence in the highest tribunal of the United States, and feel that there exists a court of

[64] 158 U.S. 629.

[65] The Chief Justice at one point tried to deny that apportionment of an income tax was impracticable, asking whether there was "any real difficulty in doing so." Later he declared that such considerations "could not be allowed to influence the conclusion." Finally, he fell back upon "the sober second thought" of the amendment process, if the government thought it really must have the power (*ibid.*, pp. 632–633, 635).

[66] *Ibid.*, p. 637.

spotless character and notable ability to stand between them and
the enactment of vicious statutes aimed at one class of individuals.[67]

Joining with the Chief Justice on the 5-4 decision were
Justices Field, Brewer, Shiras, and Gray. Each of the other four
Justices, Harlan, Brown, Jackson, and White, delivered forceful
dissents. All four dissenting Justices sharply condemned the
Court for its cavalier reversal of precedent. More unexpectedly,
all four severely criticized various social and political aspects
of the Court's decision.

The most impassioned of the four dissenters was John Marshall Harlan, who now confirmed his role as the Court's champion of the legal progressives. Reading his hour-long opinion
with a strong voice, and punctuating his language with emphatic gestures, Justice Harlan bombarded the majority opinion
from all directions.[68] He even went back to the Court's first
decision, which he called a "judicial revolution that may sow
the seeds of hate and distrust among the people of different
sections of our common country." As for the present decision,
it might "well excite the gravest apprehensions . . . in that it
denies to the general government a power which is, or may become, vital to the very existence and preservation of the Union
in a national emergency." [69] Harlan was particularly angry that
the Court had abrogated all the *tax* provisions of the Wilson Act
while leaving untouched its *tariff* provisions. This Harlan de-
cried as a "disaster to the country," the effect of which was

[67] *Albany Law Journal*, 51 (May 25, 1895), 321.

[68] The directness of Harlan's critique and the vehemence of his delivery evoked from a conservative press a torrent of abuse for Harlan
and his "Marx gospel." For some choice samples, see Ellis, "Public
Opinion and the Income Tax," pp. 241–242; Farrelly, *op. cit.*, p. 177. The
Harlan letter to his sons, which is printed in Professor Farrelly's article,
pp. 178–181, rebukes the unfairness of much of the newspaper criticism,
which represented Harlan as gesticulating in the face of the Chief Justice.
Harlan said he wasn't surprised at the attacks, since they emanated from
"large newspapers with vast incomes."

[69] 158 U.S. 665, 671.

to give to certain kinds of property a position of favoritism and advantage . . . and to invest them with power and influence that may be perilous to that portion of the American people upon whom rests the larger part of the burdens of the government.[70]

Almost equally outraged was the dissent of the moderate Justice Henry B. Brown. Brown, it may be remembered, had voiced no objection in the first decision to the income-from-rents gambit, which had then become the entering wedge to overthrow the entire tax. Now, perhaps seeing the full consequences of this initial concession to opponents of the tax, the pragmatic Brown reversed his stand and dissented from Fuller on this ground too.[71] Brown's closing indictment of the Court's decision was as bitter as anything of Harlan's. The outcome of the *Pollock* case, he charged,

involves nothing less than a surrender of the taxing power to the moneyed class. . . . Even the spectre of socialism is conjured up

[70] *Ibid.*, p. 685. The legal attack upon the income tax had treated the tax as if it were a separate legislative enactment and had totally ignored the tariff provisions of the same law (the Wilson Act).

[71] Willard L. King, in his biography of Fuller, pp. 215–217, attributes Brown's dissent, and particularly his reversal on rents, to the influence of Justice Jackson, who had helped secure Brown's appointment in 1890, and to the "relatively low" per capita wealth of Michigan, Brown's home state. King sees the per capita wealth of the Justices' home states, together with their sectional origins in North or South, as the determining factors in their votes. Brown, after retiring from the bench, gave his own explanation, writing in 1908 that he dissented because the Court's decision was "judicial legislation where the law has been settled by a series of adjudications" (Kent, *Memoir*, p. 95). This tells us nothing, however, about Brown's switch on the question of rentals, or of the possibility according to a recent suggestion by Professor Corwin (in Shiras, *op. cit.*, p. 182), that on the major issues he may have abstained from voting altogether at the first hearing. To my mind, Brown's initial indecision, and then his full affirmation of the tax (except as pertaining to municipal and state bonds) may be seen as perfectly consonant with the man's social attitudes and judicial career. An independent conservative who held a middle ground, but inclined to antimonopolism and capable of a realistic appraisal of social forces, Brown stiffened rather than broke under the pressure of the second hearing.

to frighten Congress from laying taxes upon the people in proportion to their ability to pay them. It is certainly a strange commentary . . . that Congress has no power to lay a tax which is one of the main sources of revenue of nearly every civilized State. . . . I hope it may not prove the first step toward the submergence of the liberties of the people in a sordid despotism of wealth.[72]

The dissents of Justices Jackson and White, coming after Harlan and Brown, were mild by comparison. Both Jackson and White, traditional legal conservatives, hinged their opinions on the strictly constitutional and judicial aspects of the case. Jackson thought that the precedents, even if not conclusive, "certainly raise such a doubt on the subject as should restrain the court from declaring the act unconstitutional." He rejected indignantly the doctrine of counsel and the Court that the inequality of the apportionment system had been intentional on the part of the Founding Fathers, a device of theirs to protect property owners as a class. "Where does such an idea find support or countenance under a constitution framed and adopted to 'promote justice'?"[73] For Justice Jackson, who had attended the hearing at great physical cost in the belief—false as it turned out—that his vote would be decisive, this dissent was his swan song. He weakened rapidly afterwards and died less than three months later, to some extent a sacrifice or martyr to the *Pollock* case.[74]

White had dissented at length to the first *Pollock* decision, and his contribution here was a listing of "21 points" of detailed, precise rebuttal to counsel's arguments on rehearing and to Fuller's second opinion. Newspapers of the time gave much space to White's warning that, should the government ever attempt to enforce an income tax apportioned by population, "the red

---

[72] 158 U.S. 695.   [73] *Ibid.*, pp. 699, 704.

[74] Jackson's reading of his dissent was described as "slow and painful to hear," accompanied by "paroxysms of coughing" (Ingersoll, *op. cit.*, p. 175). For Jackson's obituary, see the *Albany Law Journal*, 52 (Aug. 17, 1895), 99.

spectre of revolution would shake our institutions to their foundations." [75]

But the crowning sensation of the tax case was the actual
line-up of the Justices, a line-up which at once provoked a
storm of controversy in the public press and in later years a
scholars' debate that is still unsettled. Chief Justice Fuller had
announced in the first *Pollock* decision that on three major
questions, including whether the tax on income from personal
property was a direct tax, the Court was equally divided. Justice
Jackson, returning for the rehearing, had voted that no part of
the tax was direct—and yet the Court had decided 5-4 that the
tax on personal property *was* a direct tax. Obviously, one of the
Justices originally holding the negative view on this issue had
changed his mind, thereby annulling the entire income tax. The
opinions of the Court nowhere indicated which Justice had done
the switching. On the basis of an apparently authentic newspaper report, however, everyone assumed that it was Justice
George Shiras, Jr., a mild-mannered, moderate-minded Pennsyl-
vanian appointed in 1892 and until the second *Pollock* decision
not very conspicuous on the Court.[76] None of the Justices con-
tradicted this assumption, and Shiras was soon subjected to an
outpouring of violent obloquy by the supporters of the income
tax, furious that one man's vacillation should have wrecked the
whole tax.

What was the real significance of this voting alignment? Was
public opinion justified in placing the blame for the final debacle
of the income tax on one man? Was the assumption concerning
Shiras correct? For many years constitutional historians accepted
the contemporary version. Evidence steadily accumulated, however, to indicate that Justice Shiras was probably not "the
vacillating jurist" after all—at least not as the term had been

[75] 158 U.S. 714.
[76] See Shiras, *op. cit.*, pp. 122–127, 138–159, 184–196, for Justice Shiras'
personality and work on the Court, and pp. 169–170 for the best account
of the newspaper report incident.

commonly used—and speculation shifted to other possibilities.[77]

At the present time students of the problem offer three different explanations that have both plausibility and some degree of evidence. The first of the three—in order of publication—selects Justice Horace Gray, a careful student of the law and one of the most respected jurists on the Fuller Court,[78] as the man who switched his vote on the rehearing from favoring generally the constitutionality of the income tax to opposing it.[79] The second explanation, more subtle and more complicated, involves both Shiras and Gray and depends on a theory of different voting alignments on the undecided issues of the original hearing. According to this view, once the income from rents had been voted out, Gray was ready to declare the whole income tax invalid at the first hearing on the grounds of inseparability. But he was not then in favor of specifically invalidating the tax on personal property, presumably because such a decision would

[77] Nevins, *op. cit.*, pp. 778–779; Corwin, *Court over Constitution*, pp. 197–200; Ratner, *op. cit.*, pp. 209–210. Among the items tending to absolve Shiras was a statement of Charles Evans Hughes that there was "good reason to believe that the charge was without foundation" (*Supreme Court*, p. 54).

[78] For an estimate of Gray's contribution to the Fuller Court and an analysis of his judicial attitudes, see Elbridge Davis and Harold A. Davis, "Mr. Justice Horace Gray: Some Aspects of His Judicial Career," *American Bar Association Journal*, 41 (May, 1955), 421–428, 268–271.

[79] Professor Corwin was the first to single out Gray as the most likely vacillator (*Court over Constitution*, pp. 199–200). The heart of Corwin's argument was the incongruity of the strongly nationalist and precedent-minded Gray having voted against the tax at any time. Corwin also stated that he had information "from first hand sources" that the tradition of the Court held Gray as the vacillating Justice. Davis and Davis, though registering disbelief that a man of Gray's "integrity and forthrightness" would have remained silent and permitted Shiras to bear the brunt of the criticisms, agree that Corwin's analysis seems sound (*op. cit.*, p. 470). Willard L. King, on the other hand, who bases his views on a note from Gray to Fuller in which Gray commends the first Fuller opinion very highly and is apparently not averse to going "a little further," condemns the Corwin thesis as "impossible" (*op. cit.*, p. 219). The note is on p. 204. But Gray's note is hardly as definitive as King asserts; it still leaves to speculation that Justice's stand on the major issues.

necessitate a direct reversal of established precedents. Shiras, on the other hand, though holding the tax on personal property invalid at the first as well as the second hearing, would not on the basis of the rents alone annul the tax *in toto*. At the second hearing, Gray moved over to the Shiras view on personal property, and the income tax was invalidated.[80] The latest of the three explanations, and to this writer the most likely, is really a modern variation of the old view. It holds that while Shiras did not actually change his vote, he deferred his decision on the personal property issue or on all the undecided issues at the first hearing, with the Chief Justice counting him in on the sustaining side just the same, perhaps in order to leave the way open for a rehearing.[81]

[80] Advanced by King, p. 220, this explanation is ingenious and a distinct contribution to the solution of the problem. King has apparently put together the old newspaper story which had Shiras voting "to sustain the law as a whole" with the evidence concerning Gray. King's approach to the question is unfortunate, however. He begins his discussion with a quotation from Gustavus Myers' *History of the Supreme Court of the United States* (London, 1912), describes Myers—correctly—as a "frank Marxist," and then not very subtly proceeds to insinuate Corwin, Ratner, and indeed all the critics of the tax case into this pejorative context (pp. 218, 221).

[81] The first part of this explanation was suggested by Corwin on the basis of certain veiled statements in a recently discovered draft letter composed by the retired Justice Shiras in his eighty-third year for publication in the *Yale Law Journal*. The essence of the letter, which was never mailed, is an attempt by Shiras to clear himself from the charge of having changed his mind, but without saying outright what exactly happened (Shiras, *op. cit.*, pp. 180–183). The latter part of this explanation, as to why Fuller counted Shiras in as part of an "equally divided" Court—something which both Corwin and Mr. Shiras find difficulty in accounting for—is mine. I suggest that if we accept the thesis that Shiras could not, or would not, make up his mind on the main issues, Fuller's action may be explicable on the ground that it would be extremely unseemly for the Court to decide such great questions by a 4-3 vote with one Justice abstaining. By announcing the Court as equally divided, the tactful Fuller may have hoped he would relieve the hesitant Shiras of direct pressure and turn the issue over to an anticipated rehearing and Justice Jackson. This explanation has the added value of accounting for

Which of the three alternatives is assuredly the correct one seems impossible to say at this time.[82] Leaving this question aside for the moment, however, more important for the purposes of this inquiry is the prime fact that the final stand of both Shiras and Gray, by whatever route arrived at, was solidly against the tax. That the right-wing laissez-faireists, Field, Brewer, and Fuller, would be found against the income tax, could be taken for granted. The fact that to overthrow the tax would require a major new interpretation of the Constitution and the reversal of one hundred years of precedent could hardly be expected to deter right-wing conservatism—the development of the labor injunction in 1893–1894 had made clear enough that radical means would be no bar to effecting conservative ends. But the position of Shiras and Gray among the five Justices overturning the tax was more revealing. Moderates both, traditionalists both, both as much concerned with judicial propriety and constitutional regularity as with the rights of property,[83] Shiras and Gray had nonetheless swung the balance against the tax, against the popular prerogative. The conservative fear of the restless demos, of

---

the absolute silence of the Court despite every provocation, since to reveal the whole truth would have embarrassed the Chief Justice.

[82] Other explanations are still in order of course. A novel one is that of Prof. George D. Braden, formerly of Yale Law School, who substitutes Field for Gray in Willard King's Shiras-Gray thesis on the ground that Field may have been hesitant at first to reverse his participation in the *Springer* case, thus accounting for his emphatic argument on uniformity but relative reticence on personal property (Braden's letter printed in Shiras, *op. cit.*, pp. 178–179). But internal evidence in Field's concurring opinion weighs against the Braden idea: Field did not hesitate to disparage the *Springer* case, 157 U.S. 589; and he stated later that the tax on real estate constitutes *"part* of the direct tax" (*ibid.*, p. 608 [italics mine]). Field may not have expounded on the personal property issue in his opinion because, as Professor Braden says, it might have been embarrassing; but he could still have voted against the tax in conference.

[83] For Shiras' middle-of-the-road opinions on substantive due process, see Shiras, *op. cit.*, ch. ix. For Gray's devotion to legal scholarship and his reputation as a precedent-judge abjuring obiter dicta, see King, *op. cit.*, pp. 132–133; Davis and Davis, *op. cit.*, *passim.*

an unmanageable populism endangering with unlimited fiscal powers the patterns of the ordered society, had overcome in the end the commitment to judicial traditionalism.[84]

The real significance of the different voting alignments on the first and second hearings—no matter which of the three explanations we choose—now emerges. In the first decision, on the income-from-rents question, both Shiras and Gray (and Brown, too, of the moderates) had gone along with the Fuller opinion, a plausible ruling which would weaken the tax and yet avoid too direct a confrontation with *stare decisis*. But on the crucial issue involving *stare decisis*, the income from personal property, only one of the two, Shiras or Gray, had come over to the antitax position all at once; the other had hesitated, either withholding his vote (Shiras) or seeking another way out (Gray). On the second hearing, as the pressure reached its climax, the other had also yielded, adding—or switching—his vote to the right-wing bloc on personal property and the final death of the income tax. The vacillating vote on the second hearing, therefore, only dramatized, though in a singularly vivid way, the critical factors underlying the tax case, factors going back at least to the turn of the decade—the growing pressure on legal conservatism of an age of tension, and then, under the impact of crisis psychology, a major break to the right within the ranks of the moderate center.[85]

[84] In the words of Carl Brent Swisher, "Perhaps the larger consistency of giving protection to the existing order seemed of greater worth to them (the majority Justices) than the meticulous pursuit of the line of their own decisions" (*op. cit.*, p. 407).

[85] The line-up of the four Justices sustaining the tax is explainable within the same frame of reference. Harlan, the Court progressive of the period, following the course expected. The final stand of the free-wheeling Brown in favor of the tax on all principal grounds has been discussed *supra*, note 71. The strong-minded White was one legal traditionalist who did not "break" at any time. Both his dissenting opinions were basically conservative, emphasizing precedent and judiciality. Jackson, the moderate conservative from Tennessee, ill at home most of the Court term, had escaped the atmosphere of crisis built up by the Northeastern press and by the drama of the first hearing.

The overturn of the income tax was only one phase, if the most decisive and dramatic, of the advance of judicial supremacy in the spring of 1895. On March 14 the steady expansion of freedom of contract [86] had reached its extreme limit with an Illinois decision striking down an eight-hour law for women in garment manufacturing.[87] And on May 27, one week after the *Pollock* decision, the Supreme Court handed down its opinion in the *Debs* case, bestowing its official sanction on the new uses of the labor injunction.[88] Considered together with the *Reagan* case of the previous May and the *E. C. Knight* case of January, the judicial developments of the spring of 1895 marked at last the acceptance of that judicial guardianship so determinedly advocated by right-wing conservatism. State regulation

[86] The two 1893 decisions have been noted *supra*, ch. v, n. 1. In 1894, these cases were decided: *Leep* v. *Railway Company*, 58 Ark. 407, rejecting if applied to "natural" persons a law requiring railroads to pay employees on the day of discharge but affirming same when applied to corporations under the "reserved" clause of the state constitution; *Low* v. *Rees Printing Co.*, 41 Neb. 127, invalidating a Nebraska eight-hour law for mechanics and laborers, the first of its kind in the nation; and *Wallace* v. *Georgia, Carolina and Northern Ry. Co.*, 94 Ga. 732, voiding as contrary to "liberty of silence" a law requiring employers to give employees a statement in writing of reasons for discharge. In Jan., 1895, the Supreme Court of Colorado advised the legislature that a proposed coal "screening" law and an eight-hour law for mining and manufacturing would be unconstitutional: *In re House Bill 203*, 21 Col. 27, and *In re Eight-Hour Bill*, 21 Col. 29. In Feb., 1895, a county judge in Pennsylvania told a jury to ignore as manifestly unconstitutional the state's "scrip" act of 1891: *Hamilton* v. *C. Jutte & Co.*, reported in 1 *Lackawanna Legal News*, 173.

[87] *Ritchie* v. *People*, 155 Ill. 98. Roscoe Pound has called this case "the high-water mark of academic individualism" ("Liberty of Contract," p. 475). A ten-hour law for women had been upheld in 1876 by the Massachusetts Supreme Court in a strong opinion, *Commonwealth* v. *Hamilton Manufacturing Co.*, 120 Mass. 383.

[88] *In re Debs*, 158 U.S. 564. Justice Brewer's opinion for the unanimous Court not only upheld the injunctions of July, 1894, as properly obtained under the government's power to regulate commerce and protect its interest in the mails but also commended the government for its resort to judicial proceedings. See esp. pp. 583, 597–599.

of railroad rates,[89] the campaign against the trusts, organized labor and its use of the strike, the social legislation of the states,[90] and even the taxing power of the federal government had all been subjected to the judicial aegis. The new judicialism was complete.

[89] Important cases involving federal regulation of railroad rates under the Interstate Commerce Act of 1887 were decided by the Supreme Court in 1896 and 1897, both unfavorably to the Commission: *Cincinnati, New Orleans and Texas Pacific Ry. Co.* v. *Interstate Commerce Commission,* 162 U.S. 184, and *Interstate Commerce Commission* v. *Alabama Midland Ry. Co.,* 168 U.S. 144.

[90] State labor laws challenged under freedom of contract did not reach the United States Supreme Court till the socially less anxious years of the late 1890's, and all were upheld until 1905. See infra, ch. x, n. 15.

X

Conservatism and the Judiciary:

An Appraisal

THE triumphant advance of the new judicialism in the spring of 1895 was not unchallenged. Within the legal profession a sharp revolt broke out as the progressives and many moderates launched a vigorous attack upon judicial interventionism. Seymour D. Thompson, redoubtable foe of judicial pretensions, charged the Supreme Court in the *American Law Review* with "continually encroaching upon the legislative power of the States, on the one hand, and upon that of the general government, on the other; and . . . doing it in almost every case in the interest of the rich and powerful and against the rights and interests of the masses of the people." In a stinging critique of "Government by Lawyers" at the Texas Bar Association, he warned that unless the profession became more responsive to the people some mighty "popular tempest" could well bring down the entire fabric of law and government.[1] At the Tennessee Bar Association a former president of the association concluded a

[1] *American Law Review*, 29 (Sept.–Oct., 1895), 742–745; Seymour D. Thompson, "Government by Lawyers," *Proceedings of the Fifteenth Annual Session of the Texas Bar Association* (1896), pp. 64–85.

dramatic recounting of the income tax case with this ominous parallel:

Forty years ago the owners of peculiar property in the South appealed to the Federal courts for protection against the aggressive agitation of the dominant sentiment of the Christian world . . . and the Dred Scott decision became famous on two continents. But the contention involved in that case could not abide such judicial decision; agitation increased and it was settled on appeal to arms and by wager of battles. . . . In 1895 the owners of vast property in the North appealed to the Federal courts for protection against the popular demand that they who get the benefits of government shall bear their just share of its expenses; and they get it in this decision of the Supreme Court in the income tax cases; Dives wins, Plebs loses. Is the contention settled? [2]

Although the income tax decision bore the brunt of the insurgents' wrath, the anger of the legal dissidents was turned also upon the stream of freedom-of-contract cases, and in particular the *Ritchie* case annulling the Illinois eight-hour law for women. In the words of one writer, the courts had "disregarded elementary principles of constitutional construction"; another accused the courts of enforcing the "dungeon" of the sweatshop and overturning laws which were "the very bulwark of liberty." [3] The unanimous *Debs* decision too, though seldom criti-

[2] Ingersoll, "The Revolution of 20th May, 1895," p. 180. For a similar comparison with the Dred Scott case, see the paper of David E. Bailey, "Stare Decisis," *Proceedings of the Washington State Bar Association* (1895), pp. 72–83, and the discussion that followed, reported at pp. 26–31. Other criticisms of the income tax decision: *American Lawyer*, 3 (June, 1895), 228–229; *Harvard Law Review*, 9 (Oct., 1895), 198–210; *Proceedings of the Nineteenth Annual Meeting of the Alabama State Bar Association* (1896), pp. 7–10, and Appendix, xxii–xlvi.

[3] S. S. Gregory, "Constitutional Limitations on the Police Power," *North Western Law Review*, 4 (Nov., 1895), 50; Darius H. Pingree, "The Anti-Truck Laws, and Some Other Laws—A Legal Criticism," *American Lawyer*, 3 (Sept., 1895), 387. See also *Chicago Legal News*, 27 (March 30, 1895), 274; *American Law Review*, 29 (March–April, 1895), 236–266; and (Sept.–Oct., 1895), 766–768.

cized in its own right (as noted previously, practically the entire profession had opposed the Pullman boycott), was unfavorably regarded for its striking contrast to the *E. C. Knight* and *Pollock* cases: a clear demonstration, it was asserted, of judicial one-sidedness in behalf of the wealthy classes.[4]

Accompanying these attacks upon specific aspects of the new judicial supremacy was the emergence in 1895–1896 of a wave of constitutional radicalism. In a series of articles in the *American Law Review*, Sylvester Pennoyer, former Democratic-Populist governor of Oregon, characterized the system of judicial review as "usurpation" by "judicial oligarchy," first instigated by the "plausible sophistries" of John Marshall. Congress should impeach the majority Justices in the tax case, he declared, teach the Court a well-deserved lesson, and thus restore the Constitution to its original purity.[5] Pennoyer was soon joined by Justice Walter Clark of the North Carolina Supreme Court, who advocated amendments which would make elective, and for a term only, all federal judges.[6] Although most legal critics of the Supreme Court stopped short of supporting this radical program, the mere fact of its appearance, in conjunction with the more conventional attacks upon the judiciary, indicated the extent of professional unrest in 1895–1896.[7]

[4] Percy L. Edwards, "The Federal Judiciary and Its Attitude towards the People," *Michigan Law Journal*, 5 (June, 1896), 183–194; Jackson Gray, "Trusts and Monopolies. The Anti-Monopoly Act: A Review of the Decisions Affecting It," *Virginia Law Register*, 1 (Feb., 1896), 707–725.

[5] *American Law Review*, 29 (July–Aug., 1895), 550–558; (Nov.–Dec., 1895), 856–863; 30 (March–April, 1896), 188–202. Pennoyer's highly nonconformist political career is summarized in the *Dictionary of American Biography*, XIV, 445–446.

[6] Walter Clark, "Constitutional Changes Which Are Foreshadowed," *American Law Review*, 30 (Sept.–Oct., 1896), 702–709. Clark remained on the North Carolina Supreme Court till his death in 1924, always steadfast in his program of advanced progressive reform and a radically democratized Constitution (Aubrey L. Brooks, *Walter Clark, Fighting Judge* [Chapel Hill, 1944]).

[7] Most scholars have overlooked or minimized the legal dissidents of

The expanding professional protest against the new judicialism was but one facet of the developing political crisis of 1896. The deepening of the depression in 1894 and early 1895 had intensified the grievances of Southern and Midwestern farmers, labor unionists, the unemployed and partially employed, and thousands of bankrupt and failing businessmen.[8] President Cleveland's handling of the financial panic in 1893–1895 (the repeal of the Sherman Silver Purchase Act and the bond sales through Wall Street syndicates) and his vigorous suppression of the Pullman strike had alienated a large section of the Democratic party. While the silver miners flooded the country with free-silver propaganda as a ready panacea for all evils, both the Populists and the left-wing Democrats gained strength, the latter preparing to capture the Democracy for silver and thoroughgoing antimonopolism in 1896. Into this seething political scene was thrown the *E. C. Knight* opinion emasculating the antitrust act, the income tax decision, and the *Debs* ruling. A surge of resentment swept through the protesting forces everywhere, adding strength to the growing radicalism. Populist and Democratic members of Congress, led by such Southern fire-eaters as Senator Benjamin R. ("Pitchfork Ben") Tillman of South Carolina, arose to denounce the Supreme Court in the harshest terms. Farmers and merchants, already smarting under federal railroad receiverships and other judicial devices interfering with state regulation, were now sure the Supreme Court itself had succumbed to the plutocracy. And Illinois Governor John P. Altgeld, who had bitterly denounced Cleveland's intervention in the Pullman strike

---

these two years, as well as of the 1890's generally: Fine, *Laissez Faire and the General-Welfare State*, pp. 126–132; John P. Roche, "Judicial Self-Restraint," *American Political Science Review*, 49 (Sept., 1955), 764, n. 6; Twiss, *Lawyers and the Constitution*, pp. 141, 142, 172. But see Warren, *The Supreme Court*, III, 421–426.

[8] Charles Hoffmann, "The Depression of the Nineties," *Journal of Economic History*, 15 (June, 1956), 137–164, contains comprehensive summaries of prices, unemployment, income, and business failures during the depression.

as "government by injunction," added the Supreme Court to the list of people's oppressors and "lackeys of capitalism." He soon became perhaps the most powerful figure in the Democratic intraparty conflict.[9]

The success of the Democratic insurgents in capturing the Chicago convention and nominating William Jennings Bryan on a free-silver anti–Wall Street platform has long been a celebrated episode in American political history. Less noticed by historians have been the three separate anticourt planks contained in the platform: one plank criticized the income tax decision and hinted that the Supreme Court might well be packed to secure a reversal, another denounced government by injunction as a form of judicial "oppression," and a third opposed life tenure in the public service except as provided in the Constitution.[10] The impact of these planks was considerable; for with traditional symbols, constitutional and monetary, under joint challenge the conservative defense became especially fierce, and proved effective. In the legal profession, men of both parties joined against Bryan, isolating the advanced progressives.[11]

[9] Harold V. Faulkner, *Politics, Reform and Expansion 1890–1900* (New York, 1959), pp. 147–157; Alan F. Westin, "The Supreme Court, the Populist Movement and the Campaign of 1896," *Journal of Politics,* 15 (Feb., 1953), 3–41; *American Law Review,* 30 (March–April, 1896), 266; Harvey Wish, "John P. Altgeld and the Background of the Campaign of 1896," *Mississippi Valley Historical Review,* 24 (March, 1938), 503–518; Ginger, *Altgeld's America,* pp. 174–176.

[10] Thomas H. McKee, *The National Conventions and Platforms of All Political Parties 1789 to 1904* (Baltimore, 1904), pp. 294–295, 296, 297. The plank on life tenure would affect district and circuit court judges.

[11] See Westin, *op. cit.,* pp. 32–39, for quotations from a variety of conservative sources indicating the excitement generated by the anticourt planks. Concerted anti-Bryan activity within the legal profession is evidenced in the *Albany Law Journal,* 54 (July 18, 1896), 33; (July 25, 1896), 49; (Oct. 31, 1896), 278; (Nov. 7, 1896), 289; King, *Melville Weston Fuller,* pp. 234–235; Swaine, *The Cravath Firm,* I, 557–559. Seymour D. Thompson illustrates the dilemma that must have confronted many legal progressives. To begin with, he approved of only part of the judiciary plank, opposing the attack on the injunction (*American Law Review,* 30 [July–Aug., 1896], 579). Later he stated he was voting

The defeat of Bryan—who had emphasized the silver question above all others, thus obscuring the broader issues from much of the urban public [12]—was a great victory for American conservatism. It was especially satisfying to right-wing legal conservatism, and the congratulatory notice of the *Albany Law Journal* was well taken:

With the covert threat against the United States Supreme Court which was inserted in the platform of the defeated party, with the wild theories which were advanced against the so-called principle of "government by injunction," and with the abuse which was heaped upon the laws of our country, it would seem that the lawyers had the greatest concern, and almost as a body they have responded to the emergency, and have done their full share in the work, and that without respect to partisanship or prejudice.[13]

The judicial triumph of conservatism in the spring of 1895 had been confirmed by the political triumph of 1896. The conservative crisis of the 1890's was over.

Toward the end of 1897 the business cycle turned upward

for McKinley because he disliked Bryan's monetary position (*ibid.* [Sept.–Oct., 1896], 757). J. C. Rosenberger, mildly progressive editor of the *Kansas City Bar Monthly,* was outraged by the anticourt planks (1 [Aug., 1896], 193).

[12] James A. Barnes, "Myths of the Bryan Campaign," *Mississippi Valley Historical Review,* 34 (Dec., 1947), 367–404. William Diamond's thesis, explaining the distribution of the vote on the basis of historical urban-rural antagonisms aggravated by the tensions of the Bryan campaign ("Urban and Rural Voting in 1896," *American Historical Review,* 46 [Jan., 1941], 281–305), is strongly challenged by Lee Benson's critique in Mirra Komarovsky, ed., *Common Frontiers of the Social Sciences* (Glencoe, 1957), pp. 155–171. Benson's work offers new evidence for the view that Bryan's free-silver crusade cost him potential labor support, even traditionally Democratic labor support. Gilbert C. Fite has shown recently that many farmers too were unimpressed by the free-silver emphasis ("Republican Strategy and the Farm Vote in the Presidential Campaign of 1896," *American Historical Review,* 65 [July, 1960], 787–806).

[13] *Albany Law Journal,* 54 (Nov. 7, 1896), 289.

again, and the next year public attention was absorbed in the Cuban situation. Social tensions declined and domestic issues temporarily receded. But the long-range consequences of the judicial intervention of the 1890's were quite considerable. From the socioeconomic point of view, the court decisions were major contributing factors in the perpetuation of the inequalities that were accompanying the growth of American industrialism. The income tax decision permitted the continued accumulation of great wealth immune from significant federal levy for another twenty years. The sugar trust case cleared the way for a tremendous concentration of capital, unrestrained by fear of effective prosecution; by the time court views were modified in the next decade, "bigness" had become intrenched in the economy. The sanction of the labor injunction added further to the preponderant power of the large corporation vis-à-vis organized labor. And the delimitation of the police power in the name of due process of law and freedom of contract circumscribed the legislative discretion at the very time when the increasing complexities of the economy and the growing problems of the city with its masses of urban poor made imperative a greater flexibility in the regulation of business and the protection of social standards. That the cumulative imbalances of these developments contributed to the deterioration of economic resiliency precedent to the Great Depression appears likely.[14]

More readily demonstrable were the long-term political-constitutional implications of the new judicialism. For here the basic fact was the mere existence of judicial supremacy, those alternatives of interpretation available to the Court through such media as "direct" or "indirect" effects upon commerce, "reasonable" or "unreasonable" limitations on the rights of property. True, in the late 1890's the relaxation of social and economic ten-

[14] In the words of Professor Westin, the Supreme Court had given "capitalistic forces in the United States a vital period of protected incubation" (*op. cit.*, p. 40).

sions was paralleled by a more moderate trend in Supreme Court
decisions; [15] and in the Progressive era of the next two decades—
a "safe" movement under middle-class, essentially traditionalist
leadership—the Court applied its new powers only intermit-
tently.[16] But the doctrines of judicial supremacy developed
earlier were not abandoned; even the much-publicized Brandeis
brief effected no more than the concession that in the determination of reasonableness, economic and social data were admissible.[17] During the 1920's, as the atmosphere changed to "nor-
malcy" and firm conservatism, the Court quickly returned to the
harder view of the 1890's, striking down a wide variety of social
and economic legislation while elaborating more precisely the
techniques of judicial supremacy.[18] The full import of the con-

[15] In *Holden* v. *Hardy*, 169 U.S. 366 (1898), the Supreme Court sustained a Utah eight-hour law for miners. The Court also ruled favorably
on various types of labor laws frequently overturned by state courts in
the 1890's: e.g., *Knoxville Iron Co.* v. *Harbison*, 183 U.S. 13 (1901),
sustaining a "scrip" act, and *McClean* v. *Arkansas*, 211 U.S. 539 (1909),
sustaining a coal weighing law. In antitrust cases the Court twice rejected an attempt to attach the concept of reasonableness to the Sherman
Act: *United States* v. *Trans-Missouri Freight Association*, 166 U.S. 290
(1897), and *United States* v. *Joint Traffic Association*, 171 U.S. 505
(1898). In *Knowlton* v. *Moore*, 178 U.S. 41 (1900), the Court affirmed an
inheritance tax with progressive rate features. On the other hand, in
Smyth v. *Ames*, 169 U.S. 466 (1898), the Court unanimously invalidated
the railroad rate schedules of the Nebraska legislature as contrary to due
process of law; and in other cases of the late 1890's reduced the power
of the Interstate Commerce Commission.

[16] Contrast *Lochner* v. *New York*, 198 U.S. 45 (1905), with *Muller* v.
Oregon, 208 U.S. 412 (1908), and *Bunting* v. *Oregon*, 243 U.S. 426 (1917).
The comparative liberality of the Supreme Court in this period is well
surveyed in Edward R. Lewis, *A History of American Political Thought
from the Civil War to the World War* (New York, 1937), pp. 101–107.

[17] An interesting discussion of this point is in Edward Cahn, ed.,
Supreme Court and Supreme Law (Bloomington, 1954), p. 49.

[18] In the child labor case of *Hammer* v. *Dagenhart*, 247 U.S. 251 (1918),
the Supreme Court reaffirmed the narrow view of the commerce power
taken in the *E. C. Knight* case. A few years later in *Adkins* v. *Children's
Hospital*, 261 U.S. 525 (1923), Justice Sutherland for the Court limited

stitutional revolution of the 1890's was manifested in the mid-1930's in the critical days of the New Deal, when a new popular-based reformism ran up against the constitutional and legal defenses that had been erected in the 1890's against an older reformism.[19]

In one of his more frequently quoted aphorisms, the percipient Mr. Dooley had put it that "th' supreme coort follows th' iliction returns." Mr. Dooley, however, had oversimplified. For by the 1890's it was a root principle of American conservatism that in a time of social crisis, when rampant populism might threaten the established order, the Supreme Court must act as counterweight to the election returns, as defender of minority rights against majority rule. From the conservative point of view, this meant primarily the protection of property rights. In America the signpost of status was not place but property, and the denominator of the ordered society not respect for hierarchies of station but regard for differences in possessions. The great danger to be guarded against in America, so the conservative tradition ran, was a thrust from below, an upsurge of *the democracy* resentful at the growth of concentrated wealth and determined to use its majority power to effect redistribu-

---

to four carefully defined categories the power of the legislature to interfere with private property and freedom of contract. For a complete listing of state acts invalidated by the Supreme Court in the 1920's, see Felix Frankfurter's *Mr. Justice Holmes and the Constitution* (Cambridge, 1939), pp. 114–128. The labor injunction also reached its apogee in the 1920's, this despite the presumed protection to labor in Secs. 6 and 20 of the Clayton Act (Frankfurter and Greene, *The Labor Injunction*, pp. 165–182).

[19] Robert H. Jackson's *The Struggle for Judicial Supremacy* (New York, 1941) is a revealing narrative of the constitutional crisis of the New Deal by a leading participant (Solicitor General at the time) keenly aware of the long-term political and constitutional issues. It is an interesting speculation whether a similar crisis might not have arisen had Bryan won the election of 1896 and the Democrats then proceeded to attempt to carry out their platform.

tion.[20] If an age of tension should create a drawing of class lines, with property the divisive factor, and if universal suffrage should become the vehicle for legislative leveling, then only the judiciary could redress the balance, "the final breakwater . . . against the tumultuous ocean of democracy." [21]

Although the Constitutional Convention of 1787 had probably assumed some judicial review, the majority at Philadelphia had placed their main reliance for restraining the excesses of democracy upon the check-and-balance system in the broader sense, the "competing factions" of James Madison. The main body of conservatives in 1787, though seeking to dilute and channelize the Revolutionary enthusiasm for direct democracy, had not intended, for the most part, more than procedural limitations on the representative process.[22] True, in some future time of crisis, it was agreed, the work of 1787 might require a major readjustment; but so long as economic opportunity remained abundant and class tensions were readily reducible, no all-pervading judicial guardianship seemed essential.[23]

[20] The literature on the conservative tradition in America is thin. The two most recent full-length studies which deal with the subject, Rossiter's *Conservatism in America* and Louis Hartz's *The Liberal Tradition in America* (New York, 1955), though breaking valuable ground, leave much undone. Rossiter's book is frankly preceptive and hortatory, while Hartz considers conservatism only tangentially. An excellent article taking a broad look is Daniel Aaron's "Conservatism, Old and New," *American Quarterly*, 6 (Summer, 1954), 99–110. See also the stimulating discussion by leading historians, political scientists, and philosophers at the Third Newberry Library Conference on American Studies: *The Newberry Library Bulletin*, 3 (June, 1953), 73–87.

[21] Dillon, *Laws and Jurisprudence*, p. 214.

[22] The contract clause of Art. I, Sec. 10, was the principal exception not referable to the need for federal uniformity.

[23] For the kind of judicial review intended by the Convention majority, see Corwin, *Court over Constitution*, ch. i, and Edward M. Burns, *James Madison, Philosopher of the Constitution* (New Brunswick, 1938), pp. 150–162. For the significance of Madison's faction theory, see Douglass Adair's revealing article, "That Politics May Be Reduced to a Science: David Hume, James Madison, and the *Tenth Federalist*," *Huntington Library Quarterly*, 20 (Aug., 1957), 343–360. Concerning attitudes to-

The right-wing Federalists, however, led by Hamilton and later by Marshall, had early regarded the judiciary as potentially the key bulwark of conservative defense.[24] Certainly, in the Jeffersonian and Jacksonian periods the federal judiciary became the principal exponent of the conservative interest, the development of the contract clause and the vested-rights doctrine representing to conservatives just the kind of additional counterbalances deemed imperative to protect property rights and creditor claims in an era of advancing democracy and aggressive equalitarianism.[25] By the 1840's, although conservatism in America was temporarily losing its vitality (because its postulate of an aristocracy-democracy antagonism was inapplicable to the American scene), the tradition of judicial guardianship had already attained a pre-eminent place in the conservative firmament.[26]

Some forty years later, in the 1880's, with legislative regulation on the increase, with the rise of a new social tension perceptible, the constitutional and legal doctrines developed in earlier decades had lost their efficacy. The *Dartmouth College* case, that great

---

ward democracy in 1787, new light is shed on Madison's position by Arnold A. Rogow, "The Federal Convention: Madison and Yates," *American Historical Review*, 60 (Jan., 1955), 323–334; see also Richard Hofstadter's fine interpretation in his *The American Political Tradition and the Men Who Made It* (New York, 1951), ch. i. On the previsions of an age of crisis, I have used Douglass Adair's unpublished manuscript, "The Founding Fathers and History" (see *supra*, ch. viii, n. 1); see also Burns, pp. 60–74.

[24] *Federalist* No. 78; Alpheus T. Mason, "*The Federalist*—A Split Personality," *American Historical Review*, 57 (April, 1952), 625–643; Fred Rodell, *Nine Men: A Political History of the Supreme Court from 1790 to 1955* (New York, 1955), pp. 33–45.

[25] Edward S. Corwin, "The Basic Doctrine of American Constitutional Law," *Michigan Law Review*, 12 (Feb., 1914), 247–276.

[26] Rufus Choate, "The Position and Functions of the American Bar, as an Element of Conservatism in the State," *The Works of Rufus Choate with a Memoir of His Life*, Samuel G. Brown, ed. (Boston, 1862), II, 414–438; Alexis de Tocqueville, *Democracy in America* (Vintage ed.; New York, 1954), I, 102–107, 282–290.

anchor of the contract clause, had been weakened by construction and bypassed by legislation; while the old vested-rights
doctrine had withered away from disuse.[27] Nor was the new
Fourteenth Amendment, the almost desperate appeals of corporation lawyers notwithstanding,[28] proving an adequate substitute: the *Slaughter-House Cases* and *Munn* v. *Illinois* seemed to
have rendered it largely unserviceable. Even the teachings of
Herbert Spencer and the economists, unvarying though they
were in disparaging legislative interference with economic liberty, had thus far made only a small impression on the law
reports. Though Justice Field's persistence—and Roscoe Conkling's ingenuity—had extracted some concessions from the
Court in the mid-1880's, though Cooley and Tiedeman had
prescribed the patterns for restricting legislative police power
and a number of the state courts were beginning to show respon-
siveness, though equity jurisprudence was revealing new ex-
pansiveness in protection of property rights against labor unrest,
in the late 1880's all these tendencies, still unexplored and often
ambiguous, were receiving only limited application.

The pleas of corporate counsel and laissez-faire doctrinaires
for vigorous judicial interventionism, only partially answered
in the 1880's by the cautious moderates in control of the courts,
received a new hearing with the turn of the decade. To the
conservative mind the crisis of the 1890's was not merely a
matter of discrete political and economic conflicts over legislative policy and labor relations; the entire equilibrium of American society was being called into question. The long-assumed

[27] For conservative fears in respect to this weakening of old protections, see Andrew Allison, "Address of the President," *Report of the
Seventh Annual Meeting of the American Bar Association* (1884), pp.
241–256; Alfred Russell, "Status and Tendencies of the Dartmouth College
Case," *Proceedings of the Grafton and Coos Bar Association* (1895),
pp. 13–52.

[28] See Justice Miller's remark in *Davidson* v. *New Orleans*, 96 U.S.
97 (1878), at 103–104, on the pertinacity of counsel in their "strange mis-
conception" of the due process clause.

fluidity of the American class structure was seen as disappearing before the increasing concentration of wealth, the interests of capital and labor appeared more deeply antagonistic, and class struggle between the have's and the seeking-to-have's seemed a real possibility. America was creating a Rhine in its midst, lamented United States District Judge Peter S. Grosscup in a Memorial Day address of 1894, "and conflicts like those of the Teuton and the Gaul must be expected." [29]

The line of conservative thought thus emerging may well be termed a form of neo-Federalism, a recrudescence of a traditional conservatism fearful of restless majorities upsetting the social order and the rights of property.[30] The forebodings of the Federalists of 1787, that some future time of tension would severely strain the American experiment, seemed on the verge of fulfillment. What could stay the expected depredations of the propertyless? If the present tendencies continued, declaimed United States Circuit Judge William Howard Taft in June, 1894, "our boasted constitutional guaranties of property rights will not be worth the parchment upon which they were originally written." [31] The secure constitutionalism of 1787 was

[29] Grosscup's address, to the G.A.R. post at Galesburg, Ill., is printed in the *Chicago Legal News*, 26 (July 14, 1894), 367–368. See also John F. Dillon's address at the 1895 meeting of the New York State Bar Association, an excellent statement of neo-Federalist philosophy: *Proceedings of the New York State Bar Association—Eighteenth Annual Meeting* (1895), pp. 33–64.

That the conservatives of the 1890's may well have exaggerated the extent of social unrest, and in particular the potential receptiveness of the masses to radicalism, is not of course greatly to the point—except as a commentary on the responsibility of the conservative vision.

[30] Neither Hartz nor Rossiter has noted the emergence of this old-line conservatism in the 1890's, side by side with the more typical laissez-faire conservatism of the post bellum era. Rossiter uses the term laissez-faire conservatism to denote generally the American Right 1865–1933 (*op. cit.*, pp. 132–163). Hartz's main concern is with the apotheosis of Algerism that characterized "Whiggery" (big-property liberalism as Hartz sees it) from 1865–1929 (*op. cit.*, pp. 203–227).

[31] Taft's address, delivered to the law department graduates of the Uni-

collapsing. The Presidency was become a popular office, un-
balancing John Adams' mixed government; classes and parties
seemed increasingly nationalized, weakening Madison's structure
of competing factions.[32] At the same time the state police power
was rapidly expanding; the national commerce power was in-
vading immensely important economic relationships; and the
federal taxing power, innocuous since the early post-bellum
period, was being revived boldly as an incipient leveling device.
What the times demanded of a neo-Federalist conservatism was
a new period of creative constitutionalism, a refurbished Constitution brought up to date as a conservative instrument.

As the tensions of the time steadily mounted, and the demands
of laissez-faire right-wing conservatives grew more insistent
upon judicial intervention, the attitudes of the moderate center
of the legal profession, and particularly traditional legal conservatism, became decisive. This group had often held the
balance between the progressives and the right-wing conservatives in the profession. Moderate in their views on government
regulation and the rights of property, and concerned profession-
ally with preserving the traditional principles and procedures of
legal and constitutional construction, most traditional conservatives had long opposed any fundamental change in the nature
or extent of judicial power. The pressures of the 1890's, however, weakened the position of the moderates; the course of
judicial decision moved relentlessly toward increasing interposition; and as the crisis reached its height in 1894 and 1895 and

---

versity of Michigan, is printed in the *Michigan Law Journal*, 3 (Aug.,
1894), 215–233.

[32] Next to the Supreme Court, the neo-Federalist conservatism of the
1890's looked to the indirectly elected Senate as the major bulwark of
conservative defense. Said the president of the Kansas Bar Association:
"Until immigration is restricted, the naturalization laws are radically
changed, and an educational and property qualification is imposed as a
condition of enjoying the right of suffrage, we dare not remove the
safeguard which the present mode of electing Senators affords" (John
D. Milliken, "President's Annual Address," *Twelfth Annual Meeting
of the Bar Association of the State of Kansas* [1895], pp. 44–60, at 56).

conservative fears approached near panic, a major sector of the moderates finally broke from the center position, as in the *Pollock* decision, coalesced with the right wing in the burgeoning neo-Federalism, and sealed the triumph of the new judicialism.

The resultant constitutional and legal revolution was, from the conservative point of view, indeed creative, in its way as significant for the laissez-faire conservatism of the 1890's as the constitutionalism of 1787 for the conservatism of that era. Due process of law, once primarily procedural, was now solidly substantive as well; the police power, once freely malleable as adjuster of social imbalance, was now encased by freedom of contract; the ancient process of equity, once applicable only to named individuals and as safeguard for physical property, was now an instrument of public, i.e., judicial, policy and applicable to "all persons whomsoever"; the commerce power, once "plenary" under Marshall, was now divided under Fuller; and a hundred years of tax law precedent, thought inviolable by the rule of *stare decisis,* was now shattered by the *Pollock* case. Traditional legal conservatism, forced to choose between *traditionalism* and *conservatism*—ironic choice—had chosen the latter. The conservative attachment to the ordered society, demanding as it seemed the firmest judicial interposition in protection of property from social upheaval, had outranked in value the more formalistic virtues of legal tradition.

In strengthening the right-wing position on the issue of the role of the judiciary and thus promoting the advance of judicial supremacy, the traditional legal conservatism of the 1890's had also prepared the way, unintentionally, I believe, for the enshrinement of laissez-faire philosophy in constitutional law. With the various precedents and legal principles developed in the 1890's available as stepping stones, laissez-faire doctrinaires could far more easily have their way with the courts. Pre-1890 traditionalism, driven by the mid-nineties into alliance with laissez-faire doctrinairism, was largely absorbed by it; laissez-faire philosophy became, in the minds of many, *the* tradition of the courts. And progressives defending social legislation, rather than argue that the courts were exceeding their traditional functions, for the most part accepted the new conditions and tried to accomplish their aims by sustaining, in effect, the burden of proof in the matter of "reasonableness."

Whether the sweep of laissez-faire ideology would have encompassed the judiciary in the course of time without the special impetus of the 1890's is highly doubtful. A number of scholars have noted, without satisfactory explanation, the paradox that laissez-faire doctrines so thoroughly invaded the law considerably after their full effects in philosophy, politics, and economics were felt and passed and when *laissez faire* and Social Darwinism were already in full retreat in the body politic.[33] Certainly the crisis of the 1890's and the concomitant movement to right-wing conservatism forced decisively a dramatic quickening of the pace for laissez-faire constitutionalism, a sudden

[33] Thus, Benjamin F. Wright, *The Growth of American Constitutional Law* (New York, 1942), p. 98, describing the rise of substantive due process as "in some respects curiously obscure"; and Hamilton, "The Path of Due Process," pp. 188–190, falling back upon "the impulses within the social order." A variety of what I call "circular" explanations have been proposed: Twiss, *Lawyers and the Constitution*, the briefs and arguments of corporate counsel; Jacobs, *Law Writers and the Courts*, the influence of the textbook writers; Boudin, *Government by Judiciary*, and Rodell, *Nine Men*, the predilections of the judges. But as Prof. Wallace Mendelson has said, the answer must lie in "that force in the community" which gave strength to one side of the legal argument and weakened the other. "When we call it the bias or perversity of judges do we do any more than name (and thus hide) what we do not understand?" (*American Political Science Review*, 49 [June, 1955], 560). The close attention to chronology in this study offers, it is proposed, a key clue to the problem. Justice Holmes came close to it when he said in 1897: "When socialism first began to be talked about, the comfortable classes of the community were a good deal frightened. I suspect that this fear has influenced judicial action . . . and that in some courts new principles have been discovered outside the bodies of those instruments" (Oliver W. Holmes, "The Path of the Law," *Collected Legal Papers* [New York, 1920], p. 184).

overmounting of hurdles at a time when constitutional doctrine was still not assured in its direction. Had the legal and constitutional traditions overturned in the 1890's been maintained by the courts but another few years, the changed social atmosphere of the 1900's would have made unlikely, I suggest, the advanced judicial supremacy developed by the 1920's and 1930's.

As it turned out, however, the neo-Federalism of the 1890's opened the door to what was to prove in succeeding decades a full proliferation of judicial obstructionism. The Supreme Court of the United States became, instead of an instrument of constitutional democracy, an impediment to constitutional democracy. Exaggerating its powers beyond proportion in the period 1890–1937, confusing its proper role in the American scheme of government, the Court for a long while seriously weakened its real value. In the unfolding of these unfortunate developments, the bar and the bench of the 1890's, and not least the usually tradition-minded legal conservatives, had no little part.

Bibliography

PRIMARY SOURCES CITED

A. Bar Association Reports

Alabama State Bar Association (1887, 1890, 1896).
American Bar Association (1884, 1887–1889, 1891–1894).
Arkansas State Bar Association (1889).
Georgia Bar Association (1887).
Grafton and Coos Bar Association (1895).
Illinois State Bar Association (1891, 1893, 1895).
Bar Association of the State of Kansas (1889, 1892, 1895).
Mississippi Bar Association (1889).
Missouri Bar Association (1887).
National Bar Association (1890).
New York State Bar Association (1887, 1889, 1893, 1895).
Ohio State Bar Association (1888, 1894, 1896).
Southern New Hampshire Bar Association (1894).
Bar Association of Tennessee (1888, 1891, 1894–1895).
Texas Bar Association (1894, 1896).
Territorial Bar Association of Utah (1894).
Washington State Bar Association (1895).
West Virginia Bar Association (1887, 1890).

B. Law Journals

Advocate (Minneapolis), 1889–1890.
Albany Law Journal, 1892–1896.
American Law Register (Philadelphia), 1889, 1892–1895.
American Law Review (St. Louis), 1890–1896.
American Lawyer (New York), 1895.
Case and Comment (Rochester), 1895.
Central Law Journal (St. Louis), 1890, 1892, 1894–1895.
Chicago Law Journal, 1895.
Chicago Legal Advisor, 1890.
Chicago Legal News, 1892, 1894–1895.
Columbia Law Times (New York), 1889.
Current Comment and Legal Miscellany (Philadelphia), 1889.
Green Bag (Boston), 1893.
Harvard Law Review (Cambridge), 1892–1895.
Kansas City Bar Monthly, 1896.
Legal Advisor (Chicago), 1890, 1894–1895.
Michigan Law Journal (Detroit), 1894, 1896.
Minnesota Law Journal (St. Paul), 1893–1894.
North Western Law Review (Chicago), 1895.
Pennsylvania Law Series (Philadelphia), 1894.
Railway and Corporation Law Journal (New York), 1891.
Virginia Law Register (Lynchburg), 1896.
West Virginia Bar (Morgantown), 1894.
Yale Law Journal (New Haven), 1894.

C. Miscellaneous Legal Works, Memoirs, and Documentary Publications

Brown, Samuel G., ed. *The Works of Rufus Choate with a Memoir of His Life.* 2 vols. Boston: Little, Brown, 1862.

Carson, Hampton L. *The Supreme Court of the United States: Its History; and Its Centennial Celebration.* Under direction of the Judiciary Centennial Committee. Philadelphia: John Y. Huber, 1891.

Cleveland, Grover. *The Government in the Chicago Strike of 1894.* Princeton: Princeton University Press, 1913.

Congressional Record. 53d Cong., 2d sess., vol. 26 (March 2– March 6, 1894).

Cooley, Thomas M. *A Treatise on the Constitutional Limitations Which Rest upon the Legislative Power of the States of the American Union.* Boston: Little, Brown, 1868.

Dillon, John F. *The Laws and Jurisprudence of England and America.* Boston: Little, Brown, 1894.

Hamilton, Alexander, John Jay, and James Madison. *The Federalist.* Modern Library edition, with an introduction by Edward Mead Earle. New York: Random House, 1937.

Hicks, Frederick C., ed. *Arguments and Addresses of Joseph Hodges Choate.* St. Paul: West Publishing Co., 1926.

Kent, Charles A., comp. *Memoir of Henry Billings Brown.* New York: Duffield, 1915.

McKee, Thomas H. *The National Conventions and Platforms of All Political Parties 1789 to 1904.* Baltimore: Friedenwald Co., 1904.

Miller, Samuel F. *Lectures on the Constitution of the United States.* New York: Banks & Bros., 1891.

Story, Joseph. *Commentaries on the Constitution of the United States.* 5th ed. 2 vols. Boston: Little, Brown, 1891.

Tiedeman, Christopher G. *A Treatise on the Limitations of Police Power in the United States.* St. Louis: F. H. Thomas, 1886.

——. *The Unwritten Constitution of the United States.* New York: Putnam, 1890.

United States Bureau of the Census. *Historical Statistics of the United States, 1789–1945.* Washington, 1949.

—— Congress, House Judiciary Committee. *Receivership of the Northern Pacific Railroad Company.* 53d Cong., 2d sess., H. Rept. 1049. Washington, 1894.

—— Strike Commission. *Report on the Chicago Strike of June– July, 1894.* 53d Cong., 3d sess., Sen. Ex. Doc. 7. Washington, 1895.

Whitney, Edward B. "The Income Tax and the Constitution," *Harvard Law Review,* 20 (Feb., 1907), 280–296.

SECONDARY SOURCES CITED

Aaron, Daniel. "Conservatism Old and New," *American Quarterly*, 6 (Summer, 1954), 99–110.

Adair, Douglass. "That Politics May Be Reduced to a Science: David Hume, James Madison, and the *Tenth Federalist*," *Huntington Library Quarterly*, 20 (Aug., 1957), 343–360.

——. "The Tenth Federalist Revisited," *William and Mary Quarterly*, 8 (Jan., 1951), 48–67.

Barnard, Harry. *Eagle Forgotten: The Life of John Peter Altgeld*. Indianapolis: Bobbs-Merrill, 1938.

Barnes, James A. "Myths of the Bryan Campaign," *Mississippi Valley Historical Review*, 34 (Dec., 1947), 367–404.

Beth, Loren P. "Justice Harlan and the Uses of Dissent," *American Political Science Review*, 49 (Dec., 1955), 1085–1104.

Blakey, Roy G., and Gladys C. Blakey. *The Federal Income Tax*. New York: Longmans, Green, 1940.

Boudin, Louis B. *Government by Judiciary*. 2 vols. New York: William Godwin, 1932.

Brooks, Aubrey L. *Walter Clark, Fighting Judge*. Chapel Hill: University of North Carolina Press, 1944.

Burns, Edward M. *James Madison, Philosopher of the Constitution*. New Brunswick: Rutgers University Press, 1938.

Cahn, Edward, ed. *Supreme Court and Supreme Law*. Bloomington: Indiana University Press, 1954.

Commager, Henry S. *The American Mind*. New Haven: Yale University Press, 1950.

Commons, John R., and Associates. *History of Labour in the United States*. 4 vols. New York: Macmillan, 1918.

Corwin, Edward S. *Court over Constitution*. Princeton: Princeton University Press, 1938.

——. "The Basic Doctrine of American Constitutional Law," *Michigan Law Review*, 12 (Feb., 1914), 247–276.

——. *The Commerce Power v. States Rights*. Princeton: Princeton University Press, 1936.

——. "The Doctrine of Due Process before the Civil War," *Harvard Law Review*, 24 (March, 1911), 366–385; (April, 1911), 460–479.

Corwin, Edward S. *The Twilight of the Supreme Court.* New
Haven: Yale University Press, 1934.

Cummings, Homer, and Carl McFarland. *Federal Justice.* New
York: Macmillan, 1937.

David, Henry. *The History of the Haymarket Affair.* New York:
Farrar & Rinehart, 1936.

——. "Upheaval at Homestead," in Daniel Aaron, ed., *America in
Crisis.* New York: Knopf, 1952.

Davis, Elbridge, and Harold A. Davis. "Mr. Justice Horace Gray:
Some Aspects of His Judicial Career," *American Bar Association
Journal,* 41 (May, 1955), 421–424, 468–471.

Destler, Chester M. *American Radicalism, 1865–1901.* New London: Connecticut College Press, 1946.

Diamond, William. "Urban and Rural Voting in 1896," *American
Historical Review,* 46 (Jan., 1941), 281–305.

Ellis, Elmer. "Public Opinion and the Income Tax," *Mississippi
Valley Historical Review,* 27 (Sept., 1940), 225–242.

Ely, Richard T., and L. S. Merriam. "Report on Social Legislation
in the United States for 1889 and 1890," *Economic Review,* 1
(April, 1891), 234–256.

Fairman, Charles. *Mr. Justice Miller and the Supreme Court, 1862–
1890.* Cambridge: Harvard University Press, 1939.

——. "The Retirement of Federal Judges," *Harvard Law Review,*
51 (Jan., 1938), 397–443.

——. "The So-called Granger Cases, Lord Hale, and Justice Bradley," *Stanford Law Review,* 5 (July, 1953), 587–679.

——. "What Makes a Great Justice? Mr. Justice Bradley and the
Supreme Court, 1870–1892," *Boston University Law Review,* 30
(Jan., 1950), 49–102.

Farrelly, David G. "Harlan's Dissent in the Pollock Case," *Southern
California Law Review,* 24 (Feb., 1951), 175–182.

Faulkner, Harold U. *Politics, Reform and Expansion 1890–1900.*
New York: Harper, 1959.

Fine, Sidney. *Laissez Faire and the General-Welfare State: A Study
of Conflict in American Thought, 1865–1901.* Ann Arbor: University of Michigan Press, 1956.

Frankfurter, Felix. *Mr. Justice Holmes and the Constitution.* Cambridge: Harvard University Press, 1939.

——, and Nathan Greene. *The Labor Injunction.* New York: Macmillan, 1930.

Fuller, Leon W. "Colorado's Revolt against Capitalism," *Mississippi Valley Historical Review,* 21 (Dec., 1934), 343–360.

Gabriel, Ralph H. *The Course of American Democratic Thought.* New York: Ronald Press, 1940.

Ginger, Ray. *Altgeld's America: The Lincoln Ideal versus Changing Realities.* New York: Funk & Wagnalls, 1958.

——. *The Bending Cross: A Biography of Eugene Victor Debs.* New Brunswick: Rutgers University Press, 1949.

Graham, Howard J. "An Innocent Abroad: The Constitutional Corporate 'Person,'" *U.C.L.A. Law Review,* 2 (Feb., 1955), 155–211.

——. "'Builded Better than They Knew' Part I: The Framers, the Railroads and the Fourteenth Amendment," *University of Pittsburgh Law Review,* 17 (Summer, 1956), 537–584.

——. "Procedure to Substance—Extra-Judicial Rise of Due Process 1830–1860," *California Law Review,* 40 (Winter, 1952–1953), 483–500.

Grant, J. A. C. "The Natural Law Background of Due Process," *Columbia Law Review,* 31 (Jan., 1931), 56–81.

Haines, Charles G. "Judicial Review of Legislation in the United States and the Doctrine of Vested Rights and of Implied Limitations on Legislatures," *Texas Law Review,* 2 (April, 1924), 257–290; (June, 1924), 387–421; 3 (Dec., 1924), 1–43.

——. *The American Doctrine of Judicial Supremacy.* 2d ed. Berkeley: University of California Press, 1932.

——. *The Revival of Natural Law Concepts.* Cambridge: Harvard University Press, 1930.

Hamilton, Walton H. "Property—According to Locke," *Yale Law Journal,* 41 (April, 1932), 864–880.

——. "The Path of Due Process," in Conyers Read, ed., *The Constitution Reconsidered.* New York: Columbia University Press, 1938.

Hartz, Louis. *The Liberal Tradition in America.* New York: Harcourt, Brace, 1955.

Hays, Samuel P. *The Response to Industrialism 1885–1914.* Chicago: University of Chicago Press, 1957.

Hicks, John D. *The Populist Revolt.* Minneapolis: University of Minnesota Press, 1931.

Higham, John. *Strangers in the Land: Patterns of American Nativism, 1860–1925.* New Brunswick: Rutgers University Press, 1955.

Hoffman, Charles. "The Depression of the Nineties," *Journal of Economic History,* 15 (June, 1956), 137–164.

Hofstadter, Richard. *Social Darwinism in American Thought, 1860–1915.* Philadelphia: University of Pennsylvania Press, 1945.

——. *The Age of Reform: From Bryan to F. D. R.* New York: Knopf, 1956.

——. *The American Political Tradition and the Men Who Made It.* New York: Knopf, 1951.

Holmes, Oliver Wendell. *Collected Legal Papers.* New York: Harcourt, Brace, 1920.

Hughes, Charles Evans. *The Supreme Court of the United States.* New York: Columbia University Press, 1928.

Jackson, Frederick H. *Simeon Eben Baldwin.* New York: Columbia University Press, 1954.

Jackson, Robert H. *The Struggle for Judicial Supremacy.* New York: Knopf, 1941.

Jacobs, Clyde D. *Law Writers and the Courts: The Influence of Thomas M. Cooley, Christopher G. Tiedeman, and John F. Dillon upon American Constitutional Law.* Berkeley: University of California Press, 1954.

James, Henry. *Richard Olney and His Public Service.* Boston: Houghton Mifflin, 1923.

King, Willard L. *Melville Weston Fuller.* New York: Macmillan, 1950.

——. "The Debs Case," in Colston E. Warne, ed., *The Pullman Boycott of 1894: The Problem of Federal Intervention.* Boston: Heath, 1955.

Kirkland, Edward C. *A History of American Economic Life.* New York: Crofts, 1939.

Knoles, George H. *The Presidential Campaign and Election of 1892.* Palo Alto: Stanford University Press, 1942.

Komarovsky, Mirra, ed. *Common Frontiers of the Social Sciences.* Glencoe: Free Press, 1957.

Lardner, Lynford A. *The Constitutional Doctrines of Justice David*

Josiah Brewer. Unpublished Ph.D. dissertation, Princeton University, 1938.

Levy, Leonard W. *The Law of the Commonwealth and Chief Justice Shaw*. Cambridge: Harvard University Press, 1957.

Lewis, Edward R. *A History of American Political Thought from the Civil War to the World War*. New York: Macmillan, 1937.

Lindsey, Almont. *The Pullman Strike*. Chicago: University of Chicago Press, 1942.

McAllister, Breck P. "Lord Hale and Business Affected with a Public Interest," *Harvard Law Review*, 43 (March, 1930), 759–791.

McCloskey, Robert G. *American Conservatism in the Age of Enterprise*. Cambridge: Harvard University Press, 1951.

McMurry, Donald L. *Coxey's Army*. Boston: Little, Brown, 1929.

——. "Labor Policies of the General Managers' Association of Chicago, 1886–1894," *Journal of Economic History*, 13 (Spring, 1953), 160–178.

——. *The Great Burlington Strike of 1888*. Cambridge: Harvard University Press, 1956.

Martin, Edward S. *The Life of Joseph Hodges Choate*. 2 vols. New York: Scribner, 1920.

Mason, Alpheus T. *Organized Labor and the Law*. Durham: Duke University Press, 1925.

——. "*The Federalist*—A Split Personality," *American Historical Review*, 57 (April, 1952), 625–643.

Mendelson, Wallace. "A Missing Link in the Evolution of Due Process," *Vanderbilt Law Review*, 10 (Dec., 1956), 125–137.

Mott, Rodney L. *Due Process of Law*. Indianapolis: Bobbs-Merrill, 1926.

Mowry, George E. *Theodore Roosevelt and the Progressive Movement*. Madison: University of Wisconsin Press, 1947.

Nevins, Allan. *Grover Cleveland: A Study in Courage*. New York: Dodd, Mead, 1932.

Perlman, Selig. *A History of Trade Unionism in the United States*. New York: Macmillan, 1922.

Pound, Roscoe. "Liberty of Contract," *Yale Law Journal*, 18 (May, 1909), 454–487.

Pringle, Henry F. *The Life and Times of William Howard Taft.* 2 vols. New York: Farrar and Rinehart, 1939.

Ratner, Sidney. *American Taxation: Its History as a Social Force in Democracy.* New York: Norton, 1942.

Rezneck, Samuel. "Patterns of Thought and Action in an American Depression, 1882–1886," *American Historical Review,* 61 (Jan., 1956), 284–307.

———. "Unemployment, Unrest, and Relief in the United States during the Depression of 1893–1897," *Journal of Political Economy,* 61 (Aug., 1953), 324–345.

Roche, John P. "Judicial Self-Restraint," *American Political Science Review,* 49 (Sept., 1955), 762–777.

Rodell, Fred. *Nine Men: A Political History of the Supreme Court from 1790 to 1955.* New York: Random House, 1955.

Rogow, Arnold A. "The Federal Convention: Madison and Yates," *American Historical Review,* 60 (Jan., 1955), 323–335.

Rossiter, Clinton. *Conservatism in America.* New York: Knopf, 1955.

Seligman, Edwin R. A. *The Income Tax.* 2d ed. New York: Macmillan, 1914.

Shaw, William B. "Social and Economic Legislation of the States in 1890," *Quarterly Journal of Economics,* 5 (April, 1891), 385–396.

———. "Social and Economic Legislation of the States in 1891," *Quarterly Journal of Economics,* 6 (Jan., 1892), 227–242.

Shiras, George, 3d. *Justice George Shiras, Jr., of Pittsburgh.* Edited and completed by Winfield Shiras. Pittsburgh: University of Pittsburgh Press, 1953.

Studenski, Paul, and Herman C. Kroos. *Financial History of the United States.* New York: McGraw-Hill, 1952.

Swaine, Robert T. *The Cravath Firm and Its Predecessors, 1819–1947.* 2 vols. New York: privately printed, 1946.

Swisher, Carl B. *American Constitutional Development.* 2d ed. Boston: Houghton Mifflin, 1954.

———. *Stephen J. Field: Craftsman of the Law.* Washington: Brookings Institution, 1930.

[Symposium on John Marshall Harlan, 1883–1911], *Kentucky Law Journal,* 46 (Spring, 1958), 321–474.

"Third Newberry Library Conference on American Studies." (American Conservatism), *Newberry Library Bulletin*, 3 (June, 1953), 73–87.

Thorelli, Hans B. *The Federal Anti-Trust Policy: Its Origination to 1903.* Baltimore: Johns Hopkins Press, 1955.

Tocqueville, Alexis de. *Democracy in America.* 2 vols. New York: Vintage Books, 1954.

Trimble, Bruce R. *Chief Justice Waite, Defender of the Public Interest.* Princeton: Princeton University Press, 1938.

Tunell, George. "Legislative History of the Second Income Tax Law," *Journal of Political Economy*, 3 (June, 1895), 311–337.

Twiss, Benjamin R. *Lawyers and the Constitution: How Laissez Faire Came to the Supreme Court.* Princeton: Princeton University Press, 1942.

Warren, Charles. *The Supreme Court in United States History.* 3 vols. Boston: Little, Brown, 1923.

Westin, Alan F. "The Supreme Court, the Populist Movement, and the Campaign of 1896," *Journal of Politics*, 15 (Feb., 1953), 3–41.

Wish, Harvey. "John P. Altgeld and the Background of the Campaign of 1896," *Mississippi Valley Historical Review*, 24 (March, 1938), 503–518.

Wright, Benjamin F. *The Contract Clause of the Constitution.* Cambridge: Harvard University Press, 1938.

——. *The Growth of American Constitutional Law.* New York: Reynal & Hitchcock, 1942.

Table of Cases

Adair v. United States, 208 U.S. 161 (1908): 138
Adkins v. Children's Hospital, 261 U.S. 525 (1923): 228
Arthur v. Oakes, 63 Fed. 310 (C.C.A., 7th, 1894): 122, 138

Barr v. Essex Trades Council, 53 N.J. Eq. 101 (1894): 106
Beer Co. v. Massachusetts, 97 U.S. 25 (1878): 10
Blindell v. Hagan, 54 Fed. 40 (E.D. La., 1893); aff'd 56 Fed. 696
   (C.C.A., 5th, 1893): 107–108
Brace Bros. v. Evans, 5 Pa. Co. Ct. Rep. 163 (1888): 106
Braceville Coal Co. v. People, 147 Ill. 66 (1893): 83
Brass v. North Dakota, 153 U.S. 391 (1894): 84, 175–176, 178
Budd v. New York, 143 U.S. 517 (1892): 72–74, 84, 89, 91, 94, 175
Bunting v. Oregon, 243 U.S. 426 (1917): 228
Butchers' Union Co. v. Crescent City Co., 111 U.S. 746 (1884): 10,
   14, 89

Calder v. Bull, 3 Dal. 386 (1798): 89
Casey v. Cincinnati Typographical Union No. 3, 45 Fed. 135 (S.D.
   Ohio, 1891): 106
Charles River Bridge v. Warren Bridge, 11 Pet. 420 (1837): 89
Chicago, B. & Q. Ry. Co. v. Burlington, C. R. & N. Ry. Co., 34 Fed.
   481 (S.D. Iowa, 1886): 110

Chicago, Milwaukee & St. Paul Ry. Co. *v.* Minnesota, 134 U.S. 418
(1890): 39–42, 43, 44, 57, 64, 68, 71, 73, 176, 177
Chicago & N. W. Ry. Co. *v.* Dey, 35 Fed. 866 (S.D. Iowa, 1888): 42
Cincinnati, New Orleans, and Texas Pacific Ry. Co. *v.* Interstate
Commerce Commission, 162 U.S. 184 (1896): 220
Coeur d'Alene Consolidated & Mining Co. *v.* Miners' Union, 51 Fed.
260 (D. Ida., 1892): 106
Commonwealth *v.* Alger, 7 Cush. (Mass.) 53 (1851): 50
Commonwealth *v.* Hamilton Manufacturing Co., 120 Mass. 383
(1876): 219
Commonwealth *v.* Hunt, 4 Met. (Mass.) 111 (1842): 106
Commonwealth *v.* Perry, 155 Mass. 117 (1891): 47–48, 49–50

Dartmouth College *v.* Woodward, 4 Wheat. 518 (1819): 11, 44, 56,
231–232
Davidson *v.* New Orleans, 96 U.S. 97 (1878): 56, 232
Debs, *In re*, 158 U.S. 564 (1895): 219, 222

Eight-Hour Bill, *In re*, 21 Col. 29 (1895): 219

Farmers Loan & Trust Co. *v.* Northern Pacific R.R. Co., 60 Fed.
803 (E.D. Wisc., 1894): 117–122, 125, 127, 138, 150
Fertilizing Co. *v.* Hyde Park, 97 U.S. 659 (1878): 10
Fletcher *v.* Peck, 6 Cr. 87 (1810): 89, 172
Frorer *v.* People, 141 Ill. 171 (1892): 51

Gibbons *v.* Ogden, 9 Wheat. 1 (1824): 181
Godcharles *v.* Wigeman, 113 Pa. St. 431 (1886): 15–16, 46, 47, 50,
68, 90, 94

Hamilton *v.* C. Jutte & Co., 1 Lackawanna Legal News (La. Co. Ct.,
Pa.) 173 (1895): 219
Hammer *v.* Dagenhart, 247 U.S. 251 (1918): 228
Hancock *v.* Yaden, 121 Ind. 366 (1890): 46, 48
Head Money Cases, 112 U.S. 580 (1884): 171, 173
Higgins, *In re*, 27 Fed. 443 (N.D. Texas, 1886): 106
Holden *v.* Hardy, 169 U.S. 366 (1898): 84, 228

House Bill No. 203, *In re*, 21 Col. 27 (1895): 219
Hylton *v.* United States, 3 Dal. 171 (1796): 166–168, 169, 187, 194, 201, 210

Interstate Commerce Commission *v.* Alabama Midland Ry. Co., 168 U.S. 144 (1897): 220

Jacobs, In the Matter of, 98 N.Y. 98 (1885): 15
Jones *v.* People, 110 Ill. 590 (1884): 15

Knowlton *v.* Moore, 178 U.S. 41 (1900): 171, 228
Knoxville Iron Co. *v.* Harbison, 183 U.S. 13 (1901): 228
Kuback, *Ex parte*, 85 Cal. 274 (1890): 47

Leep *v.* Railway Company, 58 Ark. 407 (1894): 219
Lennon, *In re*, 166 U.S. 548 (1897): 116
Loan Association *v.* Topeka, 20 Wall. 655 (1874): 89
Lochner *v.* New York, 198 U.S. 45 (1905): 49, 73, 84, 228
Low *v.* Rees Printing Co., 41 Neb. 127 (1894): 219

McCullough *v.* Brown, 41 S.C. 220 (1894): 100
McLean *v.* Arkansas, 211 U.S. 539 (1909): 228
Marbury *v.* Madison, 1 Cr. 49 (1803): 90, 91
Millett *v.* People, 117 Ill. 294 (1886): 15
Moore *v.* Miller, 5 App. D.C. 413 (1895): 172–173, 186, 188
Mugler *v.* Kansas, 123 U.S. 623 (1887): 29–31, 34, 35, 71
Muller *v.* Oregon, 208 U.S. 412 (1908): 228
Munn *v.* Illinois, 94 U.S. 113 (1877): 8–10, 14, 41, 68–74 *passim*, 78, 175, 232

Old Dominion Steamship Co. *v.* McKenna, 30 Fed. 48 (S.D. New York, 1887): 106

Pacific Insurance Co. *v.* Soule, 7 Wall. 433 (1869): 168–169, 172, 187, 194, 201, 210
People *v.* Budd, 117 N.Y. 1 (1889): 73–74

Platt *v.* Philadelphia & Reading R.R. Co., 65 Fed. 660 (E.D. Pa., 1894): 138

Plumley *v.* Massachusetts, 155 U.S. 461 (1894): 203

Pollock *v.* Farmers' Loan and Trust Co., 157 U.S. 429 (1895); (*Rehearing*), 158 U.S. 601 (1895): 173, 185–195, 198–218, 222, 223, 235

Powell *v.* Pennsylvania, 127 U.S. 678 (1888): 31–32, 34, 35, 71, 89

Ramsey *v.* People, 142 Ill. 380 (1892): 51

Reagan *v.* Farmers' Loan and Trust Co., 154 U.S. 362 (1894): 176–178, 219

Ritchie *v.* People, 155 Ill. 98 (1895): 219, 222

San Antonio Ry. Co. *v.* Wilson, 19 S.W. (Texas) 910 (1892): 51–52

Santa Clara County *v.* Southern Pacific R.R., 118 U.S. 394 (1886): 7

Scholey *v.* Rew, 23 Wall. 331 (1874): 169

Shaffer *v.* Union Mining Co., 55 Md. 74 (1880): 16, 47

Sherry *v.* Perkins, 147 Mass. 212 (1888): 107

Slaughter-House Cases, 16 Wall. 36 (1873): 13–14, 89, 232

Smyth *v.* Ames, 169 U.S. 466 (1898): 178, 228

Southern California Ry. Co. *v.* Rutherford, 62 Fed. 796 (S.D. Cal., 1894): 139

Springer *v.* United States, 102 U.S. 586 (1881): 169–170, 172, 187, 194, 201, 210, 217

State *v.* Brown & Sharpe Mfg. Co., 18 R.I. 16 (1892): 52

State *v.* Fire Creek Coal & Coke Co., 33 W.Va. 188 (1889): 45–46

State *v.* Goodwill, 33 W.Va. 179 (1889): 45–46, 50, 53–54

State *v.* Loomis, 115 Mo. 307 (1893): 82–83

State *v.* Peel Splint Coal Co., 36 W.Va. 802 (1892): 52–53

Stone *v.* Farmers' Loan and Trust Co., 116 U.S. 307 (1886): 10–11

Stone *v.* Mississippi, 101 U.S. 814 (1880): 10

Terrett *v.* Taylor, 9 Cr. 42 (1815): 89

Thomas *v.* Cincinnati, N. O. & T. P. Ry. Co., 62 Fed. 803 (S.D. Ohio, 1894): 154

Toledo, Ann Arbor & Northern Michigan Ry. Co. *v.* Pennsylvania Co., 54 Fed. 730 and 54 Fed. 746 (N.D. Ohio, 1893): 111–116, 124, 144

United States *v.* Agler, 62 Fed. 824 (D. Ind., 1894): 154
United States *v.* Debs, 64 Fed. 724 (N.D. Ill., 1894): 153–155
United States *v.* E. C. Knight Co., 156 U.S. 1 (1895): 178–182, 183, 184, 189, 203, 219, 223, 228
United States *v.* Elliott, 62 Fed. 801 (E.D. Mo., 1894): 154
United States *v.* Joint Traffic Association, 171 U.S. 505 (1898): 228
United States *v.* Patterson, 55 Fed. 605 (D. Mass., 1893): 109
United States *v.* Trans-Missouri Freight Association, 166 U.S. 290 (1897): 228
United States *v.* Workingmen's Amalgamated Council of New Orleans, 54 Fed. 994 (E.D. La., 1893); *aff'd* 57 Fed. 85 (C.C.A., 5th, 1893): 109–110

Veazie Bank *v.* Fenno, 8 Wall. 533 (1870): 169

Wabash, St. Louis & Pacific Ry. Co. *v.* Illinois, 118 U.S. 557 (1886): 41
Walker *v.* Cronin, 107 Mass. 555 (1871): 106
Wallace *v.* Georgia, Carolina & Northern Ry. Co., 94 Ga. 732 (1894): 219
Waterhouse *v.* Comer, 55 Fed. 149 (W.D. Ga., 1893): 116–117
Wickard *v.* Filburn, 317 U.S. 111 (1942): 58
Wilkinson *v.* Leland, 2 Pet. 627 (1829): 89

Index

Advocate, 42
Albany Law Journal, 152, 195-196, 206, 210-211, 226
Allan, Charles C., 146-149
Altgeld, John P., 140-141, 224-225
American Bar Association, 4n., 8in.
American Law Register, 155; see also Lewis, William D.
American Law Review, 43, 154-155, 178n.; see also Thompson, Seymour D.
American Railway Union, 130, 133-135, 139, 142; see also Chicago railroad strike

Baldwin, Simeon E., 35-38, 164n.
Bancroft, Edgar A., 155-156
Bellamy, Edward, 64n.
Benjamin, Reuben M., 152
Benton, J. H., 100-102
Billings, Edward C., 107-110
Blatchford, Samuel, Justice, 40
Bonney, Charles C., 32-33
Boycotts, see Injunction and Strikes
Bradley, Joseph P., Justice, 40-41
Brandeis brief, 228
Brewer, David J., Justice, 42, 70-72, 74, 83, 89n., 121-122, 176, 177-178, 182, 217
Brown, Allan B., 44
Brown, Henry B., Justice, 74, 84-88, 182, 212-213, 218
Bryan, William J., 162, 225, 226

Carter, James C., 190-192, 207-208
Cary, John W., 77-78
Case and Comment, 156-157
Central Law Journal, 177-178
Chicago railroad strike: background and development, 132-142; lawyers' reactions to, 142-146, 155-157; Strike Commission report on, 153; and Debs contempt case, 153-155, 224
Choate, Joseph H., 172, 192-195, 208
Class conflict, 19-20, 37, 63, 70, 85, 233
Class legislation, 13, 191; see also Freedom of contract
Cleveland, Grover, 61, 140-141, 162, 174n., 224
Commerce, interstate, 41, 58, 180, 181; see also Interstate Commerce Act and Sherman Anti-Trust Act
Conkling, Roscoe, 7, 56n., 232
Conservatism, 27, 102, 159, 226, 229, 231; laissez-faire, 4, 8, 18, 23, 64-65, 89, 181, 233n., 235; traditional, 4-5, 18, 76, 81, 233; right-wing, 34, 70, 76, 81, 217, 219, 226, 234, 237; moderate, 35, 100, 157, 217-218; see also Legal conservatism
Constitution, U.S.: Fourteenth Amendment, 5-6, 7, 13, 93, 232; federal taxing power under, 164-165; commerce clause, 180, 181; contract clause, 230, 231-232

Constitutional Convention of 1787, *see* Founding Fathers
Constitutionalism (American), 27, 28, 37, 88, 100-102, 233-234, 235
Cooley, Thomas M., 12-13, 38n., 47, 129, 142-143, 232
Corporations, 5-8 *passim*, 11, 19, 52, 53, 55-59 *passim*, 65, 151, 152, 157, 183, 190
Coxey "armies," 128-129

Darling, Herbert H., 49-51
Darwinism, Social, 236; *see also* Spencer, Herbert
Debs, Eugene V., 134, 140-142, 145, 153; "Debs rebellion," *see* Chicago railroad strike
Declaration of Independence, 14, 71, 78, 89, 92, 95
Democracy, 5, 34, 37-38, 81, 230; *see also* Majority rule
Democratic party, 160-163 *passim*, 224-225; anticourt planks of, 225
Depression of 1893, 82, 128, 224
Dillon, John F., 28-29, 43n., 78-81, 164, 177, 183
Direct taxes, constitutional meaning of, 165-170, 186-189 *passim*, 191, 193, 198-200, 202, 203
Due process of law, 6, 12, 56; substantive due process, 7, 8, 11; see also *Laissez faire*, constitutionalism

Earl, Robert, 15
Edmunds, George F., 172-173, 188
Elliott, Byron K., 46
Equity, 105, 126-127, 146-147, 149; *see also* Injunction

Farmers' Alliances, 64n.; Farmers' Alliance of Minnesota, 42
Federalism, neo-, 160, 204, 233-235, 237
Federalists (of 1787), 159, 231, 232, 233
Field, Stephen J., Justice, 13-14, 32, 63-64, 74, 89, 182, 204-205, 217, 232
Founding Fathers, 28, 80, 100-101, 199, 203, 213, 230; *see also* Federalists
Freedom of contract: defined, 6; established by 1887, 12; first uses of, 15-16; applications in early 1890's, 45-54 *passim;* cases in 1893, 82n.; expansion of, 219; comments on, 33, 58-59, 65, 66-68, 222
Fuller, Melville W., Chief Justice, 42,

179-180, 182, 193-204, 207, 209-211, 217

General Managers' Association, 135-136, 138, 142; *see also* Chicago railroad strike
George, Henry, 20n.
Gibbons, John, 83
Gordon, Isaac M., 15-16
Government, scope of: comments on, 7, 22, 26-27, 33, 34, 36-37, 49, 58-59, 62, 66, 74, 87-88, 91, 94, 151, 152, 157; *see also* Legislature *and* Police power
"Granger" cases, see *Munn* v. *Illinois*
Gray, Horace, Justice, 41, 182, 215-218 *passim*
Grosscup, Peter S., 139, 233
Guthrie, William D., 173, 185-186

Hamilton, Alexander, 231
Harlan, John M., Justice, 30-32, 122n., 180-181, 211-212, 218n.
Haymarket riot, 20, 141n.
Hill, David B., 163, 172n.
Holmes, Oliver W., 43n., 47-48, 54n., 124-125, 236n.
Homestead strike, 75, 81n.
House Judiciary Committee, 117n., 118n., 126n.

Implied limitations, doctrine of, 78, 88-90, 97
Income tax case, 160; legal beginnings, 172-174; comments on, 195-197, 206-207, 210-211, 222; see also *Pollock* v. *Farmers' Loan and Trust Co.*
Income tax of 1894: origins, 160-162; provisions, 162; legislative debates on, 162-164; constitutionality of, 164-172 (see also *Pollock* v. *Farmers' Loan and Trust Co.*); annulled, 210
Ingersoll, Henry H., 222
Injunction, labor: origins, 104-107; applications in 1893, 107-122; against Debs *et al.*, 139-140; sanctioned by Supreme Court, 219; comments on, 123-128, 147-149, 152, 153-154, 158, 224-225
Interstate Commerce Act, 23, 220n.; applied to labor, 110-116 *passim*

Jackson, Howell E., Justice, 207, 213, 218n.

Jenkins, James G., 117-122, 127
Judicial review, 7, 92-99 *passim*, 160, 230; judicial supremacy, 2, 219, 227, 228, 237; *see also* "New judicialism"
Judiciary, role of: conservative tradition on, 229-231; comments on, 26-27, 37, 59, 63, 64, 71-72, 81, 102-103
Judson, Frederick N., 66-69

Knights of Labor, 19-20
Knowlton, Marcus P., 47-48

Laissez faire, 26, 27, 54, 235-236; constitutionalism, 8, 12-14, 16-18, 41, 92, 237; *see also* Conservatism, laissez-faire, *and* Due process of law
Lamar, Lucius Q. C., Justice, 41
Legal Advisor, 206-207
Legal conservatism, 5, 18, 21-22, 23, 27, 38n., 44, 81, 99, 101-102, 132, 155, 158, 195, 218; traditional, 5, 78, 88, 146, 184, 197, 234-237 *passim*
Legal progressivism, 4, 32-33, 42, 48, 53-54, 59-60, 182-184, 221-222, 225, 236
Legislature: limitations upon, 6, 78; powers of, 157, 175; *see also* Due process of law, Freedom of contract, Implied limitations, Police power, *and* "Reasonableness" of public regulation
Lewis, William D., 93-95, 125-126, 143, 196; see also *American Law Register*
Liberty of contract, *see* Freedom of contract
Lucas, Daniel B., 52-53

McMillin, Benton, 161, 207n.
McMurtrie, Richard C., 90-92, 94-96, 143-144
Madison, James, 230
Majority rule: fears of Federalists, 159-160; counsel in *Pollock* case on, 190, 192, 195; and the conservative tradition, 229-230; comments on, 17, 28-29, 35, 62-63, 69, 80, 100-102
Marshall, Charles C., 69-70
Marshall, John, Chief Justice, 90-91, 171-172, 181, 231
Miller, Samuel F., Justice, 40, 57n., 89n.
Monopoly, *see* Corporations *and* Sherman Anti-Trust Act
Murphy, Walter, 126-128

Nativism, 66
Natural rights, doctrine of, 24-27, 93; *see also* Declaration of Independence *and* Implied limitations
Neo-Federalism, 160, 204, 233-235, 237
New constitutionalism, see *Laissez faire*, constitutionalism
New Deal, constitutional crisis of, 229
"New judicialism": term explained, 3, 8n.; and Dillon's speech, 81; triumph of, 219-220; challenges to, 221, 224; consequences of, 227-228; and neo-Federalism, 235

Olney, Richard, 137-138, 174n., 179, 189-190, 208-209
Omaha Convention, 75, 81n.
Overmyer, David, 34-35

Paternalism: comments on, 27, 66, 74, 76-77, 151
Phelps, Edward J., 62-63
Police power: explained by Waite, 9; in Cooley, 12; in Tiedeman, 16; expansion in 1887, 29-31; defined by Shaw, 50; comments on, 35, 67-68, 71
Popular sovereignty, *see* Majority rule
Populist party, 75, 161, 224
Progressive era, 228
Property: expansion of meaning, 105-106; comments on protection of, 64, 69-74 *passim*, 77-80 *passim*, 83, 193, 229; *see also* Freedom of contract, Police power, *and* Wealth
Pullman strike, *see* Chicago railroad strike

Ramsay, William M., 65-66
"Reasonableness" of public regulation, 10, 40-43, 57, 176-178, 236; *see also* Freedom of contract
Receiverships, railroad, 117, 224
Reno, Conrad, 53-54
Republican party, 162, 163
Rerum Novarum, 59
Ricks, Augustus J., 111-113, 115-116
Rose, U. M., 123-124

Senate, 58, 234
Seward, Clarence A., 172, 186-187
Shaw, Lemuel, 50, 106

Sherman Anti-Trust Act, 2, 179, 181, 183; applied to labor, 108-110, 154
Shiras, George, Justice, 175, 182, 214-218 *passim*
Shumate, I. E., 22-23
Silver issue, 224-226 *passim*
Simkins, E. J., 52
Snyder, Adam C., 45-46
Socialism, 27, 36, 79, 86, 183, 236n.
Spencer, Herbert, 4, 22, 232
Stare decisis, 170, 193-194, 201, 210, 218
States' rights, 57, 182, 203
Stewart, Ardemus, 152n., 182-183
Strikes: comments on, 83n., 120-122, 127-128, 150, 152; *see also* Chicago railroad strike, Homestead strike, Knights of Labor, Injunction, *and* Unions
Supreme Court of the United States: cautiousness of, 7, 12; expands police power, 30, 31; changes in personnel, 42; centennial celebration, 61-64; rule of direct taxation, 166; focus of conservative crisis, 174; narrows commerce power, 181; agrees to re-hearing *Pollock* case, 207; trends after 1890's, 228, 229, 237; comments on, 42-44, 57, 178n., 183-184, 206, 210-211, 221-225 *passim*

Taft, William H., 111-115, 142n., 233
Tarlton, B. D., 149-151
Thayer, James B., 96-99

Thompson, Seymour D., 43-44, 48-49, 54-60, 72, 74n., 123, 126, 129n., 144-146, 183-184, 221, 225n.; see also *American Law Review*
Thornton, Lee, 152
Tiedeman, Christopher G., 16-18, 23-27, 52n., 232
Tucker, John R., 76-77

Uniformity, constitutional rule of, 170-171, 186, 189-190, 204
Unions, labor, 123-124, 130, 150, 152, 156; *see also* American Railway Union, Injunction, *and* Strikes
United States Strike Commission, 153

"Virtual monopoly," 10, 175

Waite, Morrison R., Chief Justice, 8-11, 42, 178
Wealth, distribution of: comments on, 63, 85-86, 101, 191; *see also* Class conflict
Western Federation of Miners, 130
White, Edward D., Justice, 182, 205-206, 213-214, 218n.
Whitney, Edward B., 174n., 187-188
Willey, Waitman T., 21-22, 197
Wilson, William L., 163
Wilson, Woodrow, 149n.
Wilson Act, *see* Income tax of 1894
Wintersteen, A. H., 33-34
Woods, William A., 139, 153-155

*Recent books published for the American Historical Association
from the income of the Albert J. Beveridge Memorial Fund*

THE AGRICULTURAL HISTORY OF THE GENESEE VALLEY.
By Neil A. McNall.

STEAM POWER ON THE AMERICAN FARM. *By Reynold M. Wik.*

HORACE GREELEY: NINETEENTH-CENTURY CRUSADER.
By Glyndon G. Van Deusen.

ERA OF THE OATH: NORTHERN LOYALTY TESTS DURING THE
CIVIL WAR AND RECONSTRUCTION. *By Harold M. Hyman.*

HISTORY OF MARSHALL FIELD & CO. *By Robert W. Twyman.*

ROBERT MORRIS: REVOLUTIONARY FINANCIER.
By Clarence L. Ver Steeg.

A HISTORY OF THE FREEDMEN'S BUREAU. *By George R. Bentley.*

THE FIRST RAPPROCHEMENT: ENGLAND AND THE UNITED STATES,
1795–1805. *By Bradford Perkins.*

MIDDLE-CLASS DEMOCRACY AND THE REVOLUTION IN MASSACHUSETTS,
1691–1780. *By Robert E. Brown.*

THE DEVELOPMENT OF AMERICAN PETROLEUM PIPELINES:
A STUDY IN PRIVATE ENTERPRISE AND PUBLIC POLICY, 1862–1906.
By Arthur Menzies Johnson.

COLONISTS FROM SCOTLAND: EMIGRATION TO NORTH AMERICA,
1707–1783. *By Ian Charles Cargill Graham.*

PROFESSORS AND PUBLIC ETHICS: STUDIES OF NORTHERN MORAL
PHILOSOPHERS BEFORE THE CIVIL WAR. *By Wilson Smith.*

THE AXIS ALLIANCE AND JAPANESE-AMERICAN RELATIONS, 1941.
By Paul W. Schroeder.

A FRONTIER STATE AT WAR: KANSAS, 1861–1865. *By Albert Castel.*

BRITISH INVESTMENTS AND THE AMERICAN MINING FRONTIER,
1860–1901. *By Clark C. Spence.*

RAILS, MINES, AND PROGRESS: SEVEN AMERICAN PROMOTERS IN MEXICO,
1867–1911. *By David M. Pletcher.*

LAGUARDIA IN CONGRESS. *By Howard Zinn.*

TOMORROW A NEW WORLD: THE NEW DEAL COMMUNITY PROGRAM.
By Paul K. Conkin.

CONSERVATIVE CRISIS AND THE RULE OF LAW: ATTITUDES OF BAR AND
BENCH, 1887–1895. *By Arnold M. Paul.*